More praise for *Surrendered Child*

"In a lyric and precise language, Karen McElmurray tells her story with unflinching honesty, insight, and compassion. She reveals not only her own past, but the darker side of youth in the 1970s. This book will be read by generations to come."
—Chris Offutt, author of *The Same River Twice*

"Courageous in its honesty, stunning in its vision. McElmurray is a writer of enormous talent who explores the consequences of loss and grace and recovery in this hauntingly beautiful story of her life."
—Gwyn Hyman Rubio, author of *Icy Sparks*

"Not only a deeply moving personal story that takes great courage to tell, but also a beautiful and haunting exploration of the nature and the meaning of motherhood and love. McElmurray's lyrical, incantatory voice casts a magic spell."
—Janice Eidus, author of *The Celibacy Club*

"In this fresh, painfully honest, but very wise and beautifully written book, Karen McElmurray tells us how deeply some decisions affect us, ever afterwards."   —Reeve Lindburgh

"Karen McElmurray presents her story with poetic clarity, stark honesty, and—above all—a resounding grace. I can't imagine a better memoir being published this year. It is heartbreaking not only because of its subject matter, but also because of its beauty."
—Silas House, author of *Clay's Quilt*

"With astonishing candor and courage, McElmurray parts the curtains of a birth mother's often secret struggles with pain, guilt, and unending loss, and, with the vision of a poet, leads us on an unforgettable journey of awakening, forgiveness, and love. This powerful memoir is a work of stunningly intimate confession transformed into lyrical brilliance, and, perhaps more importantly, gives her son—and, in turn, all adoptees—a redemptive look at a birthright lost and found."   —Jeanne Braselton, author of *A False Sense of Well-Being*

SURRENDERED CHILD

Association of Writers & Writing Programs

Award for Creative Nonfiction

Surrendered Child

Child

A BIRTH MOTHER'S

JOURNEY

KAREN

SALYER

MCELMURRAY

The University of Georgia Press | Athens

Published by the University of Georgia Press

Athens, Georgia 30602

© 2004 by Karen Salyer McElmurray

Designed by Mindy Basinger Hill

Set in 11.5/14 Walbaum MT

Printed and bound by Edwards Brothers

The paper in this book meets the guidelines for
permanence and durability of the Committee on
Production Guidelines for Book Longevity of the
Council on Library Resources.

Printed in the United States of America

08 07 06 05 04 C 5 4 3 2 1

Library of Congress Cataloging-in-Publication Data

McElmurray, Karen Salyer, 1956–

    Surrendered child : a birth mother's journey / Karen
    Salyer McElmurray.

        p. cm.

    ISBN 0-8203-2681-X (hardcover : alk. paper)

    1. McElmurray, Karen Salyer, 1956– . 2.
    Birthmothers—Kentucky—Biography. 3. Adoptees—
    Kentucky—Identification—Case studies.

    4. Adoption—Kentucky—Case studies.   I. Title.

HV874.82.M36A3 2004

362.82'98'092—dc22

[B]

                                    2001024090

British Library Cataloging-in-Publication Data available

For John, who loves the child I was

and the woman I am becoming,

and for Andrew, the son

I hope to someday truly know.

Contents

CHAPTER ONE

Birth Day

On the day I most want to remember, I'm wearing a strand of jet-black beads and a peasant dress that whips around my ankles in a late-spring wind. I'll wear that same dress months later, after I've given my son away, but on this day I'm pregnant and I'm happy and no other time exists but now. I'm with my best friend, Roslyn, and Mary Pat, a girl in junk-store overalls. Roslyn calls her "pure hippie," which is somewhere between disparaging and complimentary. Mrs. V., Mary Pat's mother, has come with us, and we've all driven down by the river to play. We're parked in a field full of flowers and mud where it rained the night before. The van's tires slide and spin and soon we're stuck there, an opportunity we don't want to miss. "It's meant to happen," Mary Pat says. She perches on the van's tailgate, her hairy legs crossed, and laughs at us as we push and jostle the van. She sits rolling a joint from the bag in her lap and soon I'm gathering daisies with Mrs. V. and Roslyn.

This day is so beautiful I can't bear to remember it, the daisies white and yellow, our laughter easy, sunlight and smoke floating past on the river. My best friend makes me a garland to wear in my hair and I dance for all of them in my bare feet on the grass. Mrs. V. tokes and exhales and watches me. "You're the prettiest sight," she says. "Just a vision of motherhood." I, myself, have had such visions. I have them, while I dance. I tell myself I'll give birth without drugs while I'm kneeling in this very field. I'll lick my son clean and whirl with him like a dervish. I'll baptize him in the river and all our sins will float past.

As I dance I lift the hem of my dress and try to kick my heels together and I slip in the damp grass. This, in itself, could have been a tragedy. Three stoned women. A fourth, free of all drugs since her sixth month of pregnancy, brought to labor a month early and only a stuck-in-the-mud van to rush her to the hospital. Fortunately, none of that happens. Mrs. V. and Roslyn scoop me up and set me on my feet, while Mary Pat lies back in the van, laughing. I am fine, but there is a true tragedy nonetheless. As I fell, I twisted my strand of beads around my fingers and they broke, scattering in the grass. They're glass beads, and they came from a dime store on Main Street in the eastern-Kentucky town where my mother was born. She wore them to high school and she wore them to work at the diner where she met my father, and I've worn them since she left us the year before. I've refused to have anything to do with my mother, and yet I kneel in the grass and hunt for each and every glass bead. "I'll string you another one," Mary Pat says, meaning one of the strands of woven love beads that are her specialty. I want nothing less than my jet-black beads and so we hunt and hunt. Before late afternoon they're restrung, the beads that are my only connection to my mother. One tragedy is thus averted.

The true tragedy is that, years later, I'm not sure this day hap-
pened at all, at least not in this particular way, in this particular
field beside a river. The tragedy is that memories collide with the
way things really were, and the way things were becomes merely
what I want to remember. And I do not, as hard as I try, remember
much about laughter and the color of flowers from the spring and
summer of 1973, the year I relinquished my son.

Later that summer, on the day before I gave birth, I was buoyant
with contractions and too little sleep and I was ready, almost, to
ride the elevator up and back down like a boy I'll call Joe and
I did at the shopping mall, when we skipped an afternoon of
school. There'd be no skipping this time. Joe was guiding my
wheelchair. He was my husband and he was one year older than
I was.

"Nothing but a baby," said a woman in the back of the elevator. She peered at me over the rims of her cat-eye glasses, and
her voice was slurred as whiskey. She was holding hands with
a little girl with lace-edged socks and she wet her forefinger,
dabbed at a deep, stitched cut near the child's eyebrow.

She didn't mean me, of that much I was sure. I was no baby,
even if I was having one. I was with it. I was in charge, steady
as we go. I'd found momentum, nine months' worth, and this
was the final showdown. I was ready to give birth as if it were
an everyday affair, casual as buttered toast or sex.

"Nothing but a baby her own self," the woman said again,
looking right at me this time.

I wasn't a baby, but I was close to it. I could remember as far
back as three years old, to a morning I hid in a closet full of boxes
and coats that smelled of cigars. I believed sometimes I could
remember the sound of water as I turned in my mother's body.
And now? I was full-to-bursting with baby, with this tumult of
flesh that had gathered in my own womb. I was a teenaged girl

married to a teenaged boy, and we had decided to give our son away at birth. I was sixteen and I was waiting for the future to happen, but it already had, in ways I'd discover for the rest of my life.

For twenty-five years, I will have only a few facts. My son, relinquished to adoption on the day he was born, was named Brian Keith McElmurray by the Kentucky Department of Social Services. I know that he was born very early in the morning, after a hard two days of labor. I know that he weighed six pounds and something when he slid from my womb, the only time I ever heard him cry. I know that I was allowed, by law, to refuse to relinquish my son to my father who, two days after the birth, told me how he'd stood looking through the hospital nursery window and wondered that such a new being could so resemble his own father, a Standard Oil service-station man who died when I was nine. I know that this is the only secondhand glimpse I ever had of my baby's face.

By 2000 I will know more than I could imagine and by 2002 I will know more than that, but in 1998 I will be told only what is permissible by Kentucky adoption law. Twenty-five years after his birth I finally will receive a letter from the Kentucky Department of Social Services, my first irrefutable proof that my son had a life beyond my own imperfect memory. The letter, dated January 15, 1998, states:

Dear Ms. McElmurray:
In response to your request to place information in the adoption/ case record of Brian Keith, this is to let you know that your letter/ request has been placed in his adoption record. To date, our agency has had no contact with him or the adoptive family since he was adopted by a Kentucky family in 1974. If he should ever contact our agency in the future seeking information about his birth family, we will advise him of your letter/request. Under Kentucky's current

adoption law, KRS 199.570, we can share the following nonidentifying information about the adoptive parents.

The adoptive father was born in 1936 and had his Ph.D. in math.
He was a professor at a large university. The adoptive mother was
born in 1938 and also had advanced degrees in math. She taught
part-time at the college level. Both enjoyed good health and had
more than adequate resources to provide for a child or children.
Brian Keith had adjusted quite well to the adoptive parents and
they to him. The adoptive mother enjoyed being a mother and
housewife. Our agency has no current information on the adoptive
family. I hope this information is helpful to you. For your information, Brian's birth date as given in our record is June 21, 1973.

> *Sincerely,*
> *Violet Nolan, Program Specialist*

By the turn of the century I will know the truth, but first there
will be years of partial truths and unconnected facts, accrued
like stray traces of dust. A paper trail that might have led, had
I known how to follow it, to irrefutable truths about what it
meant to bear a son and give him away on that long-ago day
in 1973.

The day before the birth, I woke just after midnight in a room
shadowed by the floodlights Joe's father kept on for his coon
hounds. Damian, my Siamese cat, slipped out from the bend of
my knees. We both often got out of bed at that time of night,
the cat for a midnight kitchen raid and I to stand at the window.
White and liver-spotted dog coats, night moisture on glass, all
of it gleaming and cool. Pain in my lower back woke me this
night, a tightness starting in my back and moving down, pulling
between my legs. Not sure yet that this was labor, I raised my
hand to the window. A thin hand, and in the floodlight I saw
blue. Pale blue skin, blue bones, right down to the blue, chilled
insides of me.

"Joe," I said. "Wake up. I think it might be time."

"Time?" he asked.

His chubby cheeks were bluish with a two-day beard, and his boy eyes were pale blue with bits of sleep in the corners. He rubbed his fists against them hard, and I thought of the times I'd seen those eyes wide and black, the pupils expanded and electric with acid or speed or whatever else we could drum up from the streets and medicine cabinets of our town. I wished both of us could fall into those pupils, some bottomless and safe place, and never come back again. Instead, I saw blue sparks ignite in the close bedroom air. We were both so small in that light. Blue sparks of fear, his and mine, ignited the scents of socks and sleep. What I didn't imagine yet was the stretching, my own slow opening.

"Oh my God," Joe said.

He was sitting on the edge of the bed, full lips beneath his mustache twitching. He had a habit of drawing his long mustache hairs into his mouth, sucking, especially when he was frightened or angry. I went to him, tucked his head next to my stomach, where he could hear movement. If this child could talk, I wondered, what would be the words? *I'm late, I'm late,* like the rabbit in *Alice in Wonderland. I want to stay here,* the baby might say, *in this soft place of blood.*

Joe and I had a plan of sorts down pat. We'd prearranged with his parents, Rose and Joseph, with whom we lived, to use their station wagon for the hospital run—no fooling around in the middle of the night with hot-wiring the Duster, which was now our car. We envisioned a back-road shortcut to the hospital, a screeching halt at the emergency room, a wheelchair or two and then, in the most undefined part of our plan, a fast-forward version of that thing called *labor,* a painless, tidy version that involved no excretions or wounds, nothing so fleshlike as after-birth.

The real exodus was chaos.

My water had not yet broken, but the pain was shifting lower and had developed an urgent, burning edge. Joe threw on cutoffs and a rose-colored polyester shirt and, still barefoot, opened the door, flipped on the hall switch, and flooded the room with light. Somewhere, in the piles of blue jeans, Marvel Comics, and the circuit breakers and boards that were Joe's hobby, lay a spare set of keys to the station wagon, ready for an emergency. I stood in the middle of this emergency, cradling my belly, which was lower than it had been and needed hands to hold it up.

Years later, a woman friend would describe how her husband helped her with prebirth exercises, lotions and massages and fingers inside her, helping her muscles give. Joe stood in the hall light and I noticed, as if for the first time, his duck-footed way of standing and a wisp of blond hair hiding one blue eye. As I often did, I felt for him something resembling pity, and repugnance, too, a yearning in my gut that churned, nausea settling like it would, weeks from this moment, when he'd try to make love to me again. Now there was the reality that I was contracting, *one, two, three,* . . . Hadn't they said to count the minutes in between?

"Mama," he called down the hall, and more lights came on, more doors opened.

Mama, the mother Joe mostly called Rose, came to the bedroom to look at me. Joseph came, too, and one of the plump twin sisters, Mandy or Candi, plus their fat cat, Effie. The whole, wide bunch of them came to check me out, to see if I was really in labor or faking it, or maybe if I was really still there at all. Two months before, Rose had advocated sending me to a home for unwed mothers in western Kentucky or Texas, some anonymous western place from which I could come back, mysteriously slim and babyless. Such homes reminded me of the game farm where Joe's father was a warden—a home with deceptively comforting pens from which girl-mothers, doe eyed, looked out and tried to decide which place was inside and which was outside.

Rose examined me up close, took my temperature with the back of her hand. She was a large woman with broad hips and arms and thighs. The sleeves of her flowered housecoat trailed across my face, and I could smell bath powders and sweat. I thought of the time Joe had told me about finding an unflushed toilet red with rings of Rose's menstrual blood, and of other times we'd raided her bathroom cabinet for downers or speed from her wide assortment of pills for heart or back or leg or head pain. She was a veritable medicine woman. In the eastern-Kentucky mountains, women could tell the sex of an unborn child by suspending a button on some string in front of a pregnant stomach or by touching that stomach, there or there or there. Rose's hands could touch me that way, urging the child to come out, or urging it to stay in, quiet, telling no one about its birthplace.

Another wave of pain rose, crested. Rose took charge, parting the whole family sea, the hall full of in-laws through which I was guided, an invalid, already entering space, the ozone, an altered consciousness I would never be able to clarify, revise in words or memory to the way it really was. Keys were found. Teeth were brushed, morning coffee made. My cat was banished to the basement, place of potatoes and canning jars and the room decorated by Joe with black-light posters of Hendrix and Black Sabbath. There was no mom's bag of panties, furry slippers, and ladies' magazines to take to the hospital. Instead, a sack was stuffed with a toothbrush and the shirt I'd be able to wear again, once I was small.

There were more obscure preparations, discreet asides. Joe sat with his father in the breakfast nook, receiving private instructions. "Do all you can do and that's all you can do, son." Effie licked at a bowl of cream. The plump twins made white toast laden with sugar and cinnamon and whispered and waited for my stomach to pop right on the kitchen floor. And I imagined this myself. The way I could sink down on the gold-flecked linoleum, my muslin hippie dress rising of its own accord around my knees. They'd boil water and roll bandages made of cast-off kneesocks. Rose and Joseph would each hold a leg and Joe would cut the umbilical cord, neatly, with his Swiss Army knife. They'd bury the afterbirth in the backyard and I'd plant a tree there with my own hands—a birch, my favorite—and I'd lie in bed with the windows open on fall afternoons, listening to the wind turn the clean, silver backsides of the leaves up to the sun.

And maybe I would plant a tree anyway. But that would be later. Now, it was midmorning. After a shortcut via Old Highway 60, a rushed registration at the front desk, and confusion about the fact that I did not have insurance, I was admitted and divested of my brown and gold floor-length dress. I was decked out, instead, in a paper gown and shoes. My frizzy hair was pulled back tight, pinned in place, and I surrendered all my possessions—a love-bead necklace, a wedding band, some large silver earrings—to a manila envelope with my name and address on the front. McElmurray, Karen. Female. DOB, 9/12/56. With reluctance, the on-duty nurse left me with my wire-framed glasses and I thought of rides at the county fair, signs warning you to beware of possible flying objects. I thought of shedding my clothes, walking nearly naked into a tank of warmish water, baptism.

Last, I was shaved, my pubis so efficiently and completely naked I touched myself with shame. I looked as white and vulnerable as kernels in a pod. My mother was the only one who had seen me this way, and I had tucked that time away, hidden it. I was fifteen, an ex-runaway, drug wise, and possessor, already, of lovers in the plural. Slick and shorn, I was a child in a bathtub again, waiting for her mother's hands with the soap. I was eleven and tugging at my first bristly pubic hair. My hymen could have grown back and I could have started over again, unkissed and innocent of the exploits of backseats and drive-in movies. Inside this whiteness, the two soft mounds and the exposed pink fissure, my son pressed down.

"Do you want this in here, or in there?" the nurse asked.

"This?"

She waved a plastic tube in the air, indicated the metal bedpan I'd use. An enema.

I spread my legs, let her insert, squeeze, help me to the metal toilet at the back of the prep room, one more step toward urgency. My bowels, stirred and prodded, released themselves partway before I could sit down, and I looked, again shamed, at my soiled bare legs. Though still at the threshold of birth, I was already getting it, understanding that this was a day of abstinence and release. I'd be denied all foods, water. I'd beg my stepmother, when she came to pay her respects, for the corner of a washcloth to suck on, for moisture. I'd be free of pee and shit, my bowels pristine. And I'd release more than that—words I won't recall, unrestrained shouts, screams, a curse on everything that had come before.

I sat on the toilet, feeling the last of the enema's fluid drain out. My belly, white and huge, rested on my knees and I watched the skin squirm, nudging me to get up, get on with it.

What I want to remember is that in 1973 I am part hippie and part little girl and not entirely good at either role. Vietnam is over and Watergate is in process and my biggest protests are save-the-deer campaigns during hunting season. By 1973, I've worn blue jeans with slits up the leg and fake leather inserts. I've worn them for thirty days straight, been swimming in them, worn holes in their knees. I've frizzed my hair like Janis Joplin and I've done acid in a junkyard by night, but none of that has made me belong to the sixties and its hippies any more than I will belong to disco or the eighties.

I am somewhere in between and nowhere at all, and yet at night in my room in my father's house, I try to write stories about my life that tell the truth. I write about wanting love and about headlines from the daily news. "Haight-Ashbury a Haven for Hallucinogens and Love." "Eight Slain Nurses Found Lying in a Pool of Blood in a Chicago Apartment." "Train Tracks Are Bobby Kennedy's Escort into the Next World." I write about coming of age in my generation. Divorce is our common denominator. Our lyrics? "You who are on the road, must have a code that you can live by." We idolize peace symbols and health foods. We know tofu and whole grains can offset the half-life of radiation. Roe v. Wade will determine the immediate futures of our embryos, but we think in the long term. We explore karma and the complexities of reincarnation on another planet. We have learned, by 1973, to love each other body and soul. Our bodies are given, one to another, as easily as a free lunch, our souls experienced in myriad visions called mescaline or windowpane.

Where I am is somewhere between truth and nowhere at all. The truth, distinguished from the facts, is that I do not clearly remember the date of my own son's conception, any more than I remember his birth. I know that it was autumn when I lost my virginity in the front seat of a Plymouth Valiant. I know that it was summer when I gave birth and that I often associate fireworks and July with unspecified sadness. I look at fire and light exploding in a night sky and I feel anger in my chest, desire that wants to explode in every direction, wants to name names, assign dates and responsibilities, a fire nevertheless impotent, sitting heavy and listless in my chest, translating to lethargy and directionless longing. The truth is that what I remember best and least of all is what I can never change. I gave my son away at birth, and no story can change my memory of that.

During the forty-eight hours of my labor, day became night became day, and I forgot place, ceased to recognize the people who were helping me give birth, wheeling me down a long hall. I was being carted from prep to delivery and on the way we passed the waiting room where my father, my stepmother, and my husband were waiting. No one stopped for hair-stroking or sympathies. This was 1973, and births were not as gentle as they are now. There would be no birthing room, no warm bath to slide into when transition came. No back rubs or partner to tell me, "Now, breathe in, out." No little hand mirror to see the head crowning or cameras to record the way the eyes looked the moment they opened.

Pain, at first, was manageable. I was still alert enough to compare it to a stomach disorder or a pulled muscle. A leg cramp. I pictured television sitcoms and how easy it was—camera on the mother, then one, and two, and it was the next morning, the mother luxuriating in her silk pajamas and someone bringing her tinted carnations. I even laughed about it all, tried to make jokes with the nurses about knives under the bed and pans of boiled water, but they knew why I was there. They spoke in whispers when they were near me and I caught words like *unwed, relinquish*. I caught the name of my social worker. I wanted to tell them I *was* wed, but that was beside the point and I was beginning to forget, already, what exactly the point was. My dilation was being measured. I was being given intravenous fluids. I began to beg for ice chips. I wanted my Siamese cat. I wanted my mother and I didn't.

But I was clever, daughter of a high-school math teacher. I could count—one and two and three and so forth—the minutes between my contractions. I told myself I could outwit them, could pretend the pains were alive and smaller than I was, as small as the characters I believed were real, in the back of the television set, when I was small. I would send them back behind the screen between shows and I told myself I could send away this hurting, too. I'd send it behind a room divider. I'd send it packing on a nurse's tray with the thermometers. I held my breath as long as I could between contractions, promising I wouldn't breathe again if I didn't hurt. I promised this to God. I said every prayer I'd ever known—*now I lay me down to sleep, I pray the Lord my soul to keep.* I breathed anyway and I hurt. I crashed into hurting. I panted. I rolled onto my side, held my belly like a large stuffed dog.

They didn't like this. They told me lying on my side would slow things down, discourage the birth. I obeyed but was sly, waited for the nurse to check the next patient or for the next shift and I turned again, curled up, knowing that it wouldn't matter. The birth was discouraged already, had been for weeks. I was over nine months pregnant, ten, if the doctor's calculations were correct. Inside me, the baby wouldn't let go, wanted to hold on, feared what came next. I felt him holding on to tissue and muscle, refusing to ride the next wave out, to slide down me in a current of blood. I felt small feet pointing, the small, curved arms. My son was a swimmer. He turned and shifted, treading amniotic waters, refusing all coaxing. He waited. Sonograms showed this, the wary positioning. Minutes passed like this. Hours. We were entering the next day, my son and I, and he lingered. He was afraid his world would be like his mother's. He wasn't sure he could count on his next meal or on where he'd sleep a week from now.

I was at hour twenty, twenty-one, twenty-two. I was counting ice chips and the changing of the guard. Joyce, the midwife, came in to check my stomach. She pressed down hard, located a knee or a shoulder, and I asked her how long was left. She disapproved, I could tell, of the time it was taking and I pushed down hard and she said, "Not now." She meant it was the wrong wave to ride, that I'd missed the critical point, the right rope to grab between this pain and the next. *Now?* I asked myself again and again. *Now? Never?* I'd already signed the papers that proved I didn't want this baby, and that was why he wasn't coming out. *Ever.* I rolled onto my side again, made myself smaller. The doctor came, a youngish man wearing slacks and a polo shirt and, I imagined, golf shoes with argyle socks.

He said, "What's all this I hear?"

I'd been bad. When no one was looking, I'd drunk melted ice from the bottom of a cup. I'd begged for drugs. I had persisted in lying on my side and that, he said, was what was keeping us behind schedule. He was sitting at the bottom of my bed, legs crossed, a golf-shoed foot kicking up and down. He was thinking *spinal block*. He was thinking *episiotomy*. He was thinking *run-of-the-mill, a good show, and now this*, a possible C-section at midnight. He wanted dinner and a scotch on the rocks. He wanted a clean, quick delivery, a precise snip and the baby slipping right out, then a stitch or two and it was over. But I'd been bad, had lain on my side for hours and that, he said, had made the baby turn. *Turn* made me think of meat done on one side. It made me think of pillows, fresh when you flip them over.

He smiled at me, half efficiency, half impatience. He'd read my chart. I was giving my son away and worse, I had no insurance. I wouldn't be back for the three-month checkup, for him to deliver the baby after this one and the one after that. So he ordered tests. He planned the strategy, the quickest and costliest route. I was weighed and measured, photographed from the inside out. I lay looking at the monitor where I saw my baby's heart beating on a screen right next to me, and I spread my hand over the light, fingers wide. I could almost feel him, the warm breath, the baby skin. I knew he was alive, waiting for me to ask him to come out, but I held on to him a little longer.

Hour thirty, thirty-one, thirty-two. I'd dilated to ten and they were checking between my legs regularly now, looking for the patch of scalp to emerge. They'd slipped something in my IV, a sedative maybe, and I couldn't have turned on my side now if I had wanted to. I heard screaming from a room down the hall. A woman, her voice high and sharp. But it wasn't a woman. It was me. I was screaming for my mother, screaming for Damian, my Siamese cat, the one Joe had always hated, her red eyes at night and her meow like a baby's and how I loved her more than I loved him. Pain was picking me up, taking me along for a ride I didn't love. I'd ridden down back roads in the country with Joe, the windows down in the rain and the Doors or Steppenwolf playing, and I'd opened my mouth to take it all in, water and the pure taste of acid and the colors that came next. This hurting was like that, and not. The white walls bent on each side of me. They were hands, one and one. They cut me in two, a razor-sharp memory I'd always have.

In grocery-store tabloids people die and come back and tell how they saw a tunnel of light and everyone who'd loved them, in this world and the next. In this world I was wheeled past the waiting room again and I saw Joe there. He was pacing, up and back, wearing a path in the floor. He was walking the perimeter of the room, over, over, and at the center of the room were my father, my stepmother. They were kneeling in prayer. Praying for me. "Father above, forgive her. She's nothing but a child herself. Forgive her for this sin, this relinquishment." And my mother's ghost from 1956 was there, too. She was wearing a plaid skirt and a sweater and she was leaving Forbes Air Force Base Hospital. She was holding me, a newborn. Her eyes were squinted, and she was tired and bruised where she'd spent the night before being opened from the inside out. She'd told me this, again and again. How much it hurt for me to be born. How someday I'd understand that birthing and pain are exchangeable, a fact as true as sin. She'd spent the night, she told me, screaming. Her throat ached with this screaming and mine did now, with words I couldn't say. *Relinquish. Surrender. Now.*

Hours forty and forty-one and forty-two and more. I'd changed my mind, I said. I didn't know it would be like this, me, reduced to whining. I begged for favors, for the cold wash-rag corner, for mercy. I was a low hum in my own ears. It was a chorus, a tide, my own blood churning. It was a thick music that roiled and in it I heard my heart emptying, chamber into chamber, room to room. "If I'd known band camp was like this," I said, "I'd never have come." I'd have sent my clarinet back, the one I used to play in fifth grade, the one my mother never liked. I'd have changed my mind and never let myself be touched, never have laid myself down for any man and opened my thighs, invited birth inside.

I was opening, in another room, one with nurses and masks and a bed made of steel where they tucked me in. They were telling me to push one more time, bear down hard. But I was stoned on pain and sedatives. I was floating. I was looking down on me, a body I didn't own, feet bound in stirrups, hands at my sides, palms up, as if a blessing could float down, contrition on a pretty slip of paper, right from heaven. "All I want," I told them, "is a glass of water. Someone to touch me, gently. Bearing down," I said, "is a joke." *Bearing down.* That's crayons on paper. It's trip after trip down the long path from my grandmother's, spring water that tasted sweet in a jar. My mother used to do that, carry water from a well down a long path. My body, like water, had no weight. No intent. I was a floating book of vision, a triptych, the opening of my body revealed to me frame by frame. I was a movie of someone else giving birth. *And why*, I asked, *should I give birth, should I give at all? I can pray, too.* I knew the verses. *Shall I cause to bring forth and shut the womb?* Bearing down was the final act. The finale. My son leaving me and me leaving him and the opening that was me would shut, a door to a tomb. My heart turned to stone. Me. Drowning in blood and sorrow.

Then they were propping me up. "Just a prick," they said. A sharp little pinpoint to the spine, one I'd hardly notice, but I flinched, feeling them entering me, taking away the last of what I felt. They told me to lie still, lie down and shut up. "It's what you've been wanting for hours," they said. I didn't know what I'd been wanting for hours, but I lay down. I was quiet and a good girl, and because I was good it filled me up right away, no coy drug, a wonder of numbness instead. It seeped down my spine, a cool river, and I was floating down with it, waiting. I was floating, quiet and hot in the cool river becoming me. Quiet and hot and then longer and longer, my legs and my feet far away and then gone altogether. I was nothing but above the waist. I was cut in two, cut off forever from my baby boy. I'd never know the truth of this part, how he left me. Something oozed out of my deadened lower half, *down there,* as my mother always said. I was ashamed, of what could have been shit or blood or anything undesirable, all the things you want to hide.

Horrible, you say, to go there, especially now. To describe your son and his last moments with his mother in the same context as something vile, as refuse, as waste.

I heard him crying, and then that was all. It was the last moment there was, and I felt them take him from me and I said, "Tell me. Tell me he's okay." And reluctantly, they did.

The truth is that for years after my son's birth, I can't feel a thing. I like it, the way I'm hollow enough to listen to my own sad heart. I'm breathing in, not out. I'm subject to the consequences of my own actions, but I can't pinpoint them, these actions. For which action should I seek absolution? When and where and how did I set my life in motion? I'm a leaf shivering in midair, but I can't spin to the ground of myself.

The truth is that in the summer of 1997 I went to the desk at an OB-GYN's office, the place that delivered my son, and asked them for a date. Asked? I demanded. I groveled. I made up a story about how unless I knew the truth of when I'd given birth I'd succumb to a devastating illness. A secretary found the correct file in the back room, but was still reluctant. Giving me the truth, she said, might have ramifications. She looked me up and down, sniffing out the potential dangers of giving out information about a birth that was unusual to an unfriendly participant in that birth. Me. The birth mother. She discussed this with a co-worker and, shielding the file from me in her arms, gave me a date—July 7, 1973. That was all.

The truth is that two months later I joined an Internet discussion group made up of birth parents—mostly mothers—and adoptive parents and adoptees. All of us typed in stories about the consequences of adoption in our lives. I recognized these stories of near suicides, of deep loneliness at holidays. Stories of body memories, the inexplicable uterine cramps at certain times of year, reminders of births no one discusses in the real world beyond the computer screen. I recognized myself in these anonymous stories of baby showers and birthday parties, always other people's stories about festive cakes and little shoes, sentimental reminders of birth, the one birth that happened but never did. "I can't seem to love anyone," one birth mother said. "It's like I'm already in love," she said, "with someone I'll never meet."

The truth is that in 1997 I talked on the telephone with a private investigator whose name I obtained via this same Internet group. Through her I finally contacted Kentucky's Department of Social Services. They sent me the letter and the nonidentifying information and a different date altogether—June 21, 1973.

One of these dates, July 7 or June 21, is my son's birthday, so I'm told, and for years I will celebrate both. I will dream, on those nights, of houses and cellars and unwanted babies and the children I will no longer birth. I will grow tired and sleep through those days and surrounding days, swimming through southern summer heat and grief, through flat, warm waters of a birth date I truly can't recall. Or I will summon this grief on other days, on occasions for celebrations as small as the purchase of a new pair of earrings. The truth is I will live on the cusp, in a world between fact and imagination. I will become a writer, live in the world of language.

The truth is for thirty years I will not see my son's face. I will see a face I have created. It is one I want, one I believe in, although I will not hunt down the truth by knocking on the door of unsuspecting people, one of whom may be my son. The truth is my son is a man now, a boy-turned-man walking through the streets of a city or town or along paths or riverbeds. I have been caught on the cusp, prisoner of my own making in a world in between. World of past and future. I relive them again and again, those times. The days before the birth. All the days since.

I relive again and again the time before my son's birth, the mornings I grew sick with the scent of my cat's fresh-cut liver, the days in high school where no one knew I was pregnant until my sixth month. I'd lied to myself about my body, sat in home-room, between my second and third months, feeling the kick and kick of my womb. I read my literature assignment, *The Yearling*, and said to myself, a daily mantra, *No baby, there is no baby.* I'd heard about abortion too late, and abortions, in 1973, happened in faraway places like Detroit, reached only by plane. I wore pants so tight they hurt and bulky T-shirts and sweaters. I prayed my father's live-in girlfriend wouldn't draw her own conclusions from the long-unused box of tampons under the sink in the bathroom we shared.

And after the sixth month? My life as a runaway was beds in halfway houses and free clinics and no real medical attention until after my eighth month, and after that, marriage to a boy one year my senior whom I'd never heard say the word *pregnant.* And then, ten months pregnant, according to my calculations, and I still wasn't ready to give birth. And after that?

All things passed away, and they did not, just as I was and was not a mother from that birth day on. I stayed in the hospital for the customary five days, tucked away on an upper floor with the old and the infirm, serenaded by a woman who believed it was 1887 and that she was riding the trains to her past. "Freight train," she sang, "carry me back." But there was no going back. I had decided, not Joe or my family or his, to give my son up for adoption. "How can you still be married," friends asked, "and give away your child like that?" *How*, I wanted to ask, *can I be a child and keep a child and be married to one?* This answer was inadequate, but it was all I could offer for a long while.

What I want to do is remember the truth. But what if there is no one truth? No exact date in the past? No real present, but only an accumulation of memories of the past and wishes for the future? Then there is the story. I want to remember it all like a story about family, chapter to chapter, until I reach a happy ending. A story, you say, is always more palatable than the truth. In a story, whether or not one remembers accurately, one re-creates. Voilà. If you cannot remember a place, a time, a moment, the feel of living flesh, create a world. Make one you can live with.

Because of such stories, everything should get easier. All glimpses of the past should be black and white, backdrops with the clearest images, the most obvious delineation of sunlight and shadow. No arbitrary references to this event or that, no invisible props, no sheer curtains with phantom outlines of misunderstood people or actions or thoughts. In this way of remembering, all things have a definite intent. Tastes are real, both sour and sweet. When a hand is lifted, pointing the way out, we follow, certain of where we will go, certain a new scene, clearer than the last, will always come next.

With such stories, emotions should fall into place. We should know when to love, when to feel the most pointed of dislikes. Love equals union and loss equals regret, but nothing more overwhelming. We know when to hold on, when to let go. Guilt, that amorphous, clinging creature, is tossed to the wayside, hidden as the curtain falls. A spade is a spade, a villain is a villain. With this remembering, everyone makes mistakes and when we do, they ignite, pure and startling. They burn up in the proper time, like

paper, mere script. They float up into the expectant air, ghosts ris-
ing and rising, and the audience applauds, relieved, ready to enter
the next pure moment.

Years after my son's birth, I went to the head of an eastern-
Kentucky hollow with a married artist who had become my
lover. We visited a house he called the Resurrection. The painter
who lived in this house had covered his walls with images from
the book of Revelation. Horses reared up from the red waves of
a lake. Candles larger than humans cast painted yellow light on
the faces of the drowned, the unrepentant. Angels were clothed
in cumulus clouds and they held fire in their bare hands, warning us about light and dark, about death and life and those who
do not believe.

While my artist lover and the painter talked in the front
room, I slipped down a hall, looking for the kitchen and a glass
of water. This hall was the most startling place of all. It was
painted many shades of white, from cool and shadowy to a deep
and impenetrable chalkiness I want to touch. At the end of
the hall, in an alcove before the kitchen, there was a painting
of Mary. Not regal or virginal, but Mary as she looked when
she was pregnant by God. She held her hand under her nine-
months-swollen belly and was ready to lie down in new-mown
hay in a field, ready to give birth. "God," it said at her feet,
"shall wipe away all tears from their eyes; and there shall be
no more death, neither sorrow, nor crying, neither shall there be
any more pain: for the former things are passed away."

In Joe's parents' house again after the hospital, I sat in the tub
in the afternoons and squeezed streams of mother's milk from
my breasts into the bathwater.

"What're you doing in there?" Joe asked from outside in the
hall. "What are you doing?"

I let him in, let him sit on the edge of the tub while I soaped and scrubbed. I let him wash my back and reach into the water and touch me, though I felt no trace of desire. Just once, on such an afternoon, Joe tried to talk with me.

"We need to talk," he said. *Talk.*

I felt so eager to talk, so filled with eagerness that I must have been like something white and hot, a bright light that made him shut his eyes and be silent. I wanted to gather them to me, all the lost beads of love and birth and afterbirth, string them new again on a string that would never break. I wanted to fill up all the silences we'd made, to replenish all the terrible, lost love for our son, but I had no definition for love, nor would I have one for many years to come.

ᴖ CHAPTER TWO

Mother,
Come at Night

You say that any story about motherhood should begin with our first definitions of love, our own mothers, their faces near ours as we drink from their breasts. What I remember is not my mother's face, but her hands. I have photographs that show these hands. Hands on her hips. Hands holding on to me as my father photographs the two of us on a picnic by a lake. Hands holding a bottle of Pepsi-Cola to my lips. Hands leading me down a sidewalk with the two of us wearing our Sunday best. The photographs show my mother's hands as beautiful, but they weren't beautiful at all. If I look closely at these photographs, I remember her hands as they really were. Fine cracks lined the knuckles, white skin flaked and peeled from her fingers. Sometimes her hands bled.

To remedy these hands, my mother always wore gloves to bed. Magazines advertised such beauty treatments. Gloves drenched with Estée Lauder or Avon lotion would produce lovely fingers and palms, delicate flesh. My mother wore the less expensive dime-store variety of lotion, bottle after bottle of it that never seemed to do any good, never seemed to heal her hands, wounded from sink after sink of foamy dishwater, endless floors she'd scoured, square inches of house she'd shined to gloss over our lives, the unclean, unspoken love. She believed that if the things of our lives were clean enough, beautiful enough, we would not have to look at the darkness at the center of ourselves—mistakes, desire, the mess that bodies make, the unloveliness we exuded.

And it was not only to her bed that my mother wore her gloves. It was to mine, late at night, more ordering of things, sheets, pillows, me. I remember the touch of those gloves, the snagging of dry skin inside cloth as she touched my hair, the touch of gloves against my neck as she tidied blankets and sent me into dreams she never knew. "Lie still," she'd say. "Don't kick the covers." I'd be quiet until I heard her clothed finger click off the light switch. I'd keep all of me completely still and go to my dreamed place, place of mystery, place halfway between sleep and not. It was a place my mother would never have predicted, could never have explained.

That place was a black box, a box without sides or bottom or top, a holy place without floor or ceiling or cleanliness or not, a box picked up by something I couldn't see and thrown far, very far into space or time, any place without limits. Inside that box I'd fold myself small as I could get, knees tucked, arms around myself. Inside that box I'd cease to breathe, be. I'd have blood that simply moved and a final blessed ceasing of beautiful. Sometimes I'd stay in that place all the way until morning. Until the morning and the box had dimensions, until it had edges with the feel of cloth, of gloves that smelled of lotions and cleaning fluid. I have no photograph of this safe place, or of the mother who took me there.

There are other photographs of my mother. The earliest one I've seen is from the early 1940s. Mounted in a fancy oval frame painted gold, the photograph is of my mother seated beside her sister Ruby, and they are both wearing brand-new striped dresses. My mother, in this photograph, is blonde headed and meticulous. She has wide-set eyes, small features, and she is looking at the camera in a slightly off-center, puzzled way. She has careful hair, the straps of her dress are aligned, her posture erect. Ruby, the younger of the two sisters, looks both disheveled and angry.

Their hair has been cut that very day, by my grandfather, whose method is bowl-and-scissors. They have short, uneven bangs and an above-the-ear bob. My aunt has made hers even more lopsided by tugging it into wisps and peaks. That day they have been to Prestonsburg, the largest town near Dwale, which is a post office and country store they call their hometown. They have bought supplies, and a traveling Jewel Tea man has taken their picture for twenty-five cents, paid for with my grandfather's first-of-the-month miner's pay.

In this photograph the girls show me two paths my life could take. There is Ruby, ready to fall into a future full of shadows and visions of herself as Jesus crucified. Forty years after the photo, Ruby fell into spells the family vaguely called seizures, hallucinations of the Holy Ghost carrying her off because she was an angry and thus unholy woman. The other path in this photograph is my mother's, a way pure and white, a way so clean I can almost believe there was no shadowed valley in my childhood, or in hers.

In another photograph my mother is thirteen going on twenty. The photographer has tinted her cheeks and her checked shirt, which has sleeves ironed in neat cuffs. Another picture, taken when my parents were dating, shows her wearing a wide-skirted gold dress and standing with my father by a car with fins. "Now there," my father has written at the bottom, "there is you a couple."

There are few photos of the two of them in the first year of their marriage. In 1955, he took her to what must have seemed a foreign country. From her eastern-Kentucky world of mother and father and two sisters and a brother, she landed in Kansas, wife to an Air

Force boy who once liked racier women with names like Goldie. A boy who liked a normal amount of clutter, a normal share of intimacy.

A later photo. My parents outside the Forbes Air Force Base Hospital in Topeka, Kansas, with me in their arms, new infant, capable of watery shit and spit-up, of colic and fretfulness. My father, in this photo, squints at the sun and has not shaved off the beginnings of a mustache. My mother looks ravaged, new wrinkles beside her eyes, a severe smile. Much later, I would look at this photo and hear her saying to me, "Don't. Don't let them touch you like that." Them. I knew she meant men and their desires. And giving birth? Why, it was a thing you couldn't even talk about, a thing of blood and sweat, of the squalor of imperfection.

By 1960 they had moved back to Kentucky with me, to Lexington, where my father finished a degree in education. In a photo from that time, we're home for a visit to Dwale. I love the tilt of my mother's head, her slightly flirtatious smile as she looks at my father, the picture taker. She's twenty-four and standing next to my aunt Ruth, who's holding me on her hip. I'm four. My mother is wearing pedal pushers and has her manicured hands on her hips. I can see through the crook of her elbow, up the hill to the smokehouse and the mulberry tree. Mulberries, my mother told me then, are unclean, possessed by tiny worms that eat the fruit, and you, from the inside out. Eat away at you like dirt would if your bare feet touched the ground, like the black on the palms of stranger's hands or the unnamed filth on the soles of our shoes. In 1960, you say, the world was still innocent. Love had a chance. There had not yet been missiles in Cuba, assassinations in Dallas, or riots in Mississippi, no runaways or love beads or hallucinogens. In this photograph, my mother's face still looks happy, and the only hint of anger is the way she narrows her eyes and frowns. Any shadow of anything else, why, that could be the glare of sunlight on Abbott Mountain reflected in her eyes. Behind her head is one blank window of the house where she was born.

I want to lay these photographs side by side by side and look at them until a story emerges—my mother's joyful face, my own birth, her descent into obsession. Yet there is no beginning, no definitive place called ending in the story of my family and the story of my relationship to my own mother's love. In another photo, 1963, it is irrefutable—a shadow has crossed my mother's face. Call it sunlight or clouds or presentiment. I am at the edge of this 1963 photograph. I am a slip of hand, a lock of hair, just above the roof of the car where my mother is standing. I am small, but a hand is already unclenching in my heart.

I study this photograph over and over and over, trying to see what will be born in me. I lie in the dark in my bed in the place I now call home, and I touch my own beating heart and try to remember where my story began.

By 1963 we were living in Lynch in Harlan County, where my father taught high-school algebra and geometry and trigonometry. This place was a bastion of grime. "Even the rain here," my mother said, "is thick with soot." It blacked the walls of our roadside trailer. It was in her hair and mine, and it colored the story of the world as my mother saw it. Dirt, she said, was everywhere. It was on the seats in diners, in the air we breathed. "Don't go near those Estep children," she told me when we saw the dozen or more of these Esteps, all children from one family, walking down the hill past where we live. "Snot nosed and oily haired," she said. "Whatever they have, it's catching."

Then I was set loose in this public world of other children, the soiled world of school. In school, I feared the edges of chairs, the snag, the run or tear that might travel down a leg or up a sleeve, follow me home, betray my inability to remain untouched in the outer world I now had to visit daily. I wore white tights and I feared the oiled wood school floors, the mud beneath the swings in the school yard, the accidents of glue and paints. One afternoon I did fall, smudging my white tights, ripping a large hole in one knee. I asked my first grade teacher to write me a note for home. "Please excuse," I asked her to write, "the knees of these tights that will, I'm sure, come clean in the wash." My teacher looked at me, bewildered, and I pretended I was joking. I wrote her a poem about sheep and clouds.

At home, I began to know the consequences of accidents, of things damaged. Alone in the bathroom, I spilled a bottle of fingernail polish on my lap and waited for the sound of my mother's footsteps outside the door, her hands, her voice, "Don't you know anything? Anything?" I woke in my own vomit with my mother bending over me, angry at the sheets, at me. I saw her on hands and knees on our floor, wiping away scuffs and sunlight, after a little girl named Marsha from down the street visited me with her doll carriage. We had no friends, my mother and father and I. We had each other, and so I began to create stories. At night I lay awake and wove dramas in my head, ones with heroines captured by Indians, transformed into Indian princesses. Afternoons I made up stories starring characters made from pieces of string. I trapped insects in empty pop bottles and created stories of escape from the patio where I played without touching the grass.

My father, too, was subject to my mother's desire to live in a clean world. One shirt for five days of teaching, long enough, so he said, for them to want to take up a collection. She said he should keep clean, like she did. She said he should sweat less, should pee sitting down, should keep the crotch of his underpants spotless, should control that uncontrollable phenomenon, the body. At night I heard the sounds of their lives, the voices sharp as the fragments of glass my mother feared in the bottoms of pop bottles, and in between, the sounds of lovemaking and my father's voice. "I love you," he said. "I love you like no other woman."

I remember afternoon television cliffhangers, shows about

long, sleek cars, a man in a black hat and a kidnapped woman. There were cliffs and a voice at the end of every show. "Who will survive? Who will fall?" Usually I was the one who fell, head over heels into the gray television screen, its static and snow. Sometimes there were bomb-raid warnings, or so I remember it. It was the time of the Cuban Missile Crisis, the Bay of Pigs. I remember my father rushing in the door one afternoon, his arms laden with his briefcase and unmarked student papers. He slammed the briefcase down and said, "They'll shoot us first. The teachers, they'll shoot us every one." I watched the television turn to a gray eye, a crisscross of humming lines. I waited for the falling bombs, the plunge into disaster.

Still, there were nights during this time in Harlan County when we were glad. When my father, listening to his ham radio outfit every evening at seven, called me to his desk and placed the receiver next to my ear and said, "Guess what that is." And I heard television laughter, whistling, Andy Griffith walking toward a fishing pond with Opie. "Isn't it a miracle," my father said, and he meant the miracle of television, soon to be brought to our very own trailer's living room. My miracle was the happiness of such evenings. In the kitchen my mother mixed peanut butter and spun honey in a bowl. She set me at the table with the full bowl and white bread for my supper. She bestowed gifts from her own toiletries—a packet of henna rinse with a movie star on the front for me to trace with on paper, a necklace of her jet-black beads I could wear to bed. On such evenings she was God. She was a woman with beautiful hands who tucked me in and said good night.

One Lynch night, my father wore shorts for the first time. I remember them as Bermuda-style, long, baggy, respectable, but men seldom wore them. They were khaki, and his legs beneath them were white with black dress socks. After the hero in adventure movies who wears a madras shirt and a white helmet, my mother called my father Jungle Jim. This, and her laughter, made him angry.

With this laughing, he saw himself back in Dwale, at the bottom of the road below his new sweetheart's house. He remembered how this new sweetheart, my mother, had long-fingered hands and smelled of Evening in Paris. Then, he had never so much as touched the pointy cups that held her breasts, but there was a promise. Then, she breathed against the fine hairs on his earlobes. He felt her laughter against his neck and shivered with the sound of ice in a glass when she brought him Co-Cola at the Big Y Drive-In, where she was a curbside waitress.

This laughter, now, was full of the military rigidity of dinner. He had fought a war in Korea, seen bodies lying like stick figures along rice paddies or piled in trucks he drove himself. That was not this family's militariness of hands that must not touch their food, of ties that must not be spotted, of crumbs that must not fall. "Jungle Jim, Jungle Jim," she said as her laughter fell on him. Such laughter held the weight of their marriage, its years of tidiness, of sex that left behind abhorrent fluids, stains on sheets, fecund odors of which he had long since grown ashamed. His legs in their Bermudas felt cold and girlish. He was not a man. No man in his own home.

After dinner, a television sitcom, *Ozzie and Harriet* maybe, that happy family of two and two. Peace for a while, but I saw my father's white legs twitch on the footrest of the recliner. He was restless with what he could not be and so he took power where he could find it. He took the night into his fists like hard rules he wanted to break. His feet were small and bare and he sat, studying the shape of his toenails, their rough edges, their longness, remembering the quarrels they'd had over the clipping of nails and sideburns, the possibility of debris trailing down onto her clean floors. He did it now, clipped his toenails right onto those floors, where all of us seemed to hear the fragments from his body whisper down. The clippings were small moons, tiny abominations. Already my mother was up, clean-diaper dust cloth in hand. Her knees were red from kneeling, cleaning after us, this time, later, always, and we saw this, saw what cost we were to her.

Then the night came open. Small sacrileges were not enough. My father, up from his chair, slammed his fist against a wall, threw a shoe against a metal washer, grabbed whichever way of saying no came first. The night was a jar of ink, shattered, and the words that rose up were a chaos that filled me. I was sick with them for years. Some were Bible words, man and woman words. *A man who looks not after his own household, a woman who does not obey, rules of the father.* My mother's rules, clean and white, snapped and broke like bone and she knelt at his feet, cleaning, sifting through fragments of herself. She of the sharp tongue, the unalterable way of our tidy world, was a girl again. I saw her shoulders give and I loved her, how small she was, as small as me, small and afraid. When I remembered this moment, later, I wanted to remember the girl in the photograph in the gilded frame, the girl with the bowl-cut hair and a sister who would later go mad. But she was no girl now. Her words came out, a blessing ripped inside out, a question meant to pare us all down, make us her size. "I never wanted this," she said to my father. "Never wanted you. You think you're a man?" The words took us all in, a family by television light.

And then I was carried to bed, to be kept safe. Through the cracked-open door, their shapes crossed and collided. Hours wove and unwove in the hall. A blanket settled on me, damp and heavy, and I couldn't kick it off. I dreamed I saw my mother shirtless and my father reaching for her small breasts. Later, I will remember a well at my mother's mother's house, the way a bucket careened down, and I will remember my family as a rope that burned my hands as I tried to hold on.

Later that night I went in to them again in my thin blue

nightgown. I stood between them, my mother with her red eyes and her angry mouth, my father in his chair again, his head in his hands. He came to me and settled on one knee, begging my forgiveness. "I promise you," he said. What he promised was *never again,* but *never* unfolded like a black box made of side after side. The next morning, my father drove me to school, tires spinning, racing with the aftermath of anger and the scatter of gravel in our wake. Their voices would become shadows in my memory, ones that bent over my bed, both loving me and meaning me harm.

I became her obsession, my body, its crevices and discharges, its unpredictabilities. By 1966 or 1967 we had moved to Frankfort, in central Kentucky, where my father became accountant for the public school districts. I was convinced, before we moved there, that Lexington had grass as blue as the vast sky in a child's drawing. I was convinced that in this new town, in this subdivision with the new house we'd bought, we would be happy. I was nine, going on ten. Then I was twelve, going on thirteen, and still she knelt naked beside the bathtub, cleansing me. I was a photograph to her, a long-ago baby on a bed, her hands supporting me. I was not a child become a girl soon to become a woman. I was an inconvenience, a body that refused to stay the same.

We were neighborhood oddities, the two of us. The talk of the block. She seldom left the house, hid around corners when well-meaning church ladies came calling. I left the house, but only within limits. On Saturday afternoons, I stayed on the back patio, within the exact perimeters my mother had drawn. I was not allowed to touch the grass beyond the concrete, even when other children came close, dared me. "You're weird," they said. And they were right. I had cat-eye glasses and knobby knees. I believed myself so unbeautiful that for art class I painted an oval of muddy colors with strings glued on for hair and called this me. Mrs. Moore, the art teacher, took me aside and told me the secrets of beauty. Makeup, new clothes, a dab of cologne behind an ear, she said, never realizing that these things were as impossible for me as the feel of grass beneath bare feet. I was not a child, not a young woman, not even a body, most days. I looked down on myself from a great distance. Someone else moved my legs.

In this new neighborhood, this new town, I found distance, but only from myself, from the body I inhabited but often wished to leave. On Sunday afternoons the three of us went driving, a diversion my mother loved. We drove through other people's lives, ones happier, wealthier, more expansive than our own. We drove around downtown so we could see where it was my father went in his day life away from us, the parking lot, the office. We drove around in subdivisions on the east side of town, well-groomed streets that had houses with chandeliers, immaculate patios, and goldfish ponds. My assigned spot for these outings was in the front seat between them, my father's unhappiness on one side, my mother's envy on the other. I longed for the backseat, a window, a place to make myself small, away from their voices and plans, but this was not allowed. What I allowed myself was imagining, myself running over the immaculate lawns, where I'd be happy. I'd feel the damp grass on the soles of my feet and a woman in a silk blouse would call to me from an open doorway. "You," she'd say, but she wouldn't be angry. She'd tell me I was lovely.

Another diversion for Sunday afternoons was walking. We'd walk the aisles in discount stores and malls where my mother could admire cosmetics and colognes, potential gifts my father might give her for birthdays or anniversaries, gifts doomed to fail. She seldom liked our presents, once they were in her possession. "You don't expect me to like that cheap, old thing," she'd say to the tweed slacks or the brooch shaped like a leaf my father and I had conspired to buy her. Our gifts were the wrong size, the wrong color, silver when they should have been gold, gold when they should have been pewter. And so there were afternoons of window shopping, which were a great unhappiness—everything desired, nothing desired, and the three of us unsatisfied and uncertain of what one thing, which possession, could bring us solace. Sundays were aisles and shelves to look at from a safe distance, undeserving as we were of the joy that truly possessing these things might bring, undeserving as we were of the deliverance we saw at night, in television families.

What I remember most is looking in a mirror one afternoon at a Sears store. I was that thin girl staring back. They, mother and father, were talking one aisle over. They were talking about the endless exchanges of merchandise my mother demanded. "Why," my father wanted to know, "can't one thing, one blessed thing, ever be right?" I remember this moment with great particularity, the way I stopped and saw myself, as if for the first time. I was wearing a blue coat with a huge, round collar, my hair was short, and my head seemed small, tiny, and useless atop the hugeness of the coat, my skinny legs and their kneesocks holding me up. And then there was another me, one stepping out of a mirror, taking my own hand. That was the first moment, I realized a long time later, that I truly left myself, the body I was learning to dislike.

That other girl, the mirror one, led me up and up, past the racks of ladies' nightgowns, the console stereos, designer wallpaper and paints. She led me past father, mother, both of them unaware of me, how light I'd grown, how powerful, powerful enough to rise and rise, to leave them behind. She led me out, over the asphalt parking lot full of cars, past houses with people happier than I knew how to be. She led me farther than that, over the horizon, beyond the blue, blue sky to a place where

I was particles, where I was light and far from my own body. Safe. Until a Wednesday in the middle of summer, at the start of Vacation Bible School, when my body betrayed me.

Vacation Bible School was a place my mother dreaded. It meant that even in the summer, I'd have to be made ready for the world, that unclean place my father visited daily when he went to work. During the school year, I had to stay clean and was punished when I didn't. She tested this by making me wear the same clothes again and again. Even my hair remained unwashed for days as if oil and tiny flakes of scalp were signs of what I refused to control. Because of my lack of control of the unclean world, I dreaded Bible School even more than she did, even as the hymnbooks said "Jesus loved the little children," loved them enough to give them a week of summer projects, wooden boxes to paint, shadow portraits of ourselves on the wall, volleyball in the churchyard. I dreaded the projects and the games, with a growing surety that I was inept at all things of the hands. I dreaded my Vacation Bible School peers even more, the way they were certain to laugh at me, dressed in the 1950s clothing of my mother's I was made to wear.

The morning the Bible School was to come pick me up, I sat in the bathroom at home, waiting for her to come clean me. The bathroom was no safe haven, since I was not allowed privacy there. I was not allowed to wipe myself clean, flush away my wastes, shut the door, even, and surround myself with scents, habits, secrets of my own body. I knew the rules. I must sit for ten or fifteen minutes, wait for the body to make its mess, call, "I'm finished," wait for her hands, the folds of tissue that snagged on her rough skin while she wiped my bottom.

This time, the body would not behave. My stomach felt heavy. Something inside me wouldn't lower itself, wouldn't empty me out and vanish into the water underneath me. Something felt thick in my belly, stirred and folded and stretched, leaked out of me, thick and slow. Pain was left in its place, pain tugging at what my mother called *down there*. The insides of my thighs ached. I peed, but between my legs was wetter than that. Wet and thick as the corn syrup she poured on my biscuits at breakfast, and I strained against this, waiting for what oozed out. I focused on the milky glass of the bathroom window, the sunlight. The window was made of squares of glass the size of my hand, and I had sat here often enough to know how long ten minutes took. The sun moved up or down two squares and that was fifteen minutes. I counted, *One Mississippi, two Mississippi.* The bathroom door, as always, was open, and I could see the white wall of the hallway, white enough to reveal any shadows that might be her. I listened for her feet, the wedge-soled pink slippers that she wore, ones that clopped and sucked along the wooden floor.

This particular Bible School morning, I committed a sacrilege. I did not wait. My heart beat hard while I, my body, reached, tore the bathroom tissue, moved the hand into the wetness down there. Pale slit of me, the space between my legs. *Your pretty,* she called it. But to me it was forbidden, unlovely. I looked down on this not-me, the way my hand reached in. Sweetness, syrup of me, brown-red stain on white. I sniffed the tissue, an animal marking, claiming. Scent of musk, of new blood. I want to remember this red-on-white as pretty, as roses on snow. But instead I will think of strings, clots, rings.

"Nastiness," she said.

Through the open bathroom door, her wedge-soled shoes slapped, one-two, one-two. I tried to drop the tissue down, quick, but she saw me.

"I know what you're up to," she said, "don't you think I don't."

Her hand raced around my wrist, pushed my legs open. She saw my first blood falling, refused its dignity. Refuse. Refuse, waste, she told me. What I'd be sorry for from then on. This bleeding would, she said, sometimes come from me in clots and strings. It would be tied to me from then on, tied to what all women are, what all women must become.

"This means," she said as she fastened a cloth between my legs, safety-pinned it to my cotton underpants, "you'll be good for just one thing. It's what all men want."

"And pain," she said as she tugged up my skirt, my Bible School outfit. "It's the pain I felt, having you, and what you'll feel, in time." And I'd be even more trouble, she told me. My father and I, both, with the work the body made, the unintended odors and stains that she had to scrub away until her hands were chapped and stinging.

All day, I sat on the sidelines of church children, an outcast. First there was the long bus ride where I sat by myself, hunting parts of the Bible about the bodies of women. "It is good," I read, "not to touch a woman. Women, in their uncleanness, must be set aside." Others must be turned to salt, or must become forever a mere rib, nothing but a temptation. Later, there were snacks at noon, and I drank sweet grape juice from a paper cup. I sat apart from the relay races on the grass, believing my bleeding was a sickness. My body was at its own great distance, already cursed at this moment of transformation, at this moment of terrible, sloughed-off humanness we cannot control.

What I remember is how at thirteen I lay awake at night, listening to the sound of voices, mother, father. "Why don't you. . . ?" they'd say. "Why do you always. . . ? Why do you never. . . ?" And still I said my wishes, my prayers. *Star light, star bright; if I should die before I wake, I pray the Lord my soul to take.* At thirteen, I saw myself from a greater and greater distance. I read Dostoyevsky and Melville, rode words beyond the world, and the distances I reached were tidy yet barbaric. Words were places no one saw or touched, frozen plains and oceans, the horizon. I took words out of myself and broke them open and spilled them into the dark, stories with me at their centers, ones about love and salvation.

I lay awake and made up stories in which women were heroes. I was Joan of Arc. I was an orphan who found her fortune on the stage. I was kidnapped on a ship on the high seas and I fell in love with gold doubloons and traveled to country after country with names like Morocco, Tasmania, Bali. I was a countess, a gypsy, anything but myself. I told myself stories from *Fox's Book of Martyrs*—ones about saints tied and dipped in wax and set beautifully aflame. Young girls nothing but skin and bones, so light they ascended into heaven on their own. I was that light, light as God. I imagined a box in the dark, above my body, with me inside.

I imagined a mother who could love me. Some days, this mother was my own. She emerged from the bathroom some afternoons, after her rituals and cleansing and combing, and she was transformed, her body sweet with vanilla and her own comfortable sweat. The lines between her green eyes were relaxed, her hands healed and kind. We spent the afternoon eating fruits that left stains on our fingers and our tongues and she told me secrets about menstrual blood and breasts, about the scents and tastes of sex. And I was transformed as well. "Behold," the Bible says, "her daughter came out to meet her with timbrels and with dances: and she was her only child; beside her she had neither son nor daughter."

I was not raised Catholic, but I loved the rituals, the scented smoke and chalices full of sweet wines, the acts of contrition and redemption. And I loved that Mother, the Holy Virgin. At the library, I found every representation of her I could. At some altars, she was gold-crowned and magnificent, the forgiving Queen of Heaven. Or she was plump and flaxen-haired, an ordinary country girl in a blue dress. She was the woman at the well. She was the Sacred Heart, and I imagined placing roses on her outstretched palms. I wanted to believe she came to me at night. She bent over me as I lay in the dark and said, "Sleep, sleep now." She told me about love and forgetting. "Salvation," she said, and this was a kindness.

Someday I will surround myself with images of the Holy Virgin—Our Lady of Guadalupe; the Sacred Heart; Maria Milagrosa, that Miraculous Mother. I will visit chapels whenever I can. I will buy candles for one dollar and sometimes five and light them, always at the altar of the Sacred Mother. What I will believe in is not the Immaculate Conception, but a moment in the past the imperfect color of ivory. I will see myself as a child before sleep, alone with prayers and stories, alone with a fear that gave the dark hands.

"I love you," I remember my father saying to my mother in the night. "I love you like no other woman." I, too, have loved her, woman called Mother whom I resemble. In photographs of her, I see my own tapered hands, a heart-shaped face like mine, our excellent teeth. During moments of uncertainty, I have my mother's nervous laugh. I hear myself changing subjects suddenly, in the midst of conversations, like she does. We both have a propensity for chocolates and cake, and a love of Doris Day movies. She has carried much weight in this world. First there was the responsibility of an aging mother, then of a ninety-year-old father. After they died, there was the home where she lived alone, loverless for all time. I watch my own shoulders bend and bear the weight of love I, too, often interpret as mere duty.

I can only guess at my mother's relationship to her own body. I am over forty now, and much of what I believe is based on that history the body gives us with its postures and lines. Her shoulders are slumped, arms held stiffly at her sides. Her expression is a little girl's, a look of both surprise and sadness that she has been born into a woman's body. She sleeps nervously, hands folded over her chest, always on her back. Not since my father has she held a lover's hand or had a date to the movies. When I visit her, she watches television sitcoms while brushing her teeth, exactly thirty minutes. Our embraces are stiff, bodies barely touching, an awkward pat on the shoulders. The space between our chests, during these embraces, is vast, heavy with our remembrances.

Her remembrances, a contradiction of colors. White house in Dwale, her own mother's long, black hair, the braids of it, held up with tortoiseshell combs. Sugar syrup and butter on a plate, green horsehair sofa, linoleum of gold and blue. These were the home-place things. Things of the only world she knew. And yet she wished for more. Cabinet radio in the front room and Bobby Darin. "I want a dream lover," he sang, "so I don't have to dream alone." He made her want rolled-down socks and saddle oxfords. He made her want more, and less.

Less of the way sulfur water from the well made her palms orange. Less of the row upon row of garden, hoeing until sundown, and the headless black bodies of pigs in the smokehouse and the long walk to the gray toilet down the hill. There must have been more, yet color and dark fell in on her. Dark of bedroom in the back of the house, where she slept in the little bed next to theirs, mother and father. What she might have heard at night sometimes gave the dark the shape of hands. She dreamed hands. Her father's, the nails black moons of coal dust. Her mother's, white with turning the biscuit dough, over, over.

My mother left her own body. It is back there in Dwale, in a house long ago leveled by Highway 23. Maybe it is in the back room of the house, in the bedroom, that place of secrets where, when my mother was in her early thirties, her father lay down and did not want to get up. He imagined a black hole in the center of the bedroom floor, and he called this the place into which the whole world could come crashing down, full of fire and infrequent redemption. This is the place my mother began, the place she never left. "Remembrances," her Bible reads, "like unto ashes."

>⌐ CHAPTER THREE

Hunger

My dreams of Dwale are like this. My mother and father and I are asleep in the four-poster bed in the bedroom off the living room when my father says, "It's her." It's Granny, my mother's mother, who has come in to wake us up, like she always does.

"Morning, this morning," she says. "Fine morning this morning."

The intrusion makes my father angry. "Privacy," he says. "Can't get a bit of it." But from the kitchen there's the scent of breakfast. Biscuits from an iron skillet, with a dab of butter to mix with cane syrup. Fried taters and onions, with slabs of bacon from the smokehouse. Runny eggs with pepper on top and coffee, sweet and light. Soon we're eating, full of food and words of the Lord.

"Give, O Jesus," Pa, my grandfather, prays over our plates. "Give us mercy and obedience to thy loving ways. For He causeth

the grass to grow and the bread to rise. He brings forth abundance, abundance and not, as He sees fit."

Pa prays sometimes to a full table of us. Uncles dipping their fingers in the sweetness, licking and waiting for the holiness to be done. An aunt, ready to touch up her red lipstick or powder her nose. Or my father, hands clenched beside a plate. And me, prayers playing in my head like radio songs. Now I lay me. Fine morning, this morning. Red clouds at night, sailor's delight.

Behind our feasts, our bellies aching with fullness, are times we can't forget. The time my Aunt Ruby tries, again, to take her own life. In the kitchen they boil pots of strong coffee, feed her cup after cup as they walk her, room to room. Her face is sallow and a fine thread of spit trails from her mouth. And there is Pa too, my grandfather, who goes into the back room, lies down, and refuses to get up. His whiskery cheeks are white and he has taken his teeth out, leaving the rubbery gums to slide against each other as he whispers to those waiting at his bedside. They say I am too young to know the reasons a man can come home that way, his hands and his lungs black with coal dust, and him not taking the time to wash at the sink before he curls into himself.

This day, he says, "There's a hole into forever."

"Lord have mercy," my grandmother says. "Where is there such a thing?"

"Right here, below us," he says, and he means the floor under the braided rug.

For a long time afterward, I will remember the round hollow of his mouth.

You say we are made of the stories of our childhoods, those long shadows families cast over us. It was both these stories and their absence that was at the heart of my mother's longing. My father, who loved her, uprooted her once, twice, more. He took her to the Midwest, a veritable desert a thousand miles from eastern

Kentucky. To Lexington, that central Kentucky city. "I believe I'd get lost there," her own sister said about that place of traffic and streets as mysterious as the cosines and tangents my father studied in college algebra. My father took my mother to Harlan, another wasteland, this time of mountains she recognized, but by then she was already descending into what was not exactly madness, but love. Love of cleanliness, of order, of the only way she could make the world stand still.

Her soul, the Bible told her, thirsted. Longed for home in a dry and dusty land, but still my father would not take her home for good. After a year or two at most, he moved us to the blue-grass and a subdivision on the outskirts of another city, where he disappeared days to an office she phoned again and again, with increasing desperation. Was he unfaithful? When was he coming home?

Her world grew smaller and smaller, more confined. A house in a world she feared. Rooms in a house she had not chosen. Herself inside those rooms, a world unto themselves. And always in those rooms, echo of her own mother's voice, echo of her father's visions.

Ghosts that sent her farther and farther into despair.

I remember that house, our subdivision house in central Kentucky, on a day the world turned to ice. I was twelve, going on thirteen, and since before daylight I had been in bed, waiting for her to get me up. Across from my room was theirs, and I could hear my father shaving in their bathroom. Jingles played on his transistor radio—*double your pleasure, double your fun*—and underneath that, I imagined, the scrape of razor against his cheeks. He turned the volume higher for the weather. Snow and ice were predicted before nightfall.

She came through my bedroom door, her shoes slapping one and two. This was the usual ritual—first my father shaved and dressed, then I could get up, be fed, dressed—but today was different. There was ice. She bent over me, straightened, neatened. I was to wait.

"Can't you ever," she said, "lie still?"

She was angry already, about the way I'd kicked my covers, the way my hair was mussed from sleep. She raised the blind beside my bed and that made her angry, too, the way the sky was gray, heavy with winter, the way there'd soon be an accumulation on drive and sidewalk that my father would have to shovel away, leaving his boots filthy with snow and mud. And she was angry, already, about the possible cancellations of work and school. No cancellations had been reported yet, but she could see it already, how she'd never get a thing done like she'd planned. No floors vacuumed, no hours alone to put on her face.

"Can't you ever," she said again, her warm breath beside my ear, "hush and wait?"

At school that morning, we all waited as ice began to fall, as electric lines swayed with ice and the parking lot grew dark and silvery. We hushed, listening for reports and for the drove of buses that would take us home early. That would take me home early and up the subdivision road. I planned how I'd walk carefully, my penny loafers inching between patches of snow, the care with which I'd hold my umbrella as ice fell neatly away from my coat. I'd pretend, I told myself, that we'd had lunch in the cafeteria. That there'd been snacks at recess to ward off the cold. An unexpected lunch at home, I knew, would also make her angry—the extra spoon, the unnecessary spill of cereal into a bowl, the intrusiveness of me.

At home, she was not ready. The two sharp lines between her eyes deepened as she poured my lunch, saltines in a bowl, one with a puddle of milk in the bottom where she had eaten her own cereal an hour before. She dipped peanut butter on a spoon and I ate as I must eat—spoon to cracker, cracker to lips, chew, swallow. I must never touch this food, its greasiness, its salt. I must keep my hands clean, one palm up in my lap, the other at the end of the spoon handle, far away from crumbs and particles and the untidiness made by mouth and teeth and tongue.

Ice fell. Drops frozen in midair, an unpredictability between sky and earth, ice sliding down the kitchen window. A sound to love. Smooth as music. Music inside a windup box my paternal grandfather gave me, long ago. A box with a mirror, a pretend frozen lake with a dancing ballerina. Music hissing and alive. Ice and snow came down and down and I felt comfortable and warm. My hand reached, traced first the edge of the bowl, then the tip of a cracker, made a line through the paste on the spoon. I licked this, tasting sweet and the salt of my own hand. Taste so delicious I ate, on and on, until the spoon was licked clean.

And then she was there, her strong, dry hand. She gripped my wrist, led me, a penitent, to the sink. Snow fell as she washed me, again and again.

"After all I do for you."

And she told about how, now, thanks to me, she must vacuum, she must wipe and shine—floor around the table, vast circle of disarray, crumbs and squalor I had made, and before I knew it, I said the words I meant and didn't mean. "I despise you," I said.

Despise, a word larger than me. Larger than my twelve-year-old self. My palms tingled with this word. It howled a cold wind. It filled my ears, tasted bitter, a residue of her, Mother, the one I wished for. Mother who would stroke my hair and feed me toast with jam. She scrubbed me harder, finger by finger, in between, beneath my bitten nails. She scrubbed so hard that surely they would become clear, these words we have said.

Behind these words are stories I want to know. Stories of mothers and daughters. Her mother. Her mother before that. They are passed down, these stories, mother unto mother. Ones about bad luck. Dogs that don't bark when the moon is full. Mirrors that shine too much. About what women should and shouldn't do. When to cross your legs and when not to. No hair washing when there's the curse. "And a good woman," the Bible says, "giveth meat to her household, girdeth her loins with strength. She is not afraid of the snow for her household. She openeth her mouth with wisdom and in her tongue is the law of kindness." And a woman who is not kind? A woman who is afraid? There are stories of such women.

Imagine one, you say. One woman. Your mother's great-grandmother. Farther back than that, into unnumbered generations. This woman is standing at the back of a house at the base of an eastern-Kentucky hill. Everything moves here. Wind, leaves, six black birds looking down into the grass. She touches the front of her dress, feels the unborn child.

Not now, but in a month, a son will be born to her and she will fear his skin, how transparent and pink it is. Not today, but some day, she will doubt her husband's love. The birds will not disappear, but will shake their feathers as if they are casting off veils of dark water. There will be a day that the earth and the house and the hill behind it will bend into each other and disappear, as if they had never been. Not now, but someday, a huge stone will slide down the hill and for one moment she will see it hover, a perfect shadow balanced directly above her. She will, in that way, be a witness to her own death.

There are, you say, many such women. Women subject to illness, madness, or nothing more than vulnerability. There is your mother, standing in a doorway. Dwale. She is seeing her own mother's face, its sadness. Her own mother, watching as her daughter leaves after another visit home. They watch one another as she walks the path down the hill, goes back, again and again, to a foreign land. Do stories save us from the future?

What are the stays against disaster?

Soon there were more and more eating rules, more and more need for emptiness.

I cleaned my plate at every meal. I scraped up every crumb of my day-old cake, so the plate would glow, so both my face and hers would shine back. We did not believe, in our house, in trash filled with incognito leavings, mishmash of crusts and grease and bones. What was laid out, we took in. We did not, in this house, open cabinets or drawers. I did not know what sat on the shelves of our refrigerator, what milk or jar of jam. We did not spill our food, did not make a trail of crumbs along the floor. I held bites of hot dog or bologna or chicken spread in my mouth, unable to swallow, knowing I must.

The food we now ate was heavy and often tasteless. For breakfast there were thick slabs of butterscotch brownie, unfrozen and soggy. Glasses of instant protein chocolate, with a layer that solidified on top, slimy and brown. We ate Vienna sausages, tiny cans with uniform pink units. Stews and hashes and potted meats. Potpies and dinners-in-a-bag, boxed macaroni and cheese a brilliant, unrelenting yellow. Food, that inconvenience, came in neat freezer boxes, in cans and bags and plastic cartons. Not for us, carrots with their shedding white hairs, potatoes with eyes that blossomed. No sweet corn-on-the-cob, with its messy, bursting kernels. My father brought home hamburger, double plastic-bagged, to hold back the leak, the drip of blood. I knew by heart the labels of these foods. *Miss Wisconsin. Sue Bee. Dinty Moore. Lauralea.* The foods had names, predictable and safe. I counted the letters on cereal boxes, divided by three, believed that was the magic number.

Some afternoons when I was back from school and waiting while she finished making her face, I snuck into the kitchen. I had learned how to slide my fingers in between cabinet door and frame, ease open a box of crackers. Knowing I had sinned, I placed the wafers on my tongue, chewed without a sound.

Other afternoons, my father picked me up after school and we drove downtown over what we called the "singing bridge," which seemed to hum loudly whenever we crossed it. Downtown we shopped at the A & P for day-olds. Mr. Kraft, the bakery manager, was a short man with heavy, black-framed glasses and wiry, white hairs growing from his ears. He saw us coming. *That man,* the one he'd come to know by name, *with his little girl.*

"What have you got for us today?" my father asked, arms folded over his soft middle. And we bought apple pies, doughnuts, sticky cinnamon rolls. The thumb on Mr. Kraft's right hand was missing, but he held the marker anyway, slashed through the original price.

Would this please my mother?

Our rules grew and grew. No fried chicken, no steak, nothing that splattered, spewed, strewed grease across stove or counter. Far easier to mix the cans and boxes. Fewer pots and pans that way, less need for forks and spoons to stir. We ate canned macaroni, cheese or tomato mixed with tuna, this on a piece of white bread, so the plate would stay clean. Our clothes were to stay spotless, pristine. My father heard about it, again and again, the way he had spotted his tie during lunch, the aberrant drip of coffee on a shirt sleeve. And after suppers the rules were these: He must go to her, stand, never sit, while she scrubbed the plates. He must talk.

"I did this and this and this," he said.

He shifted from foot to foot.

Until bedtime, we sat, one and one and one. Him, in the easy chair. Me, in the child's folding art chair, the one next to him, the one where I sat until I was so big it broke from my weight. Her, on one side only of the couch. No bowls of popcorn for us. No late-night candy corn or pretzels.

After supper, by the living-room light, my mother sewed trousers and my father added and subtracted, bank accounts, mortgages, tithes owed to God. They were no longer the couple in the photograph, the one where my mother wore a gold dress and my father had written, "Now there, there is you a couple."

Now, her eyes were narrow as she drew the thread up and back, counting, *One, two, three*, as if she were pulling a shadow out of the air. It settled on her, that shadow, and my mother was remade. A caul covered her face, one made of anger and a bitterness she attributed to us. We were unwashed shirts, scuffed floors, meals to be made and eaten and made. And yet we were not fed.

While they worked in the evening light, I read about the meals of saints. Catherine of Sienna ate nothing for ten years but lettuce leaves and ash. She washed the wounds of lepers and drank and drank from the water that cleaned their sores. She licked the holy road to Golgotha, sand tasting like cloves and blood. I read the story of the body of the Sacred Mother. After her holy conception, she visited no one, no mother, father, brother. She dressed in the dark so she could not see her flesh. Her body was so thin it could float, and upon her ascension, she was pure, like the air above the sky. I wanted to go there. I wanted her to take me. I wanted to feast on air.

I remember another winter, when we are going to eastern Kentucky for Christmas. I remember houses strung with lights, a yard with a manger scene, Santa with a sleigh as we drive over the mountains with our car full of words. They collide, break. They are full of anger, hot and red, and it slides into my lap. I clench my hands around it. I try to hold on, not let this anger loose again. We drive for hours, later than we intended, and I pretend to sleep, between them in the front seat. I lean against my father, but there is no softness. He grips the steering wheel tightly and I feel a long cord of muscle along his side.

"I heard about you," my mother says. "Don't you think I didn't. You and that Goldie woman, up at the diner and you, asking her out for coffee, or worse. My own sister. My own sister told me about it."

"Told you," my father says. "Did she?" He flips a cigarette

out the window and we sit, listening, as we hear the flame hiss in the snow.

We are sitting at the bottom of the hill in Dwale, at the path that goes up to my mother's house. There is wind down the hollow and then everything goes quiet, a brittle stillness that shatters with the least unexpected sound. There is light, a moon or the reflection off snow, and I watch my mother. She is trying to say more, yes or no, but only breath, frozen and sad, comes from her open lips. I picture my father, at a table with a woman with hair the color of gold. They are dipping doughnuts in coffee so hot it burns their tongues.

"You don't know the first thing," he now says. "Not the first or the last."

"Don't tell me," my mother says. "Don't you tell me."

We wait for what she will say next. The forbidden word either of them might say to make this night careen downhill, out of control, a car on an icy road. She gets out and slams the car door behind her, leans her weight against the window, catches her footing in the new snow. She is coatless since coats leave her untidy and so we watch her white shirt as she heads to the path up the hill. She does not look back. And my father and I are gone to the next county, to his parents. His and hers, the way it will be forever and ever.

I imagine that anger sparks and leaves a trail of fire behind us as we drive along the highway. I look in lit windows and think of steam from cups, of hands holding other hands. Winter. My father reaches out to me across the car seat, and I take his hand. I choose to remember that, the way that hand felt warm and large. Large enough to save us.

I began to believe in the power of food. I chewed slowly, twenty-five times each mouthful, cut my white bread into squares and triangles, folded my potpies into pouches full of peas and gravy; slowness was my key to delicious hunger. Hunger imparted lightness of the head and heart, and I wanted to be light enough to watch my thin and furtive self as I passed through the glass doors of my junior high. Made of light, I walked to the front of the class with my homework. I became invisible. In school, I slipped through doorways unnoticed. I sat in the back row where I could admire my legs, grown skinnier, the way my wrists and ankles were thinner by the day.

By then, I was in junior high and my friends were Dottie and Jackie. Dottie had pigtails and a red circle on the inside of her right forearm. Ringworm, she told me, and let me touch the ridged edges. Jackie was the only black girl in our school. She let me hold her hand during recess, and later my own palms were musty, a scent I associated with coal dust. The three of us were inseparable, but only at school. I knew nothing about the farm where Dottie lived, had never seen Jackie's three brothers. These were my day friends, separate from that other life, home. It was from them I learned food's benevolence.

Dottie brought saltines and cans of chicken spread in her sack. Jackie brought eggs, fried or pickled or boiled. These foods were no better or worse than my lunches—peanut butter, pressed ham, pickle loaf on white bread. I gave my lunches to them, nevertheless. I told them this was high tea, that we were eating toast points, savories and sweets, and gave them halves of my halved sandwiches. They, in turn, gave me iced oatmeal or raisin snack cakes, and I put these, untouched, in my own sack.

I did not tell them how I had come to love the afternoon rules of hunger. How I swallowed against my stomach's growling. How, unfolding in me already, was my body's future. Someday soon I would count calories, one hundred, two hundred, five hundred, stop. I would gauge my worth by pounds, ninety-five, ninety, eighty-seven, never too few. These rules, ready to be born, were secrets. I held them in my mouth for their wonderful taste.

Lunch was in the cafeteria, a place of long tables and cliques. Dottie, Jackie, and I ate by ourselves, but we had to walk past other tables of the elite, cheerleaders, prom queens past and present, class presidents. Gordon, a boy who often sat behind me to copy my answers to square roots and balanced equations, sat beside Brenda and Gwen, junior varsity majorettes. Gwen, it was rumored, had been practicing flame-twirling and had put a reddish rinse on her hair, to match her batons.

"Hey," she said one day, as I headed toward Jackie and Dottie.

I didn't answer, since she couldn't have meant me. I wore cat-eye glasses, apricot skirts made by my paternal grandmother, lime-green tights. In gym class, Gwen and others had quarreled about who had to choose me for volleyball.

"Hey," she said again. She nudged Brenda and they both turned in my direction.

Brenda had large teeth and a smile that showed them off. She scooted down, patted an empty space on the bench between her and Gwen.

At a distance, I saw Dottie put her hand discreetly next to her cheek, point to the empty spot. This was an opportunity I shouldn't miss.

Brenda and Gwen prodded at their lunches, chuck-wagon patties and little plastic bowls of tomato dumplings. They said the usual about cafeteria food and cardboard and stray hairs.

Brenda mashed her dumplings, stood her fork up in the paste, eyed my tuna with salad dressing and dill chips.

I pushed a sandwich half in each of their directions. I watched Gwen and then Brenda nibble at the clean edges of my sandwich. They licked at the dressing, ate my dill chips in bites of three. They pushed the little plastic bowls of dumplings toward me, gave me celery sticks and an untouched chuck wagon. I did not eat these.

They watched me, and I thought of a time my sanitary belt came unfastened as I walked down the hall, the napkin sliding from between my thighs. I thought of the days my hair went unwashed, the clothes I wore again and again, the way I was expected to keep them clean, one day, two, ad infinitum. I thought of my mother, kneeling by a tub, her hands washing me in places I would later not be able to remember.

"Thanks," they said. They smelled of cologne, something light, like roses with a whiff of tuna underneath, and they gathered their trays and books.

"Come try out," Gwen said.

She meant varsity cheerleading, and I saw how that could be, the line of pretty girls, their flounced skirts kicking up. And I saw other days on days, empty lunch sacks. I saw myself, a stick drawing of me, arms raised, pirouetting along a gymnasium floor. I could be that thin, so thin they soon would never see me at all.

I want to believe it was for the best. My mother, growing up believing in the attenuated glory of God and food, how it could save us, redeem us. Communion grape juice and tiny pieces of unsalted crackers in a dish. To have this she had to go down the aisle with everyone singing of holiness, to the preacher bending down. She had to believe he would tell her a secret. Hallelujah, amen, and her life would be transformed.

I tell myself I can see her, the girl, when she used to believe. Can see her listening to the radio, to Frank Sinatra and Pat Boone, to songs about promised love, love and its salvation. I believe that's what she thought about in church when the music rose. "Just as I am without one plea," they sang, "but that thy blood was shed for me." She did not yet know about a marriage night, her own blood being shed. She watched the choir, the open mouths praising glory. She was empty, waiting to be filled, and that sent her forward, down the long aisle. Saved. She wanted that. Wanted God and the man who would love her, both of them touching her secretly in the night. "Do this in remembrance of me," the offering

*table said. It is the secret of God that will fill us, the hollow walls
of our home.*

*When did she begin to profess another kind of faith? To speak to
me of sin, of broken mirrors and the body's excesses? I remember
her, the woman she became. The woman who leaves the house less
and less. When church ladies come to call, she doesn't answer the
door. She waits in the kitchen, peers around the corner, checking.
The ladies ask my father, later, whether my mother has been well.
On Sunday mornings she kneels beside a coffee table. She peers
underneath a couch, checking for dust. She wears gloves, new ones,
because it is Sunday. And because it is Sunday, she is gentler than
usual. Sunlight trails across the lawn, all the way from the church
where she was saved. That light, as pure as she once was, enters
our house. Her gloved finger traces the edge of an arm, the seat of
a chair. Sunday, and she prays for no trace of dust, no shadow in
our home.*

Afternoons after school I walked up the road from the bus stop
and she watched for me, raising the garage door as I came up the
drive. She'd already have the gas stove in the garage lit, the lawn
chair ready. Every afternoon, this is where I stayed, my home
away from home, the place I waited until she was ready for me
to go inside. The garage was where we could be safe, my father
and I. There, I could practice clarinet every afternoon, forbidden
spit falling on concrete. The garage was where he kept his ham
radio outfit, the tubes and transmitters that accumulated dust
and were thus not allowed in our house. The garage was where
he spent Saturdays, there and in the yard, or at the office, that
place of longer and longer hours. The garage was where I lay
upon a lawn chair waiting until I was cleansed of the outside
world.

Steps from the garage led into the kitchen, and after closing
the garage door behind me, she went on in, locking the door
behind her. I heard the clink of glasses and plates, the final hum

of vacuuming. Then I heard nothing and I knew she was down the hall, washing her face, shaping her hair. Each afternoon, she spent an hour, sometimes two with the implements of beauty, tweezers, liners, curlers, soaps, creams. An hour, sometimes two with the bathroom mirror. The mirror that we, my father and I, could not touch, had to leave clean of water spots, fingerprints, breath. She wanted this glass as undisturbed as water, like the well back in Dwale when she went out to toss the bucket down and looked after it, wanting to see a bottom. As undisturbed as Dewey Lake at night, when she and my father went driving and they had never kissed. When all they had done was circle the shore, watching the way the moon shone down. Now, glass was where she stood each afternoon counting all the lines we had made around her mouth.

In the garage, I had time alone. Every afternoon I found some new, forbidden place. I opened drawers, sifted through bolts and nails. Opened toolboxes and touched socket wrenches and claw hammers. Once, I found a knife with a wavy blade in a leather pouch and, very quietly, picked the lock to the door. In my sock feet, I slipped across the kitchen floor, opened the refrigerator, coveted the carton of milk, the box of cheese. I opened boxes and emptied their contents, then put everything back exactly as it was. In the garage I found notebooks with poems my father had written fifteen years before. "A woman," one poem read, "that mystery forever powdering her nose." I found slides from the war, held them to up to the garage ceiling light, saw a bare-breasted Asian woman dancing on a stage.

The other refuge was my father's office, where I sometimes went with him on Sunday afternoons. There we made meals from cartons of dip mixed with cans of smoked oysters or minced crab. We smuggled in fast food and ate it at his desk. We pretended we were a family, complete, having our Sunday dinner at a table. A few months later, a year, maybe two, I would discover other forbidden powers at the office. Bottles of typewriter fluid, breathed in deeply, better than hunger, and I would reel, light and with no body at all. Invisible, I would find my father at his desk, staring at a partition between his space and the next. I would watch him for a long time, memorize him, his face my first definition of *empty*.

One evening, with garage time over, she came down the steps, ready to make me clean. Since I had turned thirteen, I had insisted on bathing myself. This was trouble, and it showed in her angry face, in the nervous rubbing of her dry hands. I would bathe myself in the garage shower my father had installed so that he and I could wash ourselves, make ourselves clean enough to come inside. She still unbuttoned me, made me lean on her while my tights were stripped. "Careful," she said, "don't you drag them."

Soon, I was standing on a torn-open grocery sack on the garage floor and I was naked. It was warm with the gas stove, but even so, my small nipples wrinkled. I did not hide, did not cross my arms across my chest, did not fold my legs in. She had seen my breasts many times, seen the new hairs on my pubis and legs and under my arms. There was nowhere to hide as we crossed the concrete on a trail of paper she had made. She helped me, as if I was one of the infirm, and I stepped up into the shower.

The shower door was milky glass and I saw just a blur of her as the water started. Like always, she talked to me as I soaped and rinsed. "That stove," she said. "I can smell the gas, can't you? You just don't know what trouble you cause me. I can't even know how clean you get yourself and look at these tights. They're all kicked up to here, scuff marks here and here. You'll just have to wear them again, that's all, if you can't keep any cleaner. And did you eat your lunch today? I can smell the gas from that stove. Your father couldn't glue two sticks together right. The both of you, the trouble you cause. And your skirt, too. You must have sat in something. Don't you ever look? And did you eat your lunch today?"

Not eating my lunch was taboo, a danger to be avoided, like sidewalk cracks or black cats in the road. Every morning my mother spread neat slices of white bread with her favorite jam and folded them into plastic bags for my father and me. She protected this food as carefully as she watched our cleanliness, our shit, our vomit. It was food only she had touched. Such pure food went out into the world she seldom entered, and this made her afraid. It made her think of strange hands touching who knows what, of mouths with their unsanitary teeth, the horror of germs. I should not, I knew, give away such pure food, to who knows whom.

"Did you eat your lunch?" she asked.

The water coursed down as I stood a little longer, knowing I was hidden from her here, in this place of glass that revealed to her only an indistinct shape. I wanted the water to make me invisible, to careen down my back, fall harder, scourge me, dissolve me into fragments and shards, skin and bones and memory, send me down the drain, into the untouchable black earth beneath the house.

Outside the shower, I stood again on the torn grocery sack.

"Did you eat your lunch today?" she asked again.

"I ate my lunch," I said, and by this I meant the truth. I meant that I had eaten food all mine. Secret food. At school, when I was hungry, I tore the frayed edges off notebook paper, chewed, swallowed the paste. I swallowed my own spit against my belly's gnawing. By this time though, she had figured it out. I was lying. I had not eaten my lunch, her lunch, the food she had prepared with her own dry hands. "You didn't eat your lunch did you? After all I do for you?" She rubbed me hard with the rough towel, as if that were a punishment, and she studied me, my small breasts and hips, my girl's thighs. What did she see?

The girl she was once, the girl she no longer was? In ten years, in twenty, she would urge me toward hunger, toward a thinness she herself would desire. But that day in the garage she cleaned me of everything I'd been touched by in the world outside and prepared me, liar that I was, to go inside.

What I want to remember is that we were not always hungry, my mother and father and I. I remember how it was that at Christmas we would drive to eastern Kentucky, to my mother's family home, where we could eat and eat. Turkey, cooked good and tender, and pans of moist stuffing with celery seed and glossy onions. Mashed potato salad, bright with mustard and pickles. Pans of green beans cooked for twelve hours with fatback. Cream pies with peaked meringue, browned under the broiler. Or, on ordinary days, squirrels cooked in their own gravy and bowls of fresh salad greens drenched in bacon grease. Chicken dumplings made with lard and drops of yellow coloring. Delicacies. Frog legs kicking in the skillet, brains scrambled like eggs, sausage from a hog slaughtered only the week before.

Food, abundant, but hoarded against hard times. In the warm house, jars of pickled beets, the canning rings gone to rust, but still good enough. Milk right from the cow and tasting of green onions, but suitable for bread making or whitening coffee. Jam gone to sugar. Bread, moldy, but good with the edges trimmed away. Big wedges of commodity cheese, its muted color neither yellow nor white. And other commodities, too, large cans of peanut butter, of dried, sulfur-treated apricots, of powders that turned to milk or eggs.

After our suppers at Dwale, I sat with my mother and her sisters, Ruth and Ruby, and sometimes the sister-in-law, Betty. They were beautiful to me, their thin legs and pointy-toed flats, their hair clipped short and pin curled, washed auburn from packets of Helena Rubenstein. Ruth loved forbidden music, "Wake up, little

Susie, wake up." When she was eighteen she married a guitar-playing boy. A sin, all of it. And Ruby. At nineteen, she'd walked the five miles to town and back just to prove she could, and later wed an older, divorced man. And Betty. Thinking already of leaving. One day soon she would run off to be a dancer in love with go-go boots and skirts so short they made my uncle blush, long after she left him. Women, sitting, full of supper and cigarette smoke, and talking men.

"Men," they say, "can't tell about their wants. Don't they ever pee sitting down? And what about the things you never break them of, stains on their underwear or phone numbers on books of matches."

"Not to name," one of my aunts says, "the unmentionableness of their desires. Never enough, once or twice or more. And those things they use, unspeakable, for a quarter from the service station restroom."

"They just care about one thing," my mother says. "One."

And I will remember, later, how she said this, and at the same time, a picture of her. Standing next to a bed, the shadow of my father across her face, skirt held up to show her legs. She was smiling.

And the men all the while? Out in the living room talking football scores or the peculiar desires of their automobile engines. My father. Out in the garden sometimes, eating a tomato right off the vine, the juice running down his chin, like he could never do at home.

Hunger and longing, an elixir, a memory tasting of sweet and bitter.

After the garage made me clean, we ate. My father had brought home slices of honey-flavored ham, pre-cooked. My mother warmed these in the Teflon skillet with the lid and laid them out on paper towels to absorb the grease. We had peas and

Parkerhouse rolls baked with margarine on top. All of this was unusual, a superfluity of stirring and oven and stove top, and I was afraid it would stop, afraid she would stop, tell my father about my lunch, my lying. But she was busy, making up for the afternoon. Not for my bathing and the roughness of the towel. This feast of ham and bread had nothing to do with me, not yet. She was calmer now, almost girlish. For an added treat, she set out cartons of slaw, strawberry jelly for our rolls. She was making up, not with me, but with him, for what had happened after he came home. For their arguing, which was becoming a daily event. For their voices rising, angry, through the closed door, outside to the garage.

"Why," I had heard him say. "What I want to know is why."

That afternoon, they had fought. At first it was about me, the dishevelment of my school clothes. Then it was about him, the half hour he was late returning from work. It was about us, me and him, again, again, the ways we had ruined her life. But that afternoon came the turn of events she least expected. *Why*, he had asked.

He meant groceries, trips to the pharmacy for sanitary napkins and makeup, all the lists of items he had to purchase, because she did not leave the house on her own. He wanted to know why he had to do what a woman should do, the extra miles he drove to pick me up from school or the rides to the beauty shop or fashion store. He wanted to know why he did what a man should not, every afternoon in the garage. He refused, as I could not, to strip naked and shower right away, but he had his own rules to follow. He had to strip down to underwear and bare feet. I had often seen him be walked past me into the living room, paper bags taped to his outside-the-house, unclean feet, on the way to changing from outdoor clothes to house clothes.

That afternoon, he had refused. He had not quite gone the whole way, had not yet worn his shoes across the shine of our floors, but he had worn his office clothes into the house. He had sat on the end of the couch where no one was allowed. He had folded his arms with a defiant look. "A man," he had said. "I'm a man in my own home."

At first she had been taller than him, towered above him, red faced, her voice sharp.

"Why," she had wanted to know. "Why are you doing this?"

We knew she meant the minutiae of dirt, how it migrated, alive and multiplying from my father's office clothes to the couch, then on from there, to floor or walls, to our very skin. She meant more than that. She was afraid of this small rebellion of his, this breaking of the rules. She could see already the road out, the clean break. The house flung open, emptying itself of her. And so this night was ham and rolls and dinner like anyone else.

She laid out the plates, our ham slices dispensed according to our rank in family importance. The best went to him, only an edge of fat, the rest of the slice deep pink, glistening. To me went one only slightly more fatty, its islands of leanness divided by narrow ridges of white. Hers was mottled with fingers and threads of gristle, ripples of lard, an atonement for the quarrel they'd had. She was, she could tell us, good to us. Better to us than she was to herself.

Kitchen light settled above our table as we ate, a pure light, pale yellow and keen. It lit our faces until we seemed to be smiling. Our cheeks were plump, satisfied, like all the other families in all the other dining rooms I could imagine. We chewed and chewed.

And then came the gift. The twist, the turn in the road, the last thing to make this evening perfect.

"She did not eat her lunch," my mother said.

Then we had the recitation, the litany of that day. The diversion from their own sadness. The sandwich, its well-cut parts.

Me, who had the audacity to lie. This lie filled us, sweet as cream, sweet as pudding or tarts or chocolates. We could take this lie in our mouths, turn it over and over like hard candy. A lie made us forget everything else since lying was, after all, a sin.

"A sin," my father said to me, and I wanted to make him meet my eyes.

How easily he became a traitor, in league against me, when we had been expatriates, partners of the office, the Sunday afternoon, the garage. How easily I became their common ground, what was left of the way it had been. I was *daughter*, their one common project, whom they must raise right, dress, shelter, feed. And in this they were still united. Together, they caught at the edges of me. I was small enough for them to hold on to, one on each side.

A sin, they told me. Thou shalt not be ungrateful, unworthy, squandering of our nourishment.

I remember night and her shoes drifting away, one and two. The bathroom light clicks off down the hall. I hear them, the sheet folding back, one of them dusting off feet before sliding into bed. Bible pages. My father reading aloud their nightly verses, this night the Song of Songs.

"He brought me to the banqueting house," he reads, "and his banner over me was love. Comfort me with apples, for I am sick of love."

When he finishes, I hear them whispering and I believe I hear my name.

"Ungrateful," she says, "my own child." She recounts my sins, the food I have touched, the rules I have broken. But that night, I do not pray for forgiveness.

I pray for Her. The Sacred Mother. I pray that she will stand by my bed so that when I reach out, my hand will pass through her transparent skin. Fullness of spirit, she will tell me, can overflow into the body. I too can be filled. I can taste holiness, take God on my tongue, tasting of flour and sweetness, of wishing. I can rise above my bed, this house, above the sky itself. And from that great height, I can look back and see them, my father, my mother.

They are lying spooned in sleep. My mother's dry hands are clothed in gloves, heavy with lotion and healing. Still, my father's arm drapes across her and he presses his face to her neck. "I love you," he says, "like no other woman."

Then they are touching. Their bed gives and sighs, that steady rhythm I know, even now, is them making love.

All the next day, I will be snowed in, with her. My father will linger over breakfast, and they will talk of ashes on the road, of grocery lists and when he will be home.

"I am burning," she will say.

Burning inside, and all of us will know how she has suffered for him, the way for days she will hurt between her legs. A shadow will cross my father's face, a memory of what she does for him.

CHAPTER FOUR

Flight

Don't we all lose? you ask. Lose our past desires, our childhood selves? In my memory, I have lost nothing. Those late summer afternoons are as real to me now as when I was eight or nine. In my memory, my father is still gone to visit his own family in the next county and my mother and I are still in Dwale, with that grandmother. Afternoons, my aunt Ruby and I often walk up the road from Dwale to the country store where we buy peanuts and Co-Colas to put them in. The road goes to town in one direction, and in the other it goes to Beck's, my great-grandmother's house. These are the only two directions that exist this summer afternoon.

All morning I have wanted this walk, but we've had to put on our faces first and look, my aunt says, "like something besides haints." My mother has caught pans of rainwater to wash first her hair, then mine, and I'm told I look sweet now, with my short bangs curly and still drying. Ruby wears jeans with the cuffs rolled up and a short-sleeved blouse with a spoon pin at the collar, and my mother teases her. "Ruby's gone a-sparkin'." We all know, even I, that a divorced mechanic who claims he can steer a Chrysler with his bare feet wants to take her to drive-in movies and to the county fair. We speak about these things in hushed voices since we know Pa, my grandfather, does not approve of any carrying on between the sexes.

After our drinks, we walk as far as Beck's, a house that's abandoned now that Beck lives in town, in back of her daughter's service station. But we stand in the backyard anyway, listening to the water move in the fresh spring. My grandmother used to carry jars of this water home with her, claiming it was the softest there was, finer by far than the sulfur water in her own well. Afterward, we walk back home and sit in the green front-porch rocking chairs, from which we can see the whole world.

Behind the house are a shed, the smokehouse, and the hollow, and below us is a path to the outhouse, a stone-pear tree, and a field where I sometimes play. Ruby tells me how, when she was my age, she stood in this bottomland and dreamed of traveling, of anywhere but here, which is home. Sometimes the dirt path from house to outhouse could lead to places she'd never seen, if only she believed. In bed that night I make up stories about Ruby. I imagine she is a bird taking flight, a bird with glorious wings. I sleep and dream she is the Holy Ghost and that she flies up and hits the ceiling of the world and falls back hard.

It is this plethora of times and details of times, memory as fluid as spring water, that makes everything count. I am eight and I am walking in the hot sun, craving Co-Cola and salt. I am ten and I love the way my aunt makes peanut-butter sandwiches on white bread folded in half. I am eleven and I know that Ruby has begun to have mysterious spells. Behind her pointy glasses with rhinestones, her eyes have a myopic vagueness. She faints without cause. She falls down beside the kitchen stove with what the family calls seizures. She is unhappy for unspecified reasons and my mother and my aunt Ruth hint darkly that this unhappiness has to do with the unreasonable demands of Ruby's husband, Eppie. In my hearing, they don't use the word demand. Instead, they use words like his needs or you know, those things men like, and then hush, as if what they might say were as unsanitary as a gas-station restroom. I overhear my mother and father talking and he says, "Lost. I'll tell you what's the matter with her, she's lost, like the rest of them." My mother says, "Hush, you don't know the least thing about it."

Then I am twelve, thirteen, and I myself am lost, or I want to be. After school I watch Dark Shadows. I read gothic romances and I Have Always Lived in the Castle. I store up incantations and charms and walk softly on our hardwood floors in our Frankfort home, humming my mantra, step on a crack and you'll break your mother's back. In my diary, which my mother finds and reads, I write elaborate plans about my possible flights from home. I describe circuses and hitchhiking along oceanside roads, which I have never seen. "You'll marry the first boy who looks at you twice," she says to me. And I imagine being looked at, once and twice, and how then I could pirouette three times and vanish into the lemony air of our clean home.

When I am fourteen, I read The Bell Jar and I fall in love with madness. Madness will be cool as water in a silver cup, as simple as sleep. Mornings, all that fifteenth summer, when my mother comes to get me, I pretend I can't wake up. She shakes me, telling me not to be ridiculous, that I'm keeping her—from breakfast and dishes and her shiny, waxed surfaces. I hold on to sleep as long as I can and wish I really was crazy. If I'm crazy enough, I believe, they'll lock me inside somewhere steep and white. I sip cologne in the bathroom at night because this makes my own body seem far

*away, and I wish my childhood gone forever, wish it swirling down
the drain.*

By the time I was fourteen, my mother was losing herself for
good. I don't mean she was like a woman I met, years later, at
an art colony. The one who came to breakfast on the first day
with her cheeks and her lips and the edges of her eyelids carefully outlined with makeup, but on each of seven subsequent
days came downstairs with lines straying, colors running like
wet paint, until her face was indistinguishable in the smears of
blue and pink and brown. All the same, my mother was disappearing.

When a contingent from the Southern Baptist Church came
calling one more time, wondering why it was that only my
father and I attended Sunday morning services, my mother hid
and the church ladies asked my father, later, why they had seen
a wraith in brush rollers and house slippers peering out from
behind the kitchen door. She was not like other mothers who
worshipped on Sundays and Wednesdays and suntanned regularly at tennis. She did not work, drive a car, or grocery shop. She
did not drive me to school or to dress shops or to bargain barns,
nor was she a paragon of public service, organizer of rummage
sales, bake-offs, and Tupperware parties. She did not, as my
father later said, "fulfill the responsibilities of the wife." She
was, as the church ladies had seen, a wraith, secretive, fearful
of any world outside our house. What they didn't see was how,
as she slipped away, she held on tighter to us.

More and more we became her domain, her all in all, and she
became the keeper of all our comings and goings. More diligent
than ever, she marked our time. How long, she wanted to know,
did it take me to walk up the road from the afternoon bus? Why
was my father five minutes or ten or fifteen minutes late? More
and more we were captive, her audience in the garage, where I

stood listening to the litany of my misdeeds after school, where my father stood listening to his own inadequacies. She must, she said, watch our every move, make sure we kept our word, make sure we kept clean, inside and out. She rode in my lap when I came home on the school bus, and she rode on my father's back as he shopped for canned beef stew and bologna. She walked the halls of junior high with me, her own high-school sweaters embracing me, her plaid skirts hugging my hips. She entered my pockets and the very bottom of my book bag, aware of notes I'd written or received. I wrote poems and hid these in my school desk. They were about black-tiled rooms and her hands smelling of talc as she entered my sleep, a dancer, a clear, white dream.

She was no white dream, no beautiful mother, and she grew less so as my father and I began to transform. She was failing, and she knew it. We were becoming her lost loved ones. She grew suspicious of anything missing. Crackers missing from a box in a kitchen cabinet I wasn't allowed to open, crackers I'd stolen while she was doing her hair. Or condoms missing from their bedroom drawer, which she told us both about. She entered our phone calls, convinced that my father was communicating with old girlfriends on the sly, ones who called and hung up after saying things like, "I see your husband three nights a week and I'm insanely jealous." When I talked on the phone to my friends, Roslyn or Lisa, she screamed into the receiver, "You, gone a-sparkin'. Karen's gone a-sparkin'."

My mother and father fought now for hours in the garage, when he came from work, before he went to work. Evenings, he could never please her. She called him to the kitchen while she washed dishes and he stood there, made to talk. Talked too much. Said the wrong thing, even at night when I still heard them, once in six months, making love.

"I love you," he still said. "Like no other woman."

"Which woman?" she wanted to know. "Which other?"

And on Sunday afternoons she conjured ghosts of the past.

There was the sweetheart my father wanted more than her, the one back in eastern Kentucky with a space between her front teeth and a secret love of moonshine. The one back in Korea with bound feet and a silk camisole for every day of the week. He'd never, she said, made her happy. Never. He'd stolen her past right out from under her, her parents, her hometown, the date she almost had with a high-school football star, before she knew my father, but that didn't matter, did it?

"And you," she said, looking at me. "What about you?" I was the product of pain, of suffering. Didn't I know that was what birth was all about?

I'd find out, she said. Soon enough.

What I found, at fourteen, was a boy. I'd found them before, first in sixth grade. Gordon Penman was blond and blue eyed and liked me for my spelling homework. Or buck-toothed Mike, in seventh grade, who brought me a hand-decorated Easter egg and a note that said, "I like you, do you like me, yes or no." At fourteen, I found a real boy, one who reeked of Brut cologne and the same kind of blatant power that made my friend Lisa boast when Larry, her tenth-grade beau, left his belt on the couch in her family room after a Friday-night date.

Not that I had any pretensions, at that point, about *doing it*, as Lisa called late Friday nights, when she gave Larry a hand job, an arduous task that took so long, she said, her arm was numb into the next afternoon. A task, she said, that smelled like hot buttered popcorn. Nor did I have any assurances that I would ever be able to enter the dating world, that weekend phantasmagoria of football games and endless automobile trips around Frisch's, which had curb service and a reputation as a hotbed of necking and clandestine drug encounters.

No one in her family, my mother assured me, had ever dated before they were eighteen, if then. And even when my mother was eighteen, my father was visibly shaken at the idea of driving her up the hill to her home in Dwale where, who knows, Pa might be waiting with the squirrel rifle. My aunt Ruth had fought and lied to get to spark her future husband, the part-time radio rock 'n' roll singer. And Ruby you know about, the adventurous one. She walked to town and back, against Pa's wishes, to meet up with Eppie, and got a belting for it at the bottom of the same Dwale hill. Women in my mother's family did not *date*, nor did those in my father's family, for that matter. My great-grandmother on my father's side married at thirteen, young enough to sit on the floor a few years later with her first babies and their play pretties.

Dating was suspect hand-holding and smoldering kisses and impure acts. Women, particularly in my mother's family, married and hoed the garden and put up jars of pickled beets. Or, as my mother had done, they moved to god-knows-where with their Air Force husbands and suffered the consequences of laundry soap and sex with a man they'd hardly kissed before marriage.

"You know you can't date that boy," my mother said.

That boy became our household euphemism for what I wanted and couldn't have. Couldn't have, but pined for in my one-year diary, the one I knew my mother read. At first I wrote the expected, my abject grief at my mother's tyranny, her refusal to consider the intricacies of fourteen-year-old etiquette—what everyone did, what everyone wore, what everyone expected me to do and wear. "This boy," I wrote, "loves me a lot more than you do. He sees me for who I am." This, of course, was and wasn't true.

Joseph Thomas McElmurray did unmask me. He lifted up my overgrown bangs and saw my brown eyes. He drew me in art class, pencil sketches with "lovely woman" written at the bottom. He managed to peel away the layers of 1950s sweaters and pleated skirts, my mother's hand-me-downs, and find a girl inside, me, small breasted and skinny, but not undesirable, not anything like Buckwheat, the tenth-grade girl with frizzy black hair and an illegitimate child. Buckwheat, whom everyone used as a benchmark for unpopularity. I had possibilities, even if they were limited.

What Joseph Thomas, known as Tommy back at home, did not count on was the pitch and fervor, the degree to which my mother clung to my father and me like a spider web. Losing us, and losing me to the maturity that dating and lipstick implied, meant she was further losing herself. Waving good-bye, forever and ever, to the girl she had been, the one with pedal pushers and pointy shoes and a look of hope.

After weeks of insistence and finally silence, I was allowed an afternoon with Joe. The plan was for a Sunday, a time when I usually went with my father to his downtown office building. He worked on school-system budgets and I explored the upstairs Education Department library, both of us escaping my mother's growing irritation with us. My father, it seemed, had some faith in the dating principle, having sparked a number of girls back at home, before his service days. I believe sparking, for my father, implied a certain high-mindedness, an ethical code that probably meant hand-holding on the couch before nine and invitations to chicken-dumpling dinners, but nonetheless he had dated. Yes, he had dated, I heard my mother say after that. *Joyce, Betty, Goldie,* soft girl names they discussed afternoons in the garage.

"Goldie Short," my mother said with disdain.

The girl he still wanted, if the truth was known.

Hadn't she seen the way he'd gotten nervous, my mother said, the last visit home we'd made to eastern Kentucky?

They usually spent the nights apart, he at his parents', she at her parents', and I divided time between them. But what about that time she wanted to go with him? Surprise him for a change? Didn't that make him sweat, make him squirm and think of excuses?

Goldie, she was sure of it. That name like butterfly wings, like bleached-blonde hair and a padded bra.

"Don't tell me," my mother said, "there wasn't that time you asked her for coffee, and right in front of a whole diner back at home and my own sister, too."

Nonetheless, it was finally settled that just maybe a movie or a walk in the park, a date with Joe, wouldn't be such a bad thing, with limitations, of course. I would ride with my father to his downtown office building and meet Joe there. We were to walk the three blocks to the theater for an afternoon matinee and the three blocks back, no Cokes at the corner afterward. All encounters strictly in daylight hours. And the movie was to have no unnecessary bare skin. No movies like the Italian western that had been on recently, one with a black-haired vixen in a low-cut peasant dress with drawstrings a bandito began to untie, right before my mother screamed, as loud as she did when a snake came on television, and turned off the set.

For this date I wore blue culottes, frosted pink lipstick and my patent-leather Sunday-morning church shoes. I remember clicking down the sidewalk, the half-inch heels tapping out radio love songs, the ones my mother loved, by Frank Sinatra. "Strangers in the night, exchanging glances, wondering in the night, what were the chances." By block two-and-a-half, I'd left this song behind and I'd left my mother behind, with her last-minute admonitions about what to do when or if he, that boy, did this or that. I was walking with the boy himself, holding his cold, damp hand. We strolled past a parked van painted with Day-Glo flowers and ankhs and peace signs and I looked through the open doors at an older girl in a tank top and cutoffs, stretched out on a mattress.

I wanted to be that girl. I wanted to be one of the two biker

chicks we saw on the next corner. I wanted to be one of the hippies in Peace Park in Louisville, fifty miles away. I wanted to run
away to San Francisco, where I'd ride the streetcars and roll my
own cigarettes and hitchhike to the Golden Gate Bridge. The
possibilities, *girlfriend, hippie chick,* anyone but a girl in blue
culottes who'd go home, later, to be undressed and inspected in
the bathroom by her mother.

We circled the movie block twice, to make the date part, the
before-the-movie preview, longer. I mentally searched my dating lore, the stores of knowledge I had from *Young Miss* and
Seventeen, for the right questions. His Interests. Did he like
NASCAR racing? Fly-fishing, maybe? And My Responses to His
Questions were to be enthusiastic. I was to smile winningly, but
with enough coy distance to make him intrigued, to make him
call back for another movie, one with hot-fudge cake and a Dr.
Pepper thrown in. I was to be light on my patent-leathered toes,
but was not, under any circumstances, to show too much intel-
ligence. No boasting about my love of sines and cosines, inher-
ited from my father's math-teaching days. No hint that, just two
weeks ago, I had read D. H. Lawrence. And The Most Important
Advice of All: no references to my other life, the secret, subdivision life of housecleaning.

We circled the block twice and sweat eased down between
the cups of my bra, soaking into the Kleenexes I'd stuffed in
at the last minute in the office-building restroom. I eyed Joe's
blond hair and straggly mustache as we bought our matinee
tickets, contraband that they were. I'd had strict instructions to
see science fiction or a western, not Zefferelli's *Romeo and Juliet,*
which my mother had heard had a scene with full rear nudity.
Nevertheless, this was what we saw, and it was true. Len Whit-
ing and Olivia Hussey had a secret rendezvous in her bedroom
and Len stood, his white backside flexing in the predawn light.
My stomach and between my legs tingled, a sensation I'd had
before in the office-building library, when I'd read chapters in

a book about Theodora, a Roman harlot turned empress. That book had mentioned words like *nipples* and *erect* and I had read them again and again, especially the parts about what my mother termed *down there*. In the movie-theater dark I studied Joe's profile and, once, placed my palm against his wrist.

Later on, after the movie, we necked on the steps of my father's office building, ten floors safely below his desk, where he was adding columns of figures and, perhaps, penning wistful notes to an imaginary woman, a woman who might someday be my stepmother. We kissed in ways I was familiar with only from the dime-store novels I'd secretly read at my aunt Ruby's house, novels belonging to Eppie, with pictures of tousled schoolgirls or very helpful nurses on their covers. We kissed with teeth and tongues, with the pressure of body against body, mine all bone and knee, his a soft stomach, an uncertain but eager crotch.

I did not allow him to unzip me even an inch or touch any patch of thigh inside my wide culottes legs. I rubbed the toe of a patent-leather shoe against his jeans, gently dug a half-inch heel into the toe of his dingo boot. I let him remove my black plastic glasses, rake back my bangs. Our teeth clicked and my tongue ached, and I said good-bye a full fifteen minutes beyond the afternoon curfew. We spoke of another movie, of a secret football-game get-together, of obscure schemes and means by which we could neck again.

Upstairs, in my father's office, I stood for a long while, watching him at his desk. On a Sunday, he wore a sport coat and a striped dress shirt, collar undone. I seemed to look at him through a screen of golden summer light and new, unnamed desire. *Goldie*, I thought, and saw the name anew.

"You've been kissing, haven't you?" my father asked. "That's what you've been doing."

Goldie's name, as it hung in the air between us, was like soft dust on a dirt road in the wake of a passing car, the car my father might have driven to a lake, Goldie Short by his side for an afternoon of fishing and an occasional kiss. My father had known afternoon dates and lips against lips and a woman named Goldie whom my mother believed he had wanted, in a way I had almost tasted.

Memory makes this story selective. I soften details, add a flourish or a grin at appropriate moments. I edit, delete, expand, contract, as easily as raising or lowering a hemline. I leave out certain names, change the spelling of others, pick this event and not that one. I follow the rules for telling the truth. A story, I'm told, should be Aristotelian. It follows a logical pattern from beginning to middle to end. It is reasonable in its expectations about what can be forgiven or forgotten, gained or lost. It avoids magic and sentimentality, at any cost. It flashes forward at the correct point, steps back only when appropriate. It makes clear who is who, who is happy and who is not.

But what, you might wonder, are endings, and what are beginnings? Is an ending an afternoon in late summer, after soap operas, after my mother's daily hair grooming, long after the first movie adventure and the first, sweet boy-girl touch? An ending, the way my mother knows how I glance at the road, listen for the spin of tires, the mailman's knock, the letter dropped in the box. She knows the surreptitious look in my eyes that says, I have shifted and turned, I am leaving you now, good-bye. *The way I look at her makes her think of birth again, of before that, of the way I kicked and spun, groping for the insides of her until all the water cascaded out, until I cascaded out, slick and new and unpredictable, and of how, ever since, she has been trying to put me back. Put me back in the womb, back behind the closed door, behind the sheets and the blankets, back in the unmade bed where I began.*

How does she get me there? She searches my pockets and my notebooks, intercepts my mail, answers every phone call, grinding her teeth with bitterness. If she could, she would taste my spit for any unfamiliar trace, any evidence of the one she calls that boy.

She'd travel behind my ear, catching every echo, any sign of my betrayal, my susceptibility to loves.

An ending, then, if you must. A summer afternoon. From the living-room recliner, I watched as the mailman crossed the street. I was powerless, of course, to go out there, since we weren't allowed, my father and I, to enter or leave our house without permission. Still, my heart raced ahead of her to the mailbox and the letter I was almost certain she'd find. Her legs in their polyester slacks rolled high and her pink house-slippered feet lifted high to avoid all possible muddy places in the drive. She bent, peered into the box, extracted a letter, a thick one that she tore open on the spot. As she read, her displeasure blossomed. Her eyes narrowed and she was shaking. The letter itself was shaking as she turned back to the house.

I couldn't see any of this from the window, but I'd rehearsed the scene before as a precaution. For weeks, since our afternoon date, my mother had laid down the new law. "You know you can't see that boy again," she'd said. I hadn't seen him, but I had pretended to call girlfriends and called Joe instead, disguising my conversation with a code we had devised, words borrowed from cosmetics. "New concealer," we said, or, "highlighting the right parts." Once, I even begged to spend the night at Lisa's house and met Joe there for a night of making out, Lisa and her beau in one room, Joe and me in another.

"And now this letter," my mother said as she kicked aside her house shoes onto the paper taped beside the front door. She stood by the recliner, the letter's pages crackling in my face. "Filled with filth, with words no boy ever should, ever will, say in this house, no thank you, ma'am."

There had been another letter, intercepted when my father and I had stopped at the mailbox on the way to Wednesday-night prayer meeting and I'd retrieved the mail. Had he known as I slipped the letter into a grocery ad, then read it in the church bathroom? It had indeed been filled with forbidden words, phrases, and even pencil drawings. "Sexy," Joe had called me. His sexy, voluptuous one. He had drawn women with large busts, their bodices undone, their hair fiery and unkempt, and she had found the letter hidden in my zippered Bible. Little did my mother know that these women were heroines, the Valkyries of Marvel Comics. Joe drew them in art class during the school year. Rima, Girl of the Jungle. Catwoman. Spidergirl. Our sexuality, thus far, was as innocuous as Saturday-morning television. This afternoon, that did not matter.

She pointed to words on the page. *Luscious. Delectable. Tasteable.* "What does this mean?"

What she didn't know was that this moment had nothing at all to do with language. It had to do with my wanting what was mine. I wanted the contents of my dresser drawers, the ones in my room I'd never opened. I wanted lemonade from the refrigerator on a summer afternoon. I wanted my body all to myself when I was dressing and I wanted to touch my own menstrual blood with reverence, my own mysterious flesh. I wanted my diary back and I wanted silence and a closed bedroom door. I wanted a mother like the ones on afternoon television, mothers with pretty dresses and friends over for coffee and daughters who ask advice. I wanted love.

I met my mother halfway between recliner chair and letter, between question and answer. The letter's sheets twisted and ripped in our hands, but I held on with my wanting. I didn't tell her the letter was mine, this first love was mine, its thus-far innocence. Instead I reached, I grabbed. The letter, its thick, white sheets, tore between us, but I wanted my half. And I wanted hers.

I held and shoved, shoved against my mother's angry, frightened mouth. I became taller than her. I grew into someone else and I knew it, even when she reached down for a wedge-heeled slipper, then slammed it against my face.

I want to remember the proper ending to this part of the story. Mother discovers daughter's budding sexuality via a clandestine letter from a boy. Mother and daughter struggle, they make gestures neither understands, their eyes meet and they recognize for the first time the chasm between them, between their hearts and their definitions of desire. In that unbridgeable chasm lies history—birth and its resultant pain, the sadness of adolescence, the knowledge that the daughter's face mirrors the mother's, the mother's mirrors the daughter's, that this means the inevitability of years and the passage of time. An ending. The mirror breaks, the shoe falls, ugly truths spill out and nothing can be put back again.

What, you say, are endings and what are beginnings? A shoe strikes a teenaged girl's head and enmity blossoms in her heart. There is no stopping this emotion. It grows like a moonflower, white and insidious in the dark. It resists afternoons of sunlight and pretense. It will not believe that love is possible anymore, that mother loves daughter, that love defies. "Love," the Bible says. "Set it as a seal upon thine heart, as a seal upon thine arm, for it is as strong as death."

The Bible is full of such love. One Mary wipes the feet of Christ with her hair. Another Mary stands at the feet of the cross, blinded by love, her son suspended in midair, both dead and alive for all eternity. But love is not as strong as enmity, which grows, that seductive bloom. It has tendrils and roots that defy everything, overcome everything. Enmity grows in the heart of the girl, and in the heart of the father, and soon this enmity surpasses all. The bloom is enormous, fleshy and alive. It devours hearth and home. A beginning, as complete, as alive, as any ending.

After that summer afternoon, there were two, possibly three more months of our subdivision house. Of father and mother and daughter and grocery lists and home in the suburbs. Our lives were changing. Throughout the fall, I laid intricate plans for dates with Joe, secret meetings at football games and fast-food joints. I smoked my first cigarettes and tried them a second time, even after my mother found tobacco shavings at the bottom of my purse. My father stayed gone on a business trip with no explanation, even when my mother called his hotel and found his room empty. Rules were shattered forever. My father stamped through the house in the afternoon with his shoes on. He sat on the end of the couch where we were never allowed. He made himself a cheese sandwich and ate it standing in the living room. "How," he asked, "do you like that?"

The whole time I was laying plans for love and escape, my father was falling in love with a co-worker, a younger, red-haired woman who walked in the rain with him if he liked and who wanted his touch. He went to church at unexpected hours. He signed on for more business meetings. My mother claimed that someone was calling and hanging up. That she had found matchbooks from motels and lipstick stains, every predictable sign. I knew of this liaison of his, having found a draft of a love letter in a notebook in the car when my father stopped to buy milk and canned soup. But I kept his secrets, and mine, and they seethed, churned. Our house was full to bursting with such secrets.

She was desperate. She scurried after us, wiping, sweeping. She had made the world as safe as she could and now the doors were opening, the windows were sliding up, sunlight was pouring in, bright and merciless. "Once I had a secret love" were the words to a song in one of my mother's favorite Doris Day movies, and those lyrics had underwritten our lives. Now we were pulling back the drapes, the cobwebs of our secrecy. Our treachery was a spider, a web as huge as God, and she was in its shadow and she was afraid. For many years neither of us, my father nor I, had seen her sadness.

"My parents are divorcing," I told Joe, a declaration of all that could come—freedom on school nights, weekend dates past twelve, skipped school days and cars parked on country roads. It was never a question for me, which parent I'd stay with, which life I'd choose. My father and I were allies, after all. Allies of secret romances, wished-for alliances. We were beginning our lives.

I try to remember how such moments in time were the beginning or the end of something. How they had any logic at all, any flow, any impetus toward the all-important story, the truth. Memory, like water, refuses to be held. Events flood past, seeking a shape that matters.

I am fourteen and infatuated for the first time and my mother, who fears the outside world, warns me about the dangers of love and touch. I am fourteen and winter comes, full of cold and anger, and we go to eastern Kentucky. "Just for a visit," they tell me. Is it Christmastime, this visit? My memory refuses this truth, but let's say that we are headed home for the holidays like always. Home to eastern Kentucky, my mother to one county and my father and me to the next. Like always, I am invisible as we drive toward the mountains, our tires hushed with snow and the car too warm and words falling like ice from their mouths.

"Why?" she is saying. "Why do you treat me this way?"

She conjures ghosts with her hands. Ghosts of filth he treads upon her floor, ghosts of shirt collars she must scrub until her palms bleed. Ghosts of desire. Ghosts of joy no one is capable of giving her. I am the only one who sees these ghosts as they float to my lap in the backseat as we drive further east, toward the land of the Holy Ghost where my mother was born. And my father, trying one last time to keep us a happy family driving east, trying to keep his hands steady on the steering wheel, trying to take that curve, and the next and the next, to navigate us home like always, to keep us safe.

Trying, but his eyes are cold when he says, "Enough, I've had enough."

I looked behind us at the drift of snow rising from the road, and I believe, even now, that what I saw was a ghost, an omen of surrender. We can hear that snow falling a foot deep, the next day and the next, my father's mother and I, as we sit by the fire in the back room and work a jigsaw puzzle of the United States and its capitals. Indianapolis, Springfield, Jefferson City. I fit together all the pieces west. That is how we always spend holidays, my father and I, home away from home in eastern Kentucky, only this time Christmas day has come and gone and now my father is with my mother, taking her to our house for the last time. I believe even now he meant it all for the best when he took her back there, made her pack her bags, emptied the rooms of her. This I can only imagine. This I must translate as true or not. She says there was a gun, that he held it to his own head and said, "It's you or me." She says this, and mothers never lie.

The days and months afterward, when my father and I are alone, I believe I am glad. She had made us prisoners of her love and now we are free. I open closets, open drawers, run with bare feet on the front lawn and track mud right across the living-room floor. I step one and two, just like she used to do, and I say it then and there, like I will for five years, like I mean it, "I hate her, I hate her. I hate her and she never existed." Poof. My mother's gone. At night my father and I watch what we want on TV. We eat snacks and cold noodles right out of the can. I go back to school, after my mother's disappearance, in a peasant dress and moccasins and am thus released from my childhood, that prison of my mother's love.

Time whips by like wash on a line, like wind down Abbot Mountain where my aunt Ruby and I once went walking. At fourteen, I grew my hair long and wild and Pa said someone should hold me down, should shear me clean. But that's only hearsay, since I cut my mother and her family from my life as neatly as an envelope slit open with a knife. Back home with my father, I opened drawers and closets with abandon and threw away anything, any blouse or shoe or sock, that I didn't love. My mother, I told myself, was no mother at all. I told myself this as I sat watching television with my father, as I looked at the mothers in television commercials, the ones with aprons and munificence. I told myself this when I refused to see her, month upon month, while I ingested drugs like candy and drank vodka straight from the bottle and lost my virginity in the front seat of a car, as I listened to full-volume acid rock and told myself my new stepmother was no more a mother than my own mother had ever been.

I had sex in parked cars and in Joe's unmade bed, afternoons while his parents were at work, and by fifteen I was pregnant with a son I would give up. My mother didn't know this, or anything else about my life at fifteen, sixteen, seventeen, and more, since I continued to refuse to see her. Five years of silence. But by then my pregnancy was already hidden like a bone in the yard. "She's had a kidney infection or two. She's not too responsible and she'll probably never go to college," my father wrote in a letter my mother showed me, twenty years later, when we were speaking again. "But lots of good people aren't educated," he said, "and they do just fine." We'd opened our lives, my father and I, and then shut them up again, tight as a house, another secret we could never tell.

I try to remember that I was fourteen, sixteen at best. Twenty. Thirty-five. Time is a summer wind that smells like heat and burns everything away. By thirty-five I will have told myself all is forgiven. By then, I will have told myself I've forgotten the past and I will have gone back to my mother and her love. She will love me, blindly, the frantic love you give something beautiful you lost and found at the back of a drawer and then say, "Oh, there it is, it was there all along." She will love me like chocolates or butter-

scotch, *like all things sweet and passing, since I will come and go quickly from her house, eager, always, to take the high road out, the highway going away and away.*

Love comes and then disappears, gone without a promise of constancy. When I am thirty-five and home for visits, I realize this is the refrain they have all learned, the women in my mother's family. Love has made and unmade my mother, sent her back to eastern Kentucky for good. Love, for my mother, has become songs off a transistor radio she has set up in the kitchen, to listen to while she washes and rewashes her hands. Love is a Sandra Dee movie where the girl gets the boy and everything always comes out right. And men? Faithless, all. She sleeps, white gloved and virginal again, in the back room of the childhood home she will never again leave.

When I am thirty-five and visiting, I like my aunt Ruby the best, even though her face is empty, her voice flat as Bible pages. I see in her a ghost of what could have been, a shadow of strength that comes and recedes in her eyes. Love has defeated even Ruby, who used to dream of faraway places and of the possibility of flight.

"Tell me," she says. "Tell me about the places you've been."

And I tell her, about places she'd once imagined, other towns, maybe, or some state bordered by the ocean. Divorced now, like my mother, Ruby lives in an apartment paid for by Social Services, but stays with my mother and her parents whenever she's being visited by visions of herself crucified. She naps in the back room, turns the sheets down sometimes as early as one o'clock in the afternoon. She takes pills for this and that, for depression and random voices that sing her to sleep, voices in her own mind that sound, she says, like hymns of praise—just as I am, without one plea, but that thy blood was shed for me. *She sees God, she says, but she does not pray.*

Ruby's lone hands dream themselves movie-magazine beautiful and travel with love over lotion bottles and orange sticks at the five-and-dime. We sit in our nightgowns in the afternoon and she looks at my legs, which I do not shave above the knee. This, to her, is a mystery. Mysterious, also, that I navigate interstates, that I have a job and a car of my own.

"Tell me," she says, "about the places you've been."

*I tell about a three-day bus trip I once took up north. I tell about road signs and maps and my love of atlases of the world, but I do not tell Ruby or my mother about my secret life, its missing years. I can feel my mouth forming words—*relinquish, surren-der, now*—but I am not yet ready to tell my story. Instead, I tell of incidentals and I listen, as I will for years. I watch my mother pacing the clean rooms of her parents' home, listen to her bedroom slippers keeping time, one and two. I listen to her story of how my father abandoned her, she says, after all she did, the floors she shined, the plates she washed, for us. And I listen as Ruby tells her own version of loss and love. Unbeloved, she sings redneck blues into the dark. "That man Eppie, drove a two-tone Chevy, he's so fine, came and took my love without a word, gone without a sign." I do not tell, yet, how I have traveled places they could not imagine.*

CHAPTER FIVE

Sacred Heart

What I remember from 1972 is one luscious drug dream. Drug dreams come with taking curves on back roads to the tune of "El Conquistador" and "Spanish Eyes." Drug dreams come with sur- reptitious exchanges in bathrooms and public parks. They come with paraphernalia, head-shop pipes and bongs made of hand- blown glass. By the time I'm fifteen I'm wise, a sage, an old pro. I've held consecrated wafer of pure acid on my tongue, had my skin anointed with the sweat of my first lover. I've done speed a dozen times, acid a dozen more, and mescaline, to my regret, only twice. Pot makes me sick the first time out, until I discover that alcohol makes a toke slide down like cream and that pot can be cooked to a paste you spread like Sue Bee honey right on a pipe's screen.

We trade jokes, my friends and I, about tracers and flashbacks. We listen to songs backward to catch the drug encoding in the lyr- ics and we find the most trivial of disasters a hilarious event. My friends and I head out at midnight and push a bale of hay onto the highway from an overpass and marvel at the way the air flames up. Home alone at the end of a three-day speed high, I fire my father's derringer into the yard so I won't keep hearing the keen beating of my own heart. The world, we say, used to be one dull color, but now it's a Technicolor Dream Coat. It's Orange Sunshine and Colombian Gold. It's blotter and Panama Red. Drugs are prophecy. Drug dreams are flight. Drug dreams are light and the sheer power of infinity, a vision of the afterworld and the future world all at once. They make time one long trail of fire we can bend in the air with our bare hands. We're a jet blaze in the sky. We're everything and a marvelous, infinitesimal nothing when we do drugs. Time, we tell ourselves, matters not at all when you're stoned. Stoned, we say. Stoned again. Stone cold fox. Foxy, foxy lady.

I am, I tell myself, on the highway to hell and I love it. I love the times I slip a new toothbrush or a compact with a mirror up my coat sleeve in the supermarket, love the way you can shop for whole wardrobes when you wear a great big coat to the department store. Soon I fall into a special group of friends with names like Lefty or Poncho or Johnny Steele. For months after it happens, I can still hear the sound of the window breaking in the first deserted house we broke into. Nothing harmful, really, just hours of playing with the Rock 'Em Sock 'Em Robots someone had left behind, pans of popcorn on the camp stove one of my friends brought along, a couple of fifths of vodka. And after that? Joe and I are on a marketing plan. We steal headsets and transistors from the discount store and sell them for cash. We push prescription drugs and do well as the middlemen for drugs imported from the next town. We play Hendrix doing "The Star-Spangled Banner" full blast. We are, we tell ourselves, the American dream.

But my clearest recollections of 1972 are late afternoons and touch. A room in my father's house. No one home and stolen time from school. Rough tweed of couches, the kind with covers that *come off to make small, rollaway beds. First touch, penis in hand, my hand, his hand, who knows where. Hours later. My father, home and hanging up his tie in a closet in the same room and saying, "Who?" The room rich with the scents of cum and sweat. Or another afternoon, or another. Car seats on back roads and me and that boy, hidden and half undressed. Penis into me and hurting and me saying, "Go on, more, go on." Blood the next day.*

By then my father is in love again, with the office co-worker who not only will walk in the rain with him but will introduce him to Conway Twitty concerts and NASCAR. *Love, he will later say, made him blind. Blind to how I am sixteen and looking at the world from a spacey distance I call holy. "I'm pregnant," I tell Joe, the father of my child, and he offers me a pre-engagement ring and no plan at all. I am pregnant and my body is farther away than ever, its breasts tender and its belly swelling. I cast this self from the heights of chairs and from the top of the hope chest my mother left behind. I do not miscarry. Instead I think of road signs and distance and soon I have a plan down right.* I'll run away, *I tell myself,* run away for good. *Run away west to the tune of my own little song.* I'm leaving now, good-bye.

I run away with Phil, not the father of my baby-to-be. Phil, who wants to be Cat Stevens and write songs to change the spiritual direction of American youth but can't play the guitar. Phil, a delicious secret who has fucked me in my own bed at my father's house and climbed out the window just before we were found out. Phil tells me he is getting ready to hitchhike somewhere—Chattahoochee, Apalachee, Tallahassee. The names sound like poems and so I stuff fifty bucks and odd change into my jeans-jacket pocket, money made from pawning the watch my grandfather gave me when I was nine. I fill a paper sack with a notebook, a spare shirt, and a toothbrush I soon will leave behind at a truck stop outside of Little Rock.

On the day I leave home for good, two friends of Phil's, bikers known for giving orphans gifts at Christmastime, pull into the drive in a yellow Pontiac, windows rolled down and the radio jacked up. "Get your motor running," Steppenwolf sings, "head out on the highway, looking for adventure, and whatever comes our way." Phil, from the backseat, says, "Hey, man," meaning me, and I slide in, eyeing one of the bikers, the long blond ponytail, his leather jacket, thinking nothing of it when he compliments the moon and stars embroidered on my jeans by calling me a honky.

The air is cold and pure and I draw in deep lungfuls of it, but I'm ready to run back in and lock the doors and pull down the shades. I'm also ready to reach up front and crank the music louder and take a hit off the joint they're passing as we drive away, but that isn't the real truth of this moment. The moment when past and future shimmy and shake. I'm shrugging off the past like a dance partner I no longer want and I tell myself there's nothing left but now and trucks and cars that will take me over this horizon and on to the next.

Over my shoulder is the house of my childhood and I turn to watch it disappear around the bend and I think, Now, at last, I'm free. *I'm ready to be relieved and I'm ready to breathe out and in all on my own, no mother stepping behind me, one and two, no mother now or ever, none at all. And then I think I see something move. A shadow rising. Rising from the rooftop of that house of my mother's disappearance, spiraling through the air. Moving after us, trying to catch hold of the bumper of the car as we drive away west. Nothing but a sad thing, a sad and now lonely woman, that shadow, but I don't look back. My mother is now nothing but a shadow taking flight over the subdivision houses and lawns, taking flight toward the sun and disappearing for what I want to believe is forever.*

And it's true. I have forever in front of me. Forever and tomorrow nothing more than now. We head west from an exit ramp where the bikers left us. West on I-64, where we soon hop a semi. I watch passing lights of towns and tell myself it's back there, all of it. I renounce you, I renounce you, I say to the child I'd never been. To the father of the child I'm carrying. To the child itself, as good as back there still in my father's house, that world of hidden signs and symptoms, that world still holding its breath in the wake of my mother's ghost. We continue west as far as Louisville, Kentucky, with a truck driver who swallows black beauties with cup after cup of coffee laced with whiskey as he tells us stories about his whore of a wife and his town-to-town lovers. He lets us off near a downtown halfway house where for the first time I sleep all night with a boy, with Phil who tells me not to complain that we've eaten nothing but day-old cheese Danish served in big commodity bags in the front hall. The next day it's another truck driver, then another. With the last one, before we hit St. Louis, we hear a citizen's-band police report describing the search for some unnamed runaways and so we stay put in Columbia, Missouri, first in the apartment of some Persian students where we eat pot-laced brownies and party all night, next in some dorm room where I find Phil kissing a girl who smells of patchouli.

Then we're home free. We're in an apartment on Hitt Street, its drop-ins and junkies all the family I now have. Memory becomes a collage. Becomes hollow as pipe made of glass. Memory is vanishing smoke that tastes sweet and bitter. Memory is a late-night shadow of a naked woman in the living room, her eyes acid wide. Wardrobe in a hall with ten one-dollar bills hidden inside, just in case, the cost of an animal-tranquilizer high. Memory is me with a fever that lets me see apocalyptic horses traversing the walls until I am hospitalized with the name Leah Wheeler. Then home again to my mattress on the floor and Phil, just pretending, holding a knife to my throat while I jack him off. Phil, gone most days to steal appliances with a pimp named Slim and soon in love with some other girl with hair the color of amber. Mattress on the floor where I sleep alone and hold my stomach, feeling my skin grow tighter and tighter, touching sharp edges, the elbow, the knee, the soon-to-be-boy hiding in this body called mother.

Come winter, late 1972, the Hitt Street apartment was the place I shared with Phil, and with Marsha Wisdom, who left home at thirteen and became a heroin addict a year after that. We had other roommates, although you could hardly call any of them roommates, those drop-ins, other runaways, junkies and part-time pimps, a changing cast of characters in four rooms on a back street I came to call home. How I like to see myself in that apartment is in the kitchen. A kitchen with a three-legged thrift-store table propped up with an open drawer near a sink. Kitchen with black and white linoleum and water bugs in the soup bowls at night and one window decorated with waxed paper ironed over melted crayons. Strings of love beads were tacked around a single, bare bulb, but I was not living a life full of love.

I sat for hours in that winter kitchen, the late-afternoon light just strong enough for me to see the words I'd written. I filled up shoplifted notebooks with stories about God and drawings of human hands. The hands I drew were never alone. I drew them holding other hands or holding themselves, fingers intertwined. I drew them marked by the stigmata, palms up to receive holy light. After I'd drawn my fill, I'd pull my knees into my arms underneath some stretched-out sweater, study the list of things to do taped to the wall by the fridge. "Pick up milk and spaghetti; check Jack-in-the-Box for part-time work; allotment check; Granger?"

Let's call it one such afternoon. Someone had remembered to buy spaghetti, and it was already frothing on the stove, its oven door open where everyone was standing, for the heat. Terence's wire-rims were steamed and I could hardly see his eyes; they were as bleached out as the storefronts and warehouses in the city's back alleys. Just for someone to talk to, I wished for Marsha.

Marsha. Pretty Marsha, not quite eighteen years old. I had made up a secret rhyme for her—*Good Fairy, Glinda, Mother Mary, oh come home to me, to me.* Marsha had left the apartment early that morning, stepped into the hall in her long junk-store dress the color of plums, a velvet one with sleeves just to the elbow. *Mother Protectress, place of rest, home away from home, please don't tarry, be always wary, oh come home, come home to me.* Full skirts held out, arms spread wide, she had said, "I look lovely, don't I," and I said yes. Marsha, the mother I'd have chosen, if I could have. Marsha, gone since early morning. Who knew where?

Even she wouldn't have been able to talk to that crew, there since one-thirty and still deciding at four-thirty how to spend the day. Some days it was just Terence or Coleen or Randi, but other days it was whomever they'd met in back-alley conversation or over a coffee refill at the convenience store. Other runaways, same as me, or sometimes guys with ponytails and ripped-out jeans just like anybody else, only they had faces closed as a door, wrinkles around their eyes and mouths that made them look angry or tired.

Today, Terence came in first, with his flannel shirt, his looking-off-in-the-distance eyes, hands so big they could hold my wrists, pull me next to him so tight my bones would be like paper. Then he'd look me in the face and say, "Leah, that's your name, isn't it, sweetheart?"

"Where's Marsha?" Terence asked when he came in, slamming the kitchen door behind him.

A cold blast of outside air followed him and he stamped his foot impatiently, pretending to look at my notebook. My newest poems were mostly about people, like the woman down the hall who had three kids and wore a headscarf, galoshes, and a lime-green nylon raincoat, summer or winter.

"Pretty good," Terence said, whistling through his teeth to show how impressed he was. I knew the truth about Terence. Like how he'd left comments in the margins of this very notebook before, things like, "You, who're you trying to impress?"

Then he caught sight of the refrigerator. It was an old Frigidaire model that leaned forward, sweated and ran and refused to shut. I had decided, that very morning, there was no point keeping something plugged in when it was ready to just plain quit. The door was hanging open now, with melting frost dripping down into the empty lower compartment.

"I'll be damned," Terence said as he rushed across the room, face flushed. "Marsha know about this?"

He fished a small square of aluminum foil out of the standing water, then slammed the freezer compartment shut.

"A waste," he said. "A plain waste of a good chemical."

I bent over my drawing again, looking busy. I knew they kept neat little baggies of Jamaican and Mexican in the freezer, but I'd paid no attention to the tiny foiled squares of windowpane, under the ice trays, when I shut the fridge off. After all, I had done nothing but keep it from dying its own death with that constant thump and whir, hour after hour, like a heartbeat and rush of blood. Was I to blame for the thawing out of their drugs?

They were happy soon enough, anyway. Over the next two hours as everyone trickled in, Terence handed around a kitchen cup filled with acid-laced freezer water. They offered me some, but I shook my head. The water smelled used up, like the celery and tomatoes from, when was it, last week? It would have a bitter taste, metallic as a thermometer under the tongue. They passed the cup from hand to hand as carefully as holy water. They were waiting to get off.

"Well," Randi said as she loosened her colored scarf. "You wouldn't believe. Terence said to me, first thing this morning, he said, 'I've had it.' 'Had it with what,' I said. He rushed out the door like I'd never see him again. So mad you could taste it."

The others laughed. Someone handed her the cup and she sipped. She was standing on the kitchen chair, bowing, handing the cup on, drawing her story out, a needle pulling thread. With each word, her lipsticked mouth widened, narrowed.

"And I didn't see him again for four hours. Four whole hours."

I put down my pen.

"Then he came busting in the door. Hardly looked at me. Took me by the shoulders, threw me down on the bed, stared. And I said, 'Terence, is that all you want? Why didn't you say so?' "

Randi laughed and her feather earrings danced.

"Then I noticed the funniest thing," she said. "This little fleck of dark in his left eye. Shaped just like the state of Massachusetts."

The kitchen smelled of overcooked noodles, smoke. Randi, Terence, even Coleen, were beginning to sound a little sinister, their laughter high pitched, sharp as broken bottles. I got up, grabbed a rag from the sink and began soaking water up, squeezing the rest of their trip and its stories down the sink.

Later, when the refrigerator was dry and shiny, almost like new, I slipped out onto the fire escape. The city, three flights down, seemed farther, with everything hushed, new-fallen snow brushing the sidewalk. A man stopped under a streetlight, shook his coat. A car door slammed, its lights shone, vanished. I closed my eyes and wished really, really hard for Marsha to come home.

Eyes shut, all I could see was Marsha a couple of days before, early in the morning. She was in the window seat of the other bedroom, staring down at the park bordering Hitt Street. Traffic was still quiet and she was combing her long, dark hair with her fingers, her face with that look—wanting to remember something she couldn't, yards, houses, rooms, hands letting go. I took a brush from the dresser, began to untangle her hair. Neither of us said anything and after a while Marsha put her arms around me. She smelled sweet, like cinnamon or fresh air.

"Hey, you all right?"

I jumped, opened my eyes. I didn't have my coat on and realized how cold it was on the fire escape. I smiled at Coleen. She was twenty, nearly five years older, and she took the time to look out for me.

Coleen was also pregnant, and went with me on alternate Thursdays to the University Medical Center for the free Swiss cheese on rye they gave pregnant women in the cafeteria. Usually, while we waited for noon, we visited the nursery. We could stand for hours with our foreheads pressed against the display window, wondering that our huge bellies could transform into what we saw inside the incubators. The tiniest ones were hardly babies at all, nothing but elbows, knees, fingers wrapped in layers of cotton. With some of them you couldn't even see their eyes.

One Thursday we took a wrong corridor onto the east wing, instead of maternity. Past some double swinging doors there was a hall lit by fresh paint, bulbs behind glass-covered shelves lining the walls. Coleen stopped in front of large jars crowding these shelves.

"Leah," Coleen said that day, calling me by the name I'd adopted for my life in this city, in my life as a runaway.

"Man," she said. "Just what do you think this shit is, anyway?"

She touched the glass, comparing finger lengths with a jar in which floated a hand, its palms white and soft looking, like it had scrubbed too many floors. Another jar held a neatly severed left foot and ankle belonging to a good-sized man, while others contained tongues, ears, most any part of the human body you could imagine.

Voices came from an office down the hall.

"Hey, Brian," someone said. "You think it's time, buddy?"

Light shone through Coleen's fingers and her face looked solemn and respectful, like it did when we came in for the Tuesday-morning obstetrics clinic and they put the stethoscope up to her ears. I wanted that, too. I wanted to put my ear to this glass, listen to what she called the sanctity of life.

Now, I shivered and Coleen reached for my hand.

"I want to show you something," she said.

She took my hand, pulled it toward her and inside, next to layers of shirts and sweaters and behind the unbuttoned band of her old jeans. I felt movement, so slight I could have imagined it, like touching the wall, inside, down at the railway station just before the train passed.

"Isn't it the most amazing thing?" she asked, squeezing my arm.

"Yes," I said, though this was pretty far from the truth. I was seven months along and Coleen was due in only a few weeks, and I knew that the definition of amazing had settled in us in different ways. I held still, feeling the pulse of skin, thinking of how her bare stomach must look, with the veins stretched next to the surface, the shifting of knees or a foot.

From inside the kitchen, a new voice. Granger, Marsha's friend.

"What's all this?" he asked.

Through the window I saw, already, the mixture of awe and awkwardness he created in a room, almost like being near Marsha herself, as if she were sitting with them, at that very kitchen table. How many times had I heard it, absolute silence until Marsha's hand slid across, started up his arm. Coleen had asked a million times, "What, just what does she see in him?"

That's what I thought too, when Marsha brought him home for the first time, from the Corner Market, where she'd seen him lifting snack cakes and powdered aspirin. He was pale, so pale his hair was silver, his eyes pinkish blue, his silences long, white and flat. Silences they filled up with anything, straight whiskey shots, futile attempts at love. Granger seemed to prefer to wrap his arms around himself, feel his own thinness.

Now, Granger took the kitchen cup, tossed it toward the corner. It broke neatly.

"Chemicals," he said. "You want chemicals?"

He took a tiny bottle out of his pocket, opened it.

Beside me, graceful and noiseless, Coleen got up, moved back inside. A cloud of warmth enveloped me as she went toward the open kitchen door.

"Me first, me first," she said. She stood near him, opened her mouth, a hungry bird, waiting, like all of them, with their used-up excitement, for one drop, some monumental blast.

None of this story is the absolute truth, of course. I did not live in an apartment with black-and-white linoleum, did not live with a Randi or a Terence. I would never have been confident enough to unplug a vital refrigeration unit, touch the stomach of a pregnant girl, or remain calm in a kitchen full of people I'd known for only a few weeks. And Marsha? Was she thirteen or eighteen or something in between? What was her favorite song? "I've seen the needle and the damage done, a little part of it in everyone."

The truth is I can stand to tell you only so much. When I was six I lived in a mobile home and my room was down the hall and I was afraid of stitched-together monsters and the dark. Against my parents' wishes I would stand up in bed and switch on the light, to save myself. Now the light is too strong. I want it pale yellow as a porch light in summer. I want it rose-colored and soft. But memory, that relentless ghost, drums at my heart and I open myself little by little, a door to my son's birth year, a door to the sheer light of myself. I can bear to let in only so much of this light of truth, the truth of what my life was, then.

The truth is that through that Columbia, Missouri, apartment passed numerous people with names I can no longer recall, with names I now invent, to give them a context in my past. There was Red, the tall, red-haired lover of a very pregnant Irish woman who lived next to where I lived. It is she I have since called Coleen. Once, at night through the thin walls, I heard Red and Coleen making love. At the time, what I believed I heard was someone crying, saying, "Oh no, please, God, no." Though I was nearly eight months pregnant, I had never heard human voices full of passion. The next day, when Coleen came over to borrow some milk, I questioned her about what had been wrong the night before. She pulled a strand of long, brown hair across her face, narrowed her green eyes, said, "Hmm, oh, that," as she looked in Marsha's direction.

There was really a Marsha, and her last name was Wisdom. It was she I once saw standing somewhere, kitchen, hallway, bedroom, her open mouth turned up, waiting for chemicals. "Lovely Marsha," said a hippie whose name I have forgotten. He played an acoustic guitar with one of its plastic strings snapped and sang songs he'd written like, "Come out, Marsha, come out and dry your hair in the sunshine." Sunshine. Orange, yellow. Windowpane and crystal meth, to help you see the color of the sky. The words I remember are as lovely and transparent as light.

I could have stopped it, you say. Stopped this chain of events before they were born, summoned a metaphoric chariot right out of the sky, called my father collect from Columbia. Could have called on some night during what was by then winter and long, icy streets, but I believed I'd be greeted with vague inquiries, conclusions as insubstantial as snow moving through air. I believed that my father had no more idea who I was than I did myself and that if I had managed to find a phone some night by eleven or twelve, his voice would have come over the line cautious and removed.

We all make our beds, *he might have said*. We all make the places and the beds we must lie in.

Such beds of which my father would never have dreamed. My father, the one I blamed for not rescuing me sooner from my childhood, during which we had both suffered. My father, blameless even so for how he moved on so quickly, racing ahead toward the blessed horizon, toward a home with the windows open beside a four-poster bed and love present, blown in gently by the winter air. My father, still living in the house of my childhood and married, only weeks after I ran away, to a new woman with the scent of hair spray and mysterious colognes. My father, blameless for how he did not realize that while he was racing forward to a life he had so long wanted, I was still suspended in time and space, recently emerged from my past, but running from its secrets and its cleanliness. My father did not realize how I was not yet released from the wicked enchantment that was my childhood, that I was still held fast by its ghosts. My father, I believed, agreed with my childhood's refrains, the ones that told me I was not clean enough yet, not yet pure enough to love.

The truth is that what I remember most of all from that Hitt Street apartment are a rocking chair, a living-room window with cloth tacked up, and a window seat. Days, I stayed hours in that rocking chair. I remember it as beige, with a ripped-out back and the foam-rubber stuffing coming through. I remember my bare feet and the feel of indoor-outdoor carpet. I remember a notebook, the first part full of ballpoint-pen drawings of hands and peace symbols and birds in flight, all of which I'd done months before in an all-night fit of speed-induced sleeplessness. "Help me," I wrote in my notebook. "Help me, help me, help me." And yet I wanted no help.

Where I was, was the center of the universe, a room and time that had no beginning and no end. I was not pregnant. It would not happen, this child as yet unnamed in me. Nights, I tried to summon the courage to roam down to the Jack-in-the-Box two streets over, where I could panhandle for spare change. Occasionally, when I went out at night, someone passing by the corner near the apartment would give me a dollar for one square Jack-in-the-Box meal. Days, where I sat was at the center of no particular story called my own. I had no father, mother, hometown. No growing belly or stretch marks; in fact, no body at all.

Nights, I could curl up on a mattress on the floor in the back room and dream myself invisible, folded and folded into a piece of black cloth made of me, so small I did not exist. Like this, I was safe.

Like then, with everyone gearing up for another Saturday night. I was at the kitchen table. Randi, at the moment, was sitting with her back against the side of the stove, legs crossed, head resting on Terence's shoulder. She was wearing a pair of jeans and a Salvation Army 1950s-style lambswool sweater, like always. It was the necklaces she changed every day, ones she called holy inspirations, once an Egyptian scarab on a thin chain, another time an artificial-garnet rosary she said she found near the confessional at the Church of the Immaculate Conception on Seventy-seventh Street. Today she was wearing a simple strand of dime-store pearls. I had to look at it just right, eyes squinted, to figure out exactly what was holy about this necklace. Then the pearls caught the pink light from overhead and took on a softened, brittle look. She drew them tenderly through her parted lips.

"Remember Las Cruces, Terry?" Randi asked.

She'd been laughing hard and her voice came out breathless, slightly enticing. Her eyes were wide, full to the brim with her dark, expanded pupils. They made me think of full moons, of eclipses, of a desert wind you could feel but not see. That's what she wanted me to see, but I knew if I touched her skin it wouldn't feel sun-warmed at all, but damp, a little delirious.

"Yes," he said. "I remember the armpit of the old South-west."

She ignored him, twirled a strand of hair around her finger.

"Have I ever told you guys about that night?" she asked. "The one I spent alone out at Copper Canyon?"

"Only about a thousand times." Terence rubbed her shoulder, fondly enough, but it was easy to see he really meant it. He was bored. He kept looking, a little longingly, in Coleen's direction. She was sitting in the chair across from me at the table, eyes closed. She was humming something that sounded like "Battle Hymn of the Republic."

Randi kept talking anyway. I glanced over at Granger to see if he was listening too, but he was only looking out the window, beyond the fire escape, at the streetlight, which reflected in his silver hair. Snow had begun falling, heavier than before, and the windowpanes were lined with thin elbows of white. Randi's voice sounded muffled and strange with a drug dream that was not ours, though she wanted it to be.

It was the same story as always about how she and Terence left New Mexico in 1969. There were some vivid references to a sunset, and we tried to imagine rose quartz or mica sparkling under a sun we hadn't seen. Cottonwood trees, ringtail cats, cliff overhangs and sleeping out. How different that was than camping on someone's floor. As if only during sleeping out did you crawl inside some sleeping bag or blanket or another person's arms and pull your own knees into your arms and feel afraid and feel about that small.

"It started about midnight," she said. "I was sleeping in an old miner's shack, due north of the canyon. Around midnight this wind came up. I was way down in my sleeping bag, but I was still tasting grit between my teeth and feeling it behind my eyelids. I kept expecting the moon to come out, but it never did. I could look out and see clouds across the moon, until there wasn't any. That's when the sounds began."

Her voice sank to a whisper.

"Pebbles falling on tin. Like that. Sounds louder and louder, a storm of them. I kept sitting up and expecting rain, but there was nothing."

She paused, repeated this last, to make sure we got it.

"Nothing."

Terence, by this time, was standing behind Coleen's chair, stroking her thin hair. There was a lot more to the recollections, stories about Indian prayer rugs, blackbirds with white feathers, kachina dolls. But we'd had enough. The desert had receded, gone one more time into memory, leaving no film of dust on our teeth. Lightning, stretching from sky to earth in one sheer and momentary flash of brilliance, was never really there. This was just a third-floor apartment, a kitchen, a stove for warmth, no one speaking.

No one could summon a word when, at the last minute, before she put on her sweater for us to go out to a diner or a coffee-house or a bar before they closed, Randi told us how a certain woman on Patterson Street aborted her baby when she was five months pregnant, how that, too, sent chills all the way into her chest, down into her fingertips, just like sounds on a tin roof in a possibly imaginary canyon, how he was perfect, a boy already, absolutely perfect.

And Coleen, who was leaning her head against Terence's stomach, was humming, not "Battle Hymn of the Republic," but "Yellow Rose of Texas."

None of us can be blamed, of course, for our seeming lack of respect for human life. For our casual dismissal of the American dream, that holy family of dinner-table conversation and television after-ward. For the fact that we found as much fascination with body parts in a jar as we did with the unborn children in our wombs.

We were all innocent, after all. We were motherless and all we wanted was a simple explanation. Where did they go, the mothers we never had, the mothers we had but lost? They were back there somewhere, of that much we were convinced. Back there, peering from behind the kitchen door and smiling, ready to fill our hungry bellies. All we wanted was to go back to the womb. I wanted that, too. To be able to hold paper up to the sun and look through a pinpoint of light and see the Holy Mother. Or something simpler, a more reasonable facsimile of love. Marsha, maybe. Mother Marsha, smoothing her thrift-store skirts and making a place for me on her lap and saying, "Listen. Let me tell you a story about a time and a place where everything was still good and true."

Like there, in Kentucky, in that little town where I was before. There, it will always be sacred. Time. It will be eleven or twelve o'clock. My father will have turned the last page in the Revised Standard Version of the Song of Solomon. His hand will reach for the bedside light at the exact moment that my stepmother will appear in the doorway of their room, barefoot, noiseless, concealed by a darkness complete, a darkness wavering for only the one moment when her hand touches the doorknob and light from the hall spills across their bed.

Downtown. Diffused lavender light will advertise fast-food specials at the all-night diner. The streets will be nearly empty. The last carloads of students from the Franklin County Falcons' midseason game will make their final rounds of the parking lots, the shopping malls, the dime stores, the diners, none of them all-night.

Nothing's all-night in this Kentucky town. Those moments in the backseats of Pontiacs or Valiants or even Oldsmobiles are all too brief. The hand hesitates partway up the thigh, the shirt is half-unbuttoned. A girl named Mary Katherine who used to be my best friend will slip into the house past curfew, will notice how soft and kissed she looks, will kiss herself, lips to lips, in the reflection in a mirror.

They are all innocent. Innocent of the nightlife of other towns,

Columbia, St. Louis, a whole chain of events reaching west on interstate after interstate. Innocent of how it is that one of us, Coleen or Randi or I, will find herself being the one to stand on some Columbia street corner near the crosswalk panhandling for a dollar bill to buy a hamburger or a cold beer we all will share. With Coleen it's easy. She leaves her coat hanging open, pushes up her sweater. They let themselves feel sorry for the vulnerability of childbirth.

Me, I back against the side of the First Federal Reserve building where we always hang out, close my eyes. I imagine a warm spot on the couch of the halfway house, imagine bags of day-old cheese Danish, think of the now-vanished boy who brought me to this city, taught me the doubtful constancy of health-food stores and love. Sometimes I get a quarter, a dollar, five, just for being there, for continuing to seem absent when they stroke my cheek, gently, and occasionally with pity.

For Randi, it is the least easy of all. They interpret her hunger in a multitude of ways. They are demanding.

"Touch me," they say. "Touch me." As if she will know exactly how and where and why.

Late night, winter, 1973, and there wasn't much doing. So we settled for an all-night pub on some street near the train station. I used to be a little nervous about places so unsettled, marked only by the regular appearance and disappearance of suitcases. Tonight, I liked it. While Terence and Randi were downing shots of tequila at the bar, I sucked on a slice of lime and engaged in pleasant conversations at the table in the corner.

The bar was as thinned down as the cup of coffee I'd ordered some time back. Coleen was sitting across from me, sipping a draft and trying to describe the current state of her hallucinations. The beer, she said, tasted as thick as honey, but pulled at you kind of like, you know, vinegar, or sadness. There was also the vacuum cleaner salesman waiting for the 2:45 who drifted over to our table and sat down with no better excuse than needing to get a closer look at himself in the glass in the swinging door leading out to the grill. He pulled out a pocket comb, reslicked his hair. He smelled of hair tonic and somebody else's old clothes.

"Where the hell is Marsha anyway?" Coleen asked.

I shook my head and leaned back against the wall. Everything in this bar was cheap velour, tiny green circles of it under your drink, long strips of it leading from the grill to the ladies' lounge. The darts Terence and Randi were tossing at the board near the dance floor landed muffled by felt. I tried to close my eyes and think of Marsha, but the closest I came to imagining her was the memory of how her hands felt when she took mine before she left the house yesterday.

"You sure don't look old enough," the vacuum-cleaner salesman said, then paused before adding, "to be in here."

By then he'd ordered a peppermint schnapps and was taking slow, cough-mediciney sips.

"She's old enough," Coleen said. She lit a cigarette, pulled in a slow draw and then suddenly burst out laughing. She was eyeing the salesman's fancy wristwatch and tiger's-eye ring and considering the possibilities this guy had to offer.

I had to agree. Even with what looked like a twenty-year-old suit he definitely displayed some opulent signs—a fairly new briefcase, an engraved fountain pen in his front pocket, clean white socks. Both of us wished he weren't so straight-looking—ducktailed hair, penny loafers, a sheepish smile.

I was staring toward the door of the bar, where Granger was standing, nose pressed to the plate-glass window. Was he thinking about Marsha? It was late and the snow was unbroken by footsteps or passing cars. I wished it would stay that way until Marsha herself stepped off the next train or rounded the corner or crossed the street. The streetlight would reflect off the rhinestones on the front of her Goodwill cashmere sweater. She would be there just for me. Hair still neatly combed, as I had left it. She would move toward me so quickly the night and the night cool wouldn't have time to lift from her skin. The clear rhinestones, icelike, would melt and vanish.

Instead, the jukebox started up, Randi's quarter for three plays, some song about wild horses or clouds, or maybe it was Canned Heat. The quiet broke. Terence and Randi had begun to move, eyes closed, hips swaying as they danced alone with pink light. Coleen had begun to shoot pool. The salesman was describing six of the new models of vacuum cleaners he had hauled everywhere from Pocatello, Idaho, to Soddy Daisy, Tennessee. I was now also sipping some schnapps and leaning closer to him, on my elbows.

And there were some strange and wonderful items in his line-up. He showed me the brochure: a five-speed upright, adjustable, with brushes for linoleum, carpet, and cement flooring; a model so lightweight and compact it would fit into the pocket of an overcoat. His wife back in Des Moines had discount-purchased one of the foldable floor models, one she could lead from room to room, phone receiver still against one ear, the afternoon soaps still on in the kitchen. His wife, he said, hand suddenly on my knee, used to love him, but now dreamed of sampler chocolates and a clean floor.

"Leah," he said, "is that your name?"

His hand, before I knew it, crept up my leg, paused in some surprise at my stomach. *Are you old enough?* I thought of empty rooms leading to long halls, of slender and flexible hoses winding around corners, creeping up stairs.

"Leah," he said, next to my ear, "I could take care of you."

And I didn't resist, the voice like some stealthy hum of air, the hesitant damp kiss.

I glanced up once, over his shoulder, to see Granger coming toward our table, that look of something important in his eyes.

I met this look. *Misplaced angel,* is that what Marsha called him? Hair with a late-night jukebox shine. Was he thinking of Marsha? He touched my hand on the salesman's suit-jacket collar.

"What time is it?" Granger said. "What time is it, anyway?"

On the center of the dance floor I saw Randi swaying, arms circling herself, some song about moon shadow. Her pearls gleamed, luminous through their thin veneer of paint.

Twenty years after these events, I am living at the head of a hollow in a mountain cabin. In one corner of the cabin a desk is heaped with books and papers and random parts of stories that will someday be a book about birth. Above my desk I have tacked photographs and poems and a diagram of a dissection. One evening the man I live with stands looking at this diagram as if he's never seen it before. His fingers trace the clean edges of cut muscle, the dark-red, exposed chambers where blood once surged and receded, alive and beating time. This is no mere drawing, but a graphic photograph, a dissection straight from a laboratory. His face looks fascinated but repulsed.

"Why?" he wants to know. "Why do you keep such things?"

He doesn't know it yet, but he's looking for signs, reasons for the inexplicable weight of my sadness, reasons to leave behind this woman haunted by a loss he cannot understand. Reasons? Does he have to look further, really, than the stories he knows, the ones about this woman's life? The stories he could tell, he'll later say to friends. Stories about her failure to sanctify love, to offer up respect to the living human heart.

No one, not even this man, has read the stories I've begun to write, stories about Hitt Street. One is about a runaway girl. But the apartment in this story is a real home away from home, a nest of loving-kindness to which Marsha, mother to us all, returns at the end of a long night. Once again dressed in evening finery, she stands in the middle of the kitchen and twirls and twirls. Her long plum skirts flare and fall and she stands still, says, "Leah," says, "Terence, Randi, Coleen, Granger. I've hit the big time."

And the big time, in this version of a happy ending, could be anything. Backstreet audition for a grassroots production of My Fair Lady. *Interview for a sales job at a junk store called Blue Moon. Successful application for public assistance, free cheese and peanut butter on alternate Wednesdays.*

"Now," she says and holds out her hands, palms up, like Mary, like Jesus himself. "Now we can all be so happy."

And happy? Why, in this version, the kitchen becomes a stage of its own. Center of family connection, pseudo and otherwise. There, in late afternoons, we smell baking bread, of the healthiest variety. There, in late afternoons, we see hand-holding, kisses on the sly, candles, dinner on time.

In this version, I am someone else. I am Leah Wheeler, no assumed name, but myself, reborn, redeemed. I give birth naturally, kneeling on the lawn in the public park. A boy, faceless but beloved, holds out his hands to receive the afterbirth and later we both eat, hungrily. I suckle my young. Wrap him in swaddling clothes, then buy tiny sweaters and thrift-store shoes with buckles of purest gold. I watch him rise and walk. I allow him great distances, miles of highway and lengths of time, but draw him back to me, again and again. The umbilical cord is never cut. Love is never lost. I give him a name no one can change.

In this version, everyone gives birth. Coleen buys a stroller and takes long walks in the park. With Terence and Randi and me and Granger standing by her mattress on the floor, she effortlessly births a bouncing baby and nurses him in winter light that lasts well into spring. Randi, transported by this turn of events, reads books on reincarnation experiences in children. She reads of souls in trees above holy rivers, of birthmarks that show the previous manner of death. The unborn, she says, have an unusual capacity for forgiveness. They can return at any time, to any family of their choice.

Her baby, she knows, that aborted boy, is out there, waiting to be reborn, this time to Randi. He's on the fire escape, in the back alley, in our hearts, she says, if we only listen.

The bar closed that night. We, Randi and Terence and Coleen and I, made our ways home just as Columbia passed the verge of sleep. End of night, with something left undone. Something no greater than a glimpse of a hand at a window as a shade was drawn, something no greater than the look on the face of a woman in fishnet stockings we passed in a doorway.

"What've you got?" she said. "What've you got?"

It was winter and her words came out frozen. I passed them and they vanished and, after all, this was what was left.

I made my way through an empty apartment, my head spinning. I felt light, weightless, held down by nothing but my belly and a child. Was it a child? The kitchen was full of things I started to clean up, overturned ashtrays, sweat rings on the wooden counter by the stove. I stopped by a left-open carton of milk, tilted it, took a few swallows. The milk was warm, gone a little sour, but I held it in. Waves of nausea replaced the lightness and I stood by the sink, felt real again.

Later, on my bed on the floor, I imagined the cold rising through the mattress, sheets, blanket. I pulled the quilt over my head, pushed myself farther down the mattress, played tent. At first they were all in there with me, just as they had been when we walked home from the bar. Coleen looked worn out, but she stopped, eyes shining, did a not-half-bad drum roll on a metal trash-can lid. Terence bowed, pantomimed some dance step he called the fish. We passed through darkness, an alleyway, streets where the lights dimmed, one by one, but I was not afraid. Someone touched my shoulder, the middle of my back. Their voices were on either side of me, were nowhere, receding, far from me, down one more street, where there were no lights.

Under the blanket I drew my knees into my arms, exhaled one long breath, tasted cigarettes, beer.

I thought of Marsha as she looked yesterday. When was it? Six, seven o'clock in the morning. She turned once and looked back at the closed door behind which Granger was still asleep, tucked in like she'd left him. She stopped in front of the mirror in the front room, smiled, raised one hand to her lips, breathed in, lightly, as if remembering some fragrance of him.

Suddenly I heard a noise, sat up, slid over the mattress, felt my way in the dark. Outside my room, Granger was standing near the window, hands on the windowsill, looking out. So close to the glass his breath made circles of steam.

"Granger," I whispered. "Can't you sleep?"

"I know," he said, something about his voice glittery, too bright.

"Know?"

"Where she is. Where she's been all this time. I've known all along."

His eyes had the look of something I'd remember forever and forever and I didn't want to. I didn't want to know who he meant, though I knew it was Marsha.

"Where?" I asked anyway, when he didn't speak again. I moved closer to him.

The darkness outside in the streets, in this room, heard us, our whispers. We were children afraid of the dark and it was listening, seeing our sleepless eyes, the sweat on our palms. It must have been like that for Marsha her last night in this apartment. She must have lain awake for hours, listening, must have pressed the pillow over her head, tight, must have still heard her own heart beating.

She'd given herself up, he said. Had decided, once and for all, to be healed. Clean. Had been sitting for two solid days in a Fifth Street Memorial Hospital room watching the way a red bedroom slipper spun around on her index finger. He said these things bitterly.

"It won't last," he said.

"She won't," he said again. "Nothing ever does."

"Granger," I said, just that, and then put my arms around him. It's all there is.

Marsha was everywhere, in the suggestion of a step down the hall, in a hand on the doorknob. She slipped between us, put her arms around us both. In the curve of one of those arms there was a touch, an open bruise so beautiful it was a flower, the lips of a lover. I had seen her a hundred times, how she would pick up the length of hose like it was a precious, live thing, tie it in an expert knot, a bowline or a double-half-hitch.

Tomorrow, like days or nights before, will she take her time? The needle will rush in, sudden, delicious, a sliver of light. She will sit in the evenings, at the table, with a razor blade, stroking the place, watching us ease out. She will gently bind the thing. She gently holds us now. We hold on tighter.

Later, when I took Granger's hand, I could hardly see the shape of him undressing in the dark. I pulled back the sheets. He knelt, moved close, tucked his cold, skinny feet near my legs. I raised my hands to his face, felt the lines under the eyes, beside the mouth, the unshaven neck beneath the beard.

Then we lay there completely still. Even though it was not necessary in this kind of darkness, I closed my eyes, listened. I knew if I listened hard enough I would hear some echo in the next room, voices at night, the sounds of touching, of Randi and Terence or Coleen or anyone at all. Is this sound laughter? Sadness?

"Tell me, Granger," I said. "Tell me."

He moved the slightest bit, not touching at all, even though all of him was touching me, his face in the space beside my neck, in the fan of my hair on the pillow. His breathing drifted into sleep. It was the end of something. Night.

Then there was a tiny tapping at the window. Tree branches, a drift of snow. *Marsha?* I held my breath, listened. At the same instant, for the first time, in the water-dark place inside me I couldn't reach, the child moved. I continued to hold my breath, wait.

At the bottom of memory, a long, dark hall and the Sacred Mother, her hand held out. She is saying what she always will, the words I most want. "I sanction," she says. "I forgive and I unremember." She opens her bright robes, takes me in one more time. Or she merely flips a light switch, opens a door through which I can run one last time, enter one more unknown car, tires spinning as I round the corner past the diner on Main Street, leave Kentucky behind at last, ready for my life to begin again, for the past to vanish without a trace.

At the other end of that hall, my father moves his hand to the place between his wife's ribs, the place where he can feel her heart. When he's half asleep, his other hand reaches across the bed, to empty air, to the chill of the room. My name lands in his upturned palm. "Are you there?" he says. He turns, nestles against a shoulder, falls deeper, unaware.

CHAPTER SIX

Frozen Niagara

It was the only real trip I took anywhere west for a long time, that trip to Mammoth Cave. My celebration of love. I still have the paraphernalia to prove it. "See Mammoth Cave," it says on a plate I bought my paternal grandmother as a souvenir. In a box of letters and papers and postcards from over the years that I've never been able to throw away, I recently found a brochure showing a mother and a father and a cavern and a tour guide. "Born 350 million years ago," the caption reads. Mammoth Cave is ten degrees south of the equator, beneath what was once a shallow sea as salty as amnion. Tourist stuff, all of it, but I remember the truth. Mammoth Cave has corridors no one has ever entered, chambers that have never seen light. The cave is a story all its own.

In my own precave story, there was Phil, who eventually was the one to turn me in. Phone calls were made from Columbia. Cops were notified. Turning me in wasn't the first sign he was freaked out by my expanding womb, of course. He'd signed out on his responsibilities as soon as we took up residence on Hitt Street. He'd taken up for real with the dorm-room patchouli girl, who wore a beret and affected the manner of an underground spy when she visited the apartment. I caught her once flipping through the pages of my writer's notebook. There was an alert look on her face, as if what she expected to find were my initials plus Phil's in a heart with an arrow thrust through it. "Is this Phil's?" she asked another time, fingering spare change on the floor by the mattress I shared with him some nights. That mattress is another story I could tell, another reason Phil finally handed me over like a knapsack full of contraband. Toward the end, before he phoned my best friend back home and she called my father and he called the cops, we'd tried a time or two to have sex on the mattress, and he'd found out that, in the space of a few weeks, I was no longer the cute girl he'd run away with. "Your ass looks strange," he said, watching me walk naked to the bathroom. If I remember my own body, its sad reflection back from a mirror, he was right. The hips and thighs I recall were no girl's. The belly of my memory was lowering itself, preparing to give birth.

The story of my return to my father and to Kentucky is this. My father has the Missouri police send a squad car over to Hitt Street to haul me in and hold on to me until he can drive west to pick me up. I remember best the moments when the cops are in the squad car in front of the building. Everyone inside is sure in no time that a runaway raid is underway. Coleen races out of her apartment next to ours with Terence behind her, tugging his jeans legs up over his boots. Phil scoots by me to alert the new couple staying with us—a boy with black, shagged hair and his girlfriend, one more hippie chick who wears a jeans jacket with the third eye and an inverted American flag embroidered on the back.

I have a plan, or so I think. I'll hide all my cash in my underwear and head to jail like a good girl. My father, I know, has to be in the works somehow, so I'll ride with him part of the way home *if I have to, then sneak out of the first public restroom window I can find.*

"They'll frisk you up one side and down the other," Colleen says. "Leave the cash with us. Call us. We'll come get you, first thing." She loops her arm through mine.

"Trust us," Granger says. My last memory of him is a glimpse of his long, beautiful hair as he slips down the fire escape toward the back alley.

They're right about the body search, at least. The cops look through my pockets, peer into the cavities in my ears. They take everything away from me, even the safety pin that holds up my jeans. Phil is there too, much to his chagrin, and they make him take his shirt off to have a look at what might be hidden in his armpits, strip him of his boots and his Army-issue money belt. In the story I tell friends back in Kentucky, the jail where they take both of us is a cave. It's certified concrete and steel, but it has a primitive feel with its sleeping ledges and dark recesses, its scent of shit and fried eggs.

Both Phil and I are on the men's side, but I'm in the lap of luxury. At least that's what Phil says when he calls over to me, since I have my own cell. Not that he's unhappy with his own arrangements, after a while. There are three of them in his cell, and they soon are fast friends. They swing from their ledges down onto their cell's bars. They howl and make ape sounds. They piss and fart with glee. At lunchtime, I give Phil my white bread and jelly and he eats and eats. When the cop comes to get me at the end of the third day, I see Phil one last time. He looks at me through his raggedy brown bangs and gives me a peace sign, and I wonder if he'll get out of jail. Maybe he'll even make it to a coffeehouse where he'll play guitar for the masses at last. I won't see him again for almost ten years. He'll stop by my desk at a library where I'm working. We'll go to a park to smoke a joint for old times' sake, and when I'm most stoned I'll look over his shoulder. I'll see a dog just walking along. I'll see it fall, twitching, its eyes wild. It will get up again and go on, and I'll go back to work and I'll never see Phil again.

It's the ride home of which I have no memory. Or take one step back from that. It's the sight of my father's face in the police station office of which I have no memory. No memory of the way I walked up some steps with a officer and entered a room where he stood, my father, my once-ally, come to cart me home. No memory of whether we embraced or stood stiffly, avoiding one another's eyes as they gave me back my belongings, a safety pin and a cloth purse with a notebook inside.

The memories I don't have, I can supply. My father is dressed more formally than usual. He wears a tie and a button-down shirt, even if he dislikes them, as his own father had. He is formal, too, at the car, where he opens the door for me like a suitor and seems uncertain of whether or not he should fasten my seat belt. He and the office co-worker, who had become my stepmother during my absence, take turns driving as we head back east, and my father asks questions. "Where did you sleep? Is that a hole in the toe of your shoe?" Despite my huge stomach, he says I look thin. Or perhaps he makes more commonplace conversation, questions a tourist would ask, as if this is nothing more than a family vacation out west. "Did you see the Gateway Arch in St. Louis? Isn't there a river somewhere?" Or maybe there's nothing. No conversation about my pregnancy, which had not been obvious before. Now I am so enormous the inside of the car is stifling. They crank the air conditioner and my stepmother puts her foot down hard on the gas, and I watch the miles east go by too fast.

We stop for dinner at a family buffet where, before we eat meat-loaf and mashed potatoes and gravy, my father prays. "Forgive, our Father," he says, "forgive us for the choices we have made. Help us to be thankful, help us drive safely." He makes no mention of a child, the one opening and closing its hands inside my womb. While he prays I do not close my eyes. I stare at my father, how white the knuckles are on his clenched hands. I stare at my stepmother's red hair, and at how her own eyes open, midprayer. Her eyes are full of pity and bewilderment, my baby as unreal to her as the acid vision Joe once had of a giant dog in a field who told him to go forth and multiply. We'd multiplied, Joe and I, but a pregnancy seems impossible, yet, for them to digest. After we eat, I say I'm going to the restroom and my father, somewhere between solicitude and suspicion, says, "Girls will be girls." With a wink, he urges my stepmother to go with me to, as he says, help me powder my nose. When we come back to the table, he is nervous and gracious as he seats me and offers me milk for dessert. And somewhere on the border of Kentucky, we stop to buy me new shoes.

I will remember these shoes longer than anything else. They're chukka boots and they're brown and they're hip and somehow they make me feel safe. I'll wear them right from the store. I'll wear them when I go back inside, lie down in the bed in a room no longer mine, one decked out with my stepmother's quilt decorated with wee lavender flowers. I'll wear them at supper, the first night, when they break out a tiny bottle of champagne and tell me they've saved it from their wedding, just for me. No matter what Jesus thinks, we drink it in three little cups and I'm high right away. I'm soaring, I'm giddy, and the baby in my gut jumps and kicks with glee. I'll wear my hip shoes when a week has passed and my father hands me an envelope full of stems and seeds he'd found in my dresser drawer and says, "Have you ever tried this stuff?" I deny that I have, and we sit at the kitchen table burning these scraps like libations in a dish. "How do they stand this stuff?" my father says, looking at me with suspicion. I'll wear my shoes when my stepmother's office friends come calling for lunch and I'm playing Joni Mitchell way up loud, "I was a free man in Paris, I felt unfettered and alive." I prop my new shoes on a chair in the living room and pretend I belong in this, my father's house, my stepmother's house, a house that has never really been mine.

No one breathes a word of what I'll do next. On the birth day. On this day. On the next.

I'll wear the shoes when I see Joe again, when he comes calling like a shy suitor on a first date. I'll wear them when we take a drive in the country again, when we sip pop and punch spiked with vodka out of a mason jar and pretend it never happened, the baby or the road out west, Phil and my other, now secret, life on the streets. We don't want to rush into marriage, even if I will soon be nine months along. I ask Joe back into my life with caution, imagining an evening in front of the television here, a walk around the subdivision block there, all of it with my father's living room as safe terrain, a place for negotiations about whether or not we'll hold hands again, whether or not to exchange class rings and plan a drive around the curb-service restaurant on Friday night.

I'm wearing my new shoes in a photo of Joe and me in which I'm sitting on his lap, when I'm pregnant enough for my water to break right there on his thighs, when my father is photographing us, happy couple that we are. Joe is glaring into the camera in fury because my father had cornered him in the produce aisle at Kroger and threatened him with a paternity suit if he didn't marry me, soon. And I'm wearing the boots on my wedding day. So there, we'd said at last, Joe and I. Had planned the whole thing without anyone's permission, gotten our signatures from the county circuit court.

And there I am, on the wedding day itself. Church bells ring in my head and I'm standing in front of a mirror while my friend Roslyn combs and curries. She's ordered the bouquet of baby's breath and the ribbons, and for old times' sake she's plucked daisies from the front yard to weave into my waist-length hair. "Something old, something new," she hums in my ear. "Something borrowed, something blue." I'm wearing something borrowed, Roslyn's cast-off blue dress, and old is the strand of jet-black beads from the jewelry box my mother left in the bedroom at my father's

house. I stare at myself in the mirror as Roslyn rubs blush on my
white cheek, tells me to smile. I stare at my shoes and think about
how they, at least, are still new.

In the only photograph I have of my wedding day, Joe and I are
standing by the closed church-house door. We aren't looking at
the person, probably my stepmother, who is taking this picture.
I'm looking at no one, or I am looking inward, as far as I could
go at sixteen. I am clutching my bouquet at the top of my belly,
I am squinting, and my face is small and pale and puffy with
pregnancy. Joe has his arm around my waist and his other hand
is tucked inside his dress shirt so he looked like a blond, plump
Napoleon. We seem to be waiting for the clink of glasses, the
hiss of confetti, although no one has thought of being celebratory. Neither of us is smiling.

There'd been no smiling earlier that morning, either. As I did
my bride's walk down the aisle that morning I remember noticing my father nervously clipping his nails. He clipped nails or
bit his cuticles or cleared his throat and coughed during church
services and at inappropriate moments in restaurants and most
especially when he was filling in an uncomfortable space in a
sentence. And my walk down the aisle was one long, uncomfortable space. Next to my father sat my stepmother, who held
a camera that she focused this way and that, without snapping
any shots. Next to her was my best friend, and next to her were
three of the five or six other people who'd come to our wedding.
One of Joe's friends. Not my mother, of course, who still knew
nothing about my pregnancy or plans to marry. The day of my
wedding, she was living with her mother and father. Even Rose,
Joe's mother, hadn't come. "Impossible," she said, when we told
her about our plans for a Sunday wedding and a trip to Mammoth Cave afterward. "You'll be sorry." Her eyes, myopic behind
their small glasses, were helpless and afraid.

And we were sorry, Joe and I, as we stood at the altar exchanging our vows. We were sorry for all the vows we'd already broken, the ones we'd broken long before we headed back down the aisle and waited for the shower of rice and the congratulations. There was the underlying vow. "The body," the Bible says, "is not for fornication, but for the Lord, and the Lord for the body." We'd certainly fornicated. The few guests could only speculate about the way we'd snuck off into bushes and into truck beds at drive-in movie theaters. They believed I'd fornicated not only with Joe, but with who-knows-whom on the streets of a span of cities I'd hitchhiked to, and what other word than *fornicate* was there for what two children did in bed, joined in holy wedlock or not?

And those weren't the only vows we'd broken. We'd chosen a Methodist church instead of a Baptist one, and a reprobate minister who was nothing more than a part-time social worker and gay, to boot, or so my father said. My father could testify all by himself about how I'd been a heathen since age twelve, when I wanted to stay home and watch *The Mighty Sons of Hercules* rather than attend Sunday school like a good girl. I was no longer a good girl, and Joe was no good boy. The ceremony proved it.

Like everyone else we knew, we'd delved into various and sundry heathen practices—séances, wearing love beads, frequenting head shops—and this wedding ceremony itself had a pagan cast. The music we'd chosen had the ring of primitive tribes and midnight sacrifices, Jimi Hendrix, Uriah Heep, and one of my particular favorites, a tune by Black Sabbath called "Something Wicked This Way Comes." For the vows themselves we'd asked that words like *husband* and *wife* be changed to something like *conscious beings*, and *obey* had been changed to *recognize needs*. We did not ask God's blessing, although we did light the usual candles, one match for our two hands and hearts, and after that I read aloud a poem I'd written while I was in Columbia. Written to an unspecified *you*, I'd described the needs I believed should be met by love. "I'll need you like oxygen," I read. "I'll need you like air." As I read this poem, Joe, my *you*, fumbled nervously with the plain gold band I'd just put on his finger. A couple of years later, my own gold band would disappear, lost forever, it must have been, down the drain at some other house, from the edge of some bathroom sink.

We had chosen a gentler tune than Led Zeppelin for the processional at the end of our nuptials. "Morning has broken, like the first morning," Cat Stevens sang as we gathered our things and shook hands and gave hugs. The minister took my hand and said, one last time, "Marriage is honorable in all." By that time, I couldn't hear it, the rest of the verse, the awkward well-wishes from Joe's one friend and mine as we shut off the record player, moved down the church steps. I was echoing with my own tune by then. *Honorable. Honorable.* The word throbbed and hummed in my ears as we paused at the door for our photograph. With whom was I to be honorable? With Joe, who clutched one of my hands so tightly my ring bit into my finger? Or with my father, as he hugged me and fumbled for his wallet so he could give us some cash for our road trip to Mammoth Cave?

"I mean the best," he whispered. "You know that, don't you?"

My ears were still humming and I didn't know much. I was also a long way from forgiving him for the push and shove in the direction of this marriage. I twisted the ribbon on my bouquet and stared at the boots poking out from under the hem of my dress, but I answered him.

"I know you do," I said as I hugged him. "I know you mean the best." He smelled like Old Spice and hair spray and he hugged me back. "I know you love me," I said to this father of mine, though love, even on my wedding day, felt like a word with an at-best dubious definition.

He hugged me one last time. "We're praying for you," he said. *Sanctity.* Was that what the Bible called it, the moment when father blesses daughter, when daughter becomes a woman and leaves forever her father's house? Neither woman nor girl, I held on to him, too.

It's the next moment I've memorialized, the one I'll remember years later. As my father stuffed a bill in my free hand, a gift for our honeymoon, I could still hear it, our wedding song. *Blackbird has spoken, like the first bird.* Other words echoed in my head. *I'll need you like daylight, I'll need you like dawn. I'll need you like twilight, if you'll only care.* A few months after the ceremony, the only needs Joe and I would be able to imagine for the weeks ahead were food stamps and how we'd live through the summer in the hot attic of his maiden aunt's house. Now, sweat trailed down my back, and as I juggled the bouquet and Cat Stevens, the record slid from its jacket, tumbled down, broke neatly in half. They grew quiet, our guests, as Roslyn knelt, picked up the broken halves and said, "Is this a sign?" Joe and I went toward the parking lot, this sign trailing us like streamers on the back of a wedding car.

Good-bye, good-bye, they waved. My father and my stepmother blew kisses while the rest of them made peace signs with their fingers and saluted us. *Good luck and farewell.* Joe and I were quiet as we cranked the engine, started out toward Mammoth Cave. By then the wedding words had also quieted in my head, but I could still hear it, another sound like water and hands. It was the sound my son made as he dove and turned inside me, dancing in celebration, he might have believed, on his parents' wedding day.

I think it was my own love of dark places that sent me there, to Mammoth Cave. Listen to the words of one of the first travelers to see the mystery of the world's largest cave: "No ray of light but the glimmer of our lamps; no sound but the echo of our own steps; nothing but dark, and inside, moistness, fecundity." This isn't entirely true. Caves have three levels of darkness. They are twilight at their entrances. Then there is a stygian blackness called the middle zone. And at last there is total darkness, a core of dark where there are blind and colorless animals, eyeless cave shrimp, blind crayfish. There are mummies four thousand years old. There are corridors that have never been entered, chambers that have never seen light at all.

At sixteen, I am a cave all my own. I remember twilight and my mother's face, her wounded hands and their white gloves. "Lie still," she says as she tucks me in, as she keeps my night world smooth and clean. I am a black box in space with just enough light inside to see myself. I am voices in a hall and the shadows of my parents moving past. "You'll marry," my mother says, "the first boy who'll have you." Then the stygian blackness takes me in, sings me mescaline lullabies that lure me west, and I do marry. I am married and sixteen and I'm looking into the frightened face of a seventeen-year-old boy and we both know we're moving forward into a darkness we can't predict. My womb is a fecund cave, and inside, my son has never seen the light of day. His hands are opening fists. Fingers that write messages on the cave walls that are me. He demands that I listen. It's almost time, *he says, and I know that he is right.*

I finished two cigarettes in a row and tossed them behind us just to see the red sparks crash along the highway. The insides of Joe's Plymouth were close with cigarette smoke and the sourish smell of carpet wet through the floorboard with days-old rain. Thirty more miles to Highway 70, our next route, and the rain was starting up again, leaving the asphalt in wet ripples of light.

It was almost seven o'clock and I was almost asleep, head against the window, feet in Joe's lap, when we pulled into a truck stop with a sign boasting a miner with a pick and shovel and a huge bat with its wings spread, sure signs we were nearing

Mammoth Cave. Bat and man danced in neon on the diner's roof, and Joe nudged me.

"Want anything?"

"I don't think I could eat."

"Milk? Pie?" he asked again, eagerly.

I suspected the eagerness wasn't necessarily about pleasing me, though to be fair this was in the mix. It was about onion rings, his favorite, or other diner food we could buy with the thirty bucks my father had given us. I was giddy with menthol cigarettes and new marriage, so I agreed. I shoved my sock feet into the moccasins I'd changed to from wedding gear and swung my legs out into the parking lot.

"OK, Je t'aime. Pie, then."

I called him *Je t'aime*. JTM, his initials, *I love you* in French, which neither of us knew.

The diner was full of jukebox tunes and fluorescents. We sat at a booth hand painted with more bats, and fish with weak-looking eyes. "Blind cave fish," Joe said as he handed me a menu, which advertised Sinkhole Burgers and Green River Filets, dredged, it said, "from the river in the depths of the world's largest cave." Near our booth, a truck driver or two sat yawning, hands circling their cups as if they were the hands of sweethearts miles back, at home.

After the food came, I watched Joe as if I were seeing him for the first time, a time I'd want to remember. He'd ordered big: eggs with shiny yolks in pools he mopped up with piece after piece of toast, hot links, fried apples, foiled wedges of grape jelly. He ate and scraped his plate and ordered coconut pie and didn't look at me, not even when the song about nights in white satin and letters came on, a song that might have played on the car radio the very night I'd gotten pregnant in the Plymouth's front seat. Did Joe love me? Was the Joe who'd been my first lover the same Joe who'd just professed to love me, signed for it with Cat Stevens playing in the background? Was the Joe who ate fried eggs the same one who was father to the child curled around itself inside me, its eyes still shut? I ate my own pie, banana cream, but the edges of the room melted and bent and moved back farther and farther, like I was tripping or just traveling, faster and farther from any place I'd known before. Nausea spread into my legs, my arms.

Back at the car, I leaned against the door, head bent over the asphalt. I wanted the growing nausea to stop. How small I felt as Joe held the back of my head. His hands felt as insignificant as the leaves rustling in the trees at the edge of the parking lot.

I tell myself that I did the best I could at sixteen as I traveled from mothered to motherless to mothering. I was riding the waves of change without a map, without any one direction to trust. And this, too, is the lesson of caves. Mammoth Cave itself is, after all, a metaphor. For a God who, in his deep and infinite wisdom, created the mystery of the earth that unfolds, layer upon layer, revealing deep chasms of complete darkness. For the presence of the holy, an echo that comes back when you stand at the entrance to a cave, shouting your greatest wish down into the darkness. But mostly, the cave is a metaphor for change. Just look at how one thing here becomes another.

Three hundred fifty million years ago, the sea left behind ghosts—the shells of tiny creatures, which accumulated by billions on the sea floor. Two hundred eighty million years ago, sea levels dropped and the continent rose, exposing layers of limestone and sandstone and this, we are told, was the advent of Mammoth Cave. The earth's crust buckled and twisted, cracked open, and waters rushed in. Microcaverns formed and enlarged as rivers cut deeper. Water tables dropped, old channels emptied and new ones opened, cavern upon cavern, a vast system of passages. The cave, a living being, formed and unformed and is still being made. Winds still shift and temperatures rise and fall. Moisture condenses on stone and soft rains fall beneath the earth. Plants inhale, exhale carbon dioxide. Organisms rise up at night from underground, steal nourishment for the living, breathing cave.

And sometimes you need no additional knowledge, no geologic terms, no brochures, not even a tour that begins midmorning with a guide and a map of all the hidden trails, to witness the lessons of all caves. You need do nothing but stand perfectly still and listen. Place one hand, gently, across your chest. Feel your blood churn and move, and at the same time place your hand, with equal reverence, against the smooth, moist wall of a cave.

The next morning we ate pancakes for breakfast at the lodge restaurant and then drove across the road to the Mammoth Cave Visitor Center. It had a campfire circle for scary cave stories and a trail that led to Mammoth Cave Church, which, I imagined, might specialize in the story of Lot's wife transformed into a stalagmite.

I stood with Joe in a large group of other wives and husbands and sundry families who were listening, as we were, to the ranger's introductory talk. This group was prepared. They'd brought cameras and highlighted maps from their automobile club. They were reading cave literature, which we didn't have, since guidebooks cost. It was midmorning, but they'd brought picnic hampers for later on, backpacks bulging with extra sweaters and film canisters and snacks. In one pack, its zipper hanging open, I saw lengths of rope and a heavy-duty lantern. The man carrying all this had new hiking boots with the tag still attached at the heel and he blinked his weak-looking eyes as he looked at me in my muslin dress and fringed moccasins. I thought of bats.

"The immediate cave area," our tour guide said, "has been populated from Paleo-Indian times." He was ruddy and white-haired from the sun, and I could imagine him as the hunter who chased a bear through the hills and stumbled on the entrance to what became Mammoth Cave.

"But Mammoth Cave was formally discovered in 1925," the guide continued. "Floyd Collins found Crystal Cave in 1917, then Sand Cave in 1925. Later that year he made his most important find: Mammoth Cave, where today," the guide concluded, "you can choose from a range of cave tours."

Travertine, he said, with just eighteen steps to climb, was nothing but a bus ride to one entrance and a quick look down at some stalagmites. At the other end of the scale was the Grand Avenue, which involved switchbacks and five hundred stairs. My legs were swelling but I wanted a midrange tour. I wanted at least the Wild Cave tour, which had small openings and tight holes and lots of crawling for which I might have to buy gloves or knee pads at the gift shop. That tour featured a series of canyons and would exit, we were told, at Frozen Niagara, which sounded like a drink and promised spectacular pits and domes and a sharp descent of some three hundred steps.

At the mention of Frozen Niagara, Joe laced his arm partway around my waist and patted protectively. Overnight, he'd become a husband. He'd opened restaurant doors and he'd ordered milk for me at breakfast and he'd signed the motel guest register Mr. and Mrs. Someday. Later he'd remind me of a boy playing GI Joes, half aggression and half make-believe hero, but right now I thought, *My husband*.

In the night he'd pushed himself inside me and I'd felt heat and wetness, but also a wall of confusion made of baby and our marriage and ambiguity. I'd pushed back and I'd felt how that wall might dissolve, pleasurably, if we would let it, but I didn't yet know the language for my own desire. At sixteen and pregnant, I'd never had an orgasm, and Joe, at seventeen and a father-to-be, experienced sex, food, and drugs as a continuum of pleasure. Now, when he thought I wasn't looking, he checked me out and sucked nervously at his lip.

Inside, the visitors' area featured the cave literature we

hadn't bought and a variety of cave paraphernalia to take back home—mugs and paperweights made of gypsum, key rings and glow-in-the-dark bats. There were also various areas that simulated, we were told, the natural cave environment. There were Styrofoam stalactites and stalagmites. There was a long tube through which children could shimmy, a fake version of a cave passage. Then, while Joe was down the hall at the drinking fountain, I entered a room behind the book sales area. It was called Look Before You Leap and promised an exact replication of cave atmosphere.

A motherly ranger with blue-tinted hair was at the door, selling tickets. While I hunted up the change, she gave me a quick look up and down, my frizzy hippie hair and an ankh on a chain around my neck.

"We're not scared of the dark, are we?" she asked.

I looked behind me, expecting a crowd, but Joe wasn't back yet and I was at the end of the line. She meant me. Or the two of me, since she was looking now at my middle, her mouth set in that way I'd come to see as surprise or disapproval or adjustment, when someone saw a girl as far along as I was.

"No," I said. "I'm not a bit scared."

I slipped in quickly, just as the door to the simulation room sealed and the last of the hall light ebbed. The inside was forty-five degrees Fahrenheit, a recording said, and in my peasant dress and bare arms I wasn't prepared for that, but I knuckled down and listened to the voice tell us about this vast, subterranean world, which in simulation smelled like old air-conditioning. *Subterranean* made me think of the center of the earth, complete with gaping cracks that opened and lava pits and molten fire and ice. This cave world, the voice continued, rose to the heights of the 192-foot Mammoth Dome and sunk to the level of the 105-foot Bottomless Pit. There were rivers, too, ones with names like Styx, and creatures called *ghostly white spiders*. I pictured rowboats and souls. I pictured long fingers of white light caressing my skin. I pictured the way the sonogram looked, the time I saw this baby's heart.

The truth is I *was* scared. Scared, or limited. I didn't yet know how much or for how long I was limited, but I'd begun to know since the advent of my life as a married girl. Just last night in the motel room, our wedding night, I'd slipped on the bathtub's daisy appliqués when I was under the shower with Joe, and I caught it for the first time, that startled look. *Pregnant,* his eyes said. *She's really pregnant after all,* as if what I'd been concealing under my dress was a figment of the imagination, his or mine. "There are three kinds of cave light," the voice said. "Twilight. Middle zone. Dark zone." I put my hand on my stomach, trying to feel the baby's movement. I closed my eyes, opened them, comparing kinds of darkness.

Cave tales, like love stories, are also about loss. They're about rivers without bottoms and black holes in space and time. Consider the story of the death of Floyd Collins, circa 1926. While exploring a new passage in Sand Cave, near Mammoth Cave, Collins slipped and a rock trapped his leg. For fourteen days, while friends and family and emergency teams drilled through the rock-facing above him, Collins waited. Newspapers and radio stations across the country reported on efforts to reach him. The nation prayed over the supper table and sent personal notes of sympathy that might well have been read aloud down into the enlarging hole above Floyd Collins's head. They were chanting for the dead, for on the fifteenth day, when rescuers reached him, it was too late. Collins had been buried alive. A cave had taken him in and refused to let go. We can only imagine the real story.

At first Collins must have been logical about his captivity. He did, after all, think like a scientist. He knew about cave animals, ones who survive their entire lives by feasting on cool and dark.

Eyeless, these animals have developed other faculties. And this was how Collins hoped to survive. He imagined painting on the cave walls, maps to the outer world. He climbed upward on ladders of desire. Memory took flight.

We can imagine Collins on days four and five and six, when he was still coherent, when he could still remember with accuracy. A leaf, for example. He was six years old and he was facing the sun and he watched the way a leaf spun and fell and spun, catching sunlight. He was eighteen and he was touching the face of a pretty girl, a particular face that for the first time revealed his own heart. Days seven and eight in the cave were less clear. One face became another. Hands took hold, tried to lift him up, baptize him, redeem him in the heart of the earth. The hands of his mother stroked underground rain from his eyes, moved inside his boot to comfort his broken bones. And after that? Days nine, ten, on into forever. He began to hallucinate. He heard sweet voices, his mother singing, Tra la la, *and another voice, Jenny Lind, caressing him with songs. That was real, wasn't it? Hadn't she visited this cave once, to bless it with music?*

Days twelve and thirteen and we know there weren't many more. He was desperate, for air and light. He could hear other sounds now, a humming deep at the heart of everything, a humming soft and coy. It wasn't his own mother anymore, it was that other mother, the Earth. She said, Hold still, listen. *And he did, to the sounds of wings, bats, angels, the sifting of stone ground down to sand. To the sound of a woman bending over him, one so beautiful he longed, one last time, for touch. She was singing, her breath the scent not of dampness, of a cave's exhalation, but of roses.* Help us, *she sang,* provide us remedies for our pain and do not abandon us.

For a while, he had hope. He felt lighter, so thin and pliable his trapped ankle could almost slide right out, release him upward. Elevate us from the depths of despair, *she sang,* protect us, with love. *He felt so light he could almost reach out, touch the face of the Miraculous Mother.*

In the end Joe and I chose the Discovery tour, a moderate three-quarter-mile descent of sixty steps, to view, we were told, the most magnificent chamber in the cave. We were standing there now and I was repeating to myself that word, *chamber, chamber,* which made me think of canopied beds.

This chamber was strung with electric lights that gave the walls a softened, insubstantial look, like they were a stage curtain the ranger might pull down to reveal the next set. This ranger, a perky blonde with barrettes and a whistle on a chain around her neck for use in case we got lost, was giving us the history of saltpeter mining operations and geologic origins. She was pointing out various formations with a hefty flashlight. A stalactite looked like a slender leg wearing a dance slipper, but was actually a formation created by vertically seeping water, she said. Just as I was imagining water droplets with miniature hands and toes, she told us how this water dissolved calcium carbonate and could redeposit it if the water dripped into an air-filled passage.

Earlier, as we descended the sixty steps, this same ranger had taken in my stomach, which was small for nine months but still a sure sign of trouble in a crevice. The others in our tour group, ten or twelve members of what seemed to be a senior citizens' hiking club, also had been solicitous of me, offering me a hand up here, a steadying grip there. At first I was resentful, but now, as I took sips of cave-chamber air, I realized I actually was unsteady. My feet throbbed as a leg or an arm pushed up hard against my ribs and my stomach was gravity itself, a living anchor.

"Underneath us," the ranger was saying, "are waterways, tributaries small and large from the River Styx and the Green

River." I imagined myself lying back, floating down and out until I reached sunlight and could breathe deeply again, child free and weightless.

I sighed and Joe said, "What was that?"

He was spooked, and he looked it as he nervously eyed the shadows the ranger was pointing to with her flashlight. He looked like he was expecting one of the twelve species of cave bats to swoop down, enormous and hungry. He had been scared already, on the way down the sixty steps.

"Are you all right?" he asked. "You really want to do this?"

He was holding my hand and he'd taken off his flannel shirt so I could drape it over myself against the chill. He was chivalrous, my new husband, but I was repeating to myself, *do this, do this,* and I was studying his face by cave light. I was sixteen and he was seventeen and he was one head taller than I was and I'd said I'd do this, this marriage, this birthing of his child. I had said it just yesterday, in a church with music and candles, and I had said it again on our wedding night as I told him I loved him, whispered words in his ear, but now I was examining the soft pouch under his chin, the insignificant and pointy nose. Above us, the cave ceiling was pitted and uneven and I had the sense of a much larger room, a planetarium, or the sky itself at night. "There's no way," the ranger said, "to know the exact dimensions of this part of the mystery we call Mammoth Cave. We know of three hundred charted miles, but it's a changing ecosystem, a world of passageways that collapse." Terminal breakdown, she called it.

Right then, the lights went out, all of them, electric bulbs and flashlights, not a light anywhere but a ghostly shimmer at the top of the sixty steps leading up. She wanted, the ranger said, to surprise us. To show us the real world of a cave. For a second I told myself it was no surprise at all, that it was like in a theater before the screen comes on or like the darkroom in art class at school. But it was darker and lighter, both at once. It was alive. It was a moist black, and I opened and closed my hands into it, felt it settle on my bare arms and legs.

"Caves," she noted, "are passageways to time."

The ancients, she said, called them the privileged place, of life and death, of light and darkness. Of creation. Of destruction. Of the miraculous. They were reliquaries and tombs. They were the dwelling places of demons and gods. Caves, she said, were sanctuaries. They were receptacles of the spirit.

I closed my eyes, opened them. Were there degrees of dark like that? There had been when I was a child. There was the dark when my mother shut off the bedroom light and I was alone. There was the dark when I stayed awake and made up stories in my head. Adventures. Love stories where everything worked out in the end. And I said prayers while I listened to my parents' voices from the next room. *Our Father who art in heaven*, I prayed. *Hail Mary, full of grace.* I'd recited prayers like mantras, like charms against the world. I closed my eyes and waited to see if I could pray now in this dark place the ranger was calling holy. And if I could pray? I wanted that prayer to travel inside me like breath, to travel past my heart, to settle in my belly. A prayer. It could hold my baby with love in my womb, his own dark cave. I shivered in this cold cave dark. I touched my face and was surprised to feel tears.

"Caves," the ranger said, "are nothing less than the womb of the entire universe."

Beside me, Joe squeezed my fingers hard. I wanted to take his hand and put it against the weight of my stomach, and say, *Here, feel your son, now, before it's too late.* I wanted Joe to put his hand *just there*, in the one right place, have him hold me up, me and him and this child, hold us firm against any disaster, any breakdown of what we had promised, to *do this*. But he couldn't feel what I was feeling—the impatient kick and kick inside me, the limbs stretching out, the body unfurling, ready to blossom, to enter the world of light and air. I wanted to keep the baby there, still and forever unborn in the dark. *I can't,* I said to my child. *I can't.* And then the ranger struck a match, held it above her head so that wavering light shone down on her face.

"Regardless of their power of the mysterious," she said, "caves are intricately tied to the outside world, dependent on that world for air and food and energy."

In the match light I could see Joe and he was looking at me, at his hand against my belly, and he looked both awed and anxious and he was saying, "What, what," and I realized I'd said it aloud. "I can't." I said it a third time, a charm, an irreversible spell in the dark, though I didn't know, quite yet, what I meant by *can't.* But that was when it came alive in me, the decision I'd make in a matter of weeks. The decision that said, *I'm a mother and I'm not a mother and I can't. I can't keep my son.*

It's not entirely true, of course. Caves are made and unmade and made again. The moment I realized I would place my son for adoption may well have been in the motel room where I spent my honeymoon night. Or it might have been weeks later, during a logical conversation over dinner. Or later still, at the moment he left my body for good.

What is true is that I won't tell anyone, even Joe, of my decision for weeks. And what's also true is that my body won't let me give birth. Unless the calculations were wrong, I was ten months pregnant before I felt my first labor pains, one day before the OB-GYN office I'd started seeing in my ninth month scheduled me for a cesarean. For those last three to four weeks of my pregnancy I felt my son in my body so acutely I wanted to curl myself around him and never let him leave the moist cavity of my womb. I felt him holding on, saying No, no, I can't either. I can't. *We both cried when he was born.*

My memories of that day of deciding to relinquish my child are made of complete darkness and silence. For years I will recall nothing at all, speak of nothing at all. When other women speak of birth, I will describe the absence of children from my life. The secret life of my son and me will remain suspended in time, and that moment when I decided to let him go will be both imaginary and complete.

For years I will not be able to recall the beauty of the cave's huge room, gypsum flowers blossoming from walls and ceiling, how white and gold, how surprising they were. I will not be able to admit to myself how beautiful that moment was, that small voice in the dark that told me I was not ready to be a mother. Nor will I be able to admit, without self-recrimination, how beautiful, how right it was that he should leave me and find a home, a family with love and enough to spare, some other, warm, safe place on earth.

Coal refinery near
Ashland, Kentucky.

Pearlie Lee Baisden,
my mother, at about
age thirteen.

My mother at the Big Y drive-in, just before her marriage.

Clarence Salyer, my father, in Korea, 1954.

Now There is You A Couple.

Dating. The caption is my father's.

My parents on their wedding day, 1955.

My mother's family, also on the wedding day. In the doorway, from left to right, are my grandfather, my aunt Ruby, and my grandmother. The two women to the left of the door are unknown to me.

Picnicking with my parents, about 1958.

My mother and her sister Ruth, about 1960.

Karen Leigh Salyer, age six.

Pearlie Lee Baisden Salyer, about
twenty-four years old.

Christmas with my father's family. From left to right are my father, my cousin David, my grandfather, me, and my grandmother.

My mother, 1968.

Me, about fourteen years old, just two years before I would give birth.

My wedding day, 1972.

My senior prom,
1974, two years after
the birth.

Me in 1999,
ready to begin
the memoir.

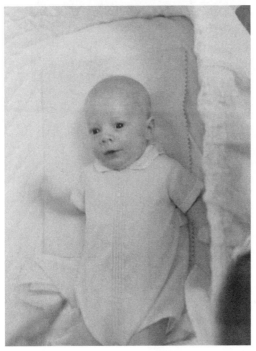

Andrew Cox,
two weeks old.
*(Photo courtesy
of Betty Cox)*

Andrew at
Christmas, 1974.
*(Photo courtesy
of Betty Cox)*

Andrew Cox,
2000.

Andrew, with his adoptive mother, Betty Cox, and his sweetheart, Jennifer Williams.

Andrew and me, 2001.

CHAPTER SEVEN

What We Remember and What We Forget

The greatest tragedy, I will come to believe, is emotional and ethical suspension. That complete inability to move forward or backward, to accept or decline, embrace or relinquish, our belief in a future. When I left the hospital in the summer of 1973, I believed in nothing at all. My body felt emptied and stretch-marked, and who I had been, that thin girl, was changed forever. My jeans with the suede triangles in the legs wouldn't zip, and the shorn hair between my legs bristled and chafed. I was wound tight, folded into myself. I was paper and on me were written the words I believed were me—*lost, unforgiven, unworthy*. I put these words under my tongue, bitter words from the mouth of God, from the God of my own father. But I was not unworthy. I was only sad. I wanted to be flame, to burn up, bright and vanishing.

Two days out of the hospital I started to shiver uncontrollably. Joe piled the covers on, sleeping bags, quilts, blankets, and I curled up under them, holding on to myself. I'd shiver again like this six weeks later when I went to work too soon as a Holiday Inn maid, but right then I was suspended in time and place. Under the covers my body felt thin and alien, and out of the covers I felt naked. I touched my belly again and again, checking, double-checking, surprised every time my hand met flatness. I felt like amputees must when they're certain the missing arm or leg, the stray foot or hand, is out there somewhere. I felt that the missing part of me was buried and lost forever, but still wanted to come back to me and my sorrowful self, which would not completely admit its loss.

I moved like an old woman, holding on to the walls when I went to the bathroom across the hall and then back again, to bed, to hiding. Mandy and Candi and Joe's parents came to my room with water glasses and chocolate cake on little plates and get-well cards drawn with crayons. They set these things inside the door and then backed out, quietly, as if my sadness were a communicable disease, something they'd touch and never be able to wash off. I shivered, my body unpregnant and fragile, shocked in the aftermath of labor, shocked to be a mother and not to be one.

To comfort me, Joe bought two hamsters. Damian, my cat, kept vigil for these hamsters, watching with her red eyes while one hamster, named Cleopatra, made a nest in the upper tubing of the cage after attacking Antony, who died, shivering and refusing water. Cleopatra, who gave birth to nothing, died soon thereafter, and I cremated both of them in the garden next to the house. I remember the white bones, teeth and tiny femurs left from the fire, and I remember how I wanted to see my own bones just that clean, the lines of my hips and my fluted rib cage.

I wanted everything to be as clean as those burned-away bones. Floors immaculate in the basement room Joe and I now shared in his parents' house. Underwear folded in all the drawers, record albums dusted and the stereo's needle sharp. When the Social Services letter came announcing the placement of my son, one Brian Keith McElmurray, for a state-supported adoption, I tossed envelope and all into the plastic tulip trash can in the corner and told myself that was the end of it. I wanted nothing extraneous, no stray socks, no clutter, and yet my life was chaos and I was being pulled down and down, drowning in a maelstrom of loss and its ordinary repercussions. The way a cup fell and shattered on the concrete floor of our room. The way pounds were gained, lost, gained, as I whittled away at myself, my after-baby thighs and gut. *If I am thin enough*, I told myself, *if only I am thin enough*. There was no end to this wish. It hung in the air, enticing and elusive, a path of clean truth away from what I had done.

In the days following the birth, my father called often. He wanted me to understand, before it was too late, that I had options. There was, of course, the option I'd disregarded from the first. No marriage, no sex. That was an essential law from God himself. "Be not born of fornication," the Bible said, a kind of warning, after the fact. The Bible, I had long noted, didn't include the word *sex* in the concordance. *Having sex* or *birth control* or *when to say no and when to say yes* were instructions I could well have used. It was too late to obey the law, but that didn't mean I didn't have options now. Lots of people, he'd tell me, married young, had children, got themselves jobs, got by. And if I couldn't be responsible enough for that, then *why*, for God's sake, couldn't I let him adopt my baby?

Late on the evening of my fourth day home, my father called and I went to the phone, which was in a short hall between kitchen and family room.

"Yes," I said. My voice sounded harsh, angry, even to myself.

"Do you know what you're doing?" he asked. "Do you?"

Television light rippled on the wall above the phone and a chair creaked. It was Joe's mother, watching her nightly game show. "That's right," a voice said. "In our bonus-points round, you can earn up to three free gifts."

"What do you mean?" I asked. I was rippling too, my head spinning, my body light enough to rise, float back down the hall, back to the safety of bed.

"You don't know?" he said. "You mean to sit there and say you don't know what I mean?"

"I'm not sure," I said.

I held on to the phone cord, wrapped it tightly around my wrist. Rose's chair creaked again and she came down the hall, walked past me without a glance, as if I were a ghost, light she could pass through.

"I saw him, you know" he said. "I saw him through the hospital window. He looks like you. He looks like my father, too. Just like him."

"I can't," I said. "I can't even take care of myself."

"I'm not asking you to."

"I'm sick," I said.

"He's your boy," he said. "And you're going to give him away?"

"I have to go now," I said.

"We'd take him," he said. "Right now. All you have to do is sign for it."

"I'm sick and I have to go now," I said.

"You'll regret this," he said. "You'll regret this for the rest of your life."

I held the receiver out from my ear, listening to the recitation of truths about my life. I'd made my bed, and I could by-god lie in it, but what about him, what about his grandson? His name, I should realize, his family name, would end here. I'd regret this, forever, and I could still, even now, change it, if only I would. I could give the boy to them to raise, to him and my stepmother. He'd be like their own child.

"How can you do this?" my father asked as I hung up. "How can you do this?"

How I could give my son away is, of course, not the question. *How* is easy enough. It's forms at a Social Services office. It's questions. *Your interests? Your family medical history? Education, please? How* is another form you sign, sometime midlabor, a form that proves you won't change your mind or come to your senses or be converted, at the last second, by certain revelations about the nature of motherly love. *Why* is the truer question, the kicker, the punch in the gut. Why not be a mother, like a mother should? Why not give my son to my father, to raise as his own? *Why* comes back to you again and again and again and it's a blank you can't fill in.

It's an accumulation of details and random memories, of truths and proofs that vanish as soon as you're sure of their existence. I have tried to subscribe motives to the past in order to understand the present. The truth is, those months following my son's birth and adoption proceedings are the times I remember least well. I can reach back in myself and take out moments of that time and sift through them, boxes full of photographs I am not in.

Why, my father wanted to know, why not give him my son to raise as his own?

As easily as he gave me options to giving up my son to adoption, I can even now supply reasons. The arrogance of a teen-aged girl. The judgment of a soon-to-be-woman who could not relegate her son's life to the very past she had just managed to escape. My son would never be my brother. Or a simpler reason, maybe. That the man I love, that father who is mine, knelt in the waiting room on the day of my son's birth and asked God for my forgiveness. Something simpler still? I would not allow my son's future to be shaped by my father's truths about what it means to be a man.

My father has told me stories of adventures, some of them his, some of them his father's or his father's father's. Once they climbed down to the river below the train trestle and went skinny-dipping in the ice-cold March water. One of them laid his clothes out on the grass and the train passed by, showering his trousers with live sparks. There were shiverees, raccoon hunts under a full moon, cows slaughtered at the first frost. And when these boys became men, they put away childish things. First touch of a woman's breast in a car's backseat at a drive-in movie. Showgirls by streetlight in the downtown of some wartime city. Back home again to marriage and a job. "The man," the Bible says, "who looketh not after his own household is worse than an infidel." Over the years, as he reflects upon his life, my father will consider this again and again—what a man can and must be.

I imagine these stories my father tells of his boy self becoming a man. Stories of nights when they hit the dirt road out of their hometown, four or five of them jammed into someone's pickup and the dogs in the back too, redbones baying at half a moon. Cold black coffee out of a quart jar to keep them awake for the hours ahead. Whoever was the driver pulling a right-angle turn into a clearing at the grove of chestnut trees, and then it was a little hike from there, with the redbones nipping and running circles ahead of them, ready to hunt the woods for foxes and squirrels. Path giving way to blackberries and catbrier, but they plunged on through, figured a right turn or a left and then they were there, at the best camping place in the county.

They had worked up a sweat by then, and they squatted, balanced on their ankles as they passed a flask one of them had pulled out of a knapsack. I imagine them as no more than sixteen or seventeen, and already they knew enough to know good, clear moonshine, none of that with oil or who-knows-what, poison, floating on the top. I imagine my father rinsing it through his teeth, swallowing hard.

This was the spot where they always came, close enough to the lake to see the water shift as if they could see down below the warm surface to icy cold and to hundreds of crappies and bass just waiting for them. My father must have felt the moonshine stir and shiver in his blood, just the way a school of fish might dart and scatter when he skipped a flat stone five times toward the other shore. He'd felt it plenty, a bass the length of my arm shimmying on a line, his trousers wet and heavy as he waded into the thick, sucking murk, and the body of that fish a frenzy he held for the space of a minute, no more, lost in a glimmer of light and the still lake.

That night they weren't there for fishing. It was dusk, then darker than that, so one of them went and rolled the truck windows down, burned the headlamps so that a ghost of light shot down through the trees. It was past supper time back at their houses and they knew it, but they held out, made a mound of pine needles and dead wood, found a match or two and told stories. You know the ones, one-armed man with a knife, little dog with its tail cut off, then three legs and then the fourth. And still that flask, tasting sweeter and sweeter, with my father and the rest of them elbowing each other and giggling like boys with something to tell and no one to tell it to. And later on, maybe, a magazine with pretty girls and a naked leg or cleavage to touch with a finger as you wet it and turned a page.

Just at pitch dark, when the cicadas and the tree frogs started up, someone reached one last time into the knapsack. Moonshine went down now like water lit by fire, sparked low and wild in their guts, and that's when I imagine it came to them, the way they could cease for all time to be boys. They'd ceased in other ways already, of course, by means of blackjack and minor bets of nickels and dimes, crew cuts they slicked back with butch wax. But they wanted something more, a sign, an irreversible bridge they'd cross to that place called *being a man*. The redbones were baying in the distance, a bark and a long howl and another that echoed from one ridge to the next, and someone said, "Yeah, that's it." I imagine them drawing straws. Or one of them tearing off half an unfiltered cigarette and holding that cigarette and another one next to his chest and saying, "Here, pick one of these." My father won the draw that night. I imagine them laughing in his direction, like boys who aren't quite men do, part jest, part bravado. They circled one another, fists raised, boxed the air. One of them whistled, two fingers against his lips, a sharp, piercing sound, and the others held their palms against their ears, rolled their eyes. In the distance the redbones yapped and raced, joyous to be called back.

There were four such redbones, all of them belonging to one of the boys. Or not even to him, but to his father. The boys were already planning what they'd say. Something implausible, perhaps, but they'd have to be believed. How the dog ran full tilt toward a stump as sharp as if it had been whittled that way. Ran and leaped and dived down, like it was ready for its own demise. How they had to do it, put the thing out of its misery. How hard that was, no gun, nothing but a pocketknife, and it too dull to cut butter. Anything but the truth, which was what they'd planned.

This first dog raced into the camp place, its legs working, long and lean and reaching, saliva white and foaming at its lips. It ran toward them like it always did, then stopped midway, tail between its legs, the correct subservience, the cowering posture, waiting for the command, the truck's tailgate slamming down, someone saying, "You there, get on up there now." That's what the dog expected.

And that was what my father almost did, even though he was the one who had been chosen. He stood back, giving them time. Time to wrestle the dog to earth, hold its strong legs, paw to paw. The dog, startled and pleased, inched itself belly-up, ready to receive the praise of boys' hands. Then it was whining, surprised at the way these hands twisted fur and flesh and held down fast. I imagine my father, he who became a gentle man, looking at the mist from that dog's breath and saying, not aloud at first, *I can't, I can't.* Moonshine twisted in his belly, painful and frightened, and he was almost at the edge of it. Edge of drunkenness, edge of a knife entering as swiftly as sex, blood pouring out pungent and rich, blood that would make him a man.

That was the determining moment. The glitch in time when my father chose once and for all. Or did not choose, as you define this story. Watched, instead. Was or was not a man. Watched how easily the dog gave up, that first dog to return to the camp, its throat slit so easily, strung up by its paws. Watched as something sour and shameful forced its way up out of him, something that sounded too much like *no.* He crouched on his knees, as if in prayer, saying to himself the whole time, *That's right son, that's the way, now take it like a man.*

My father became a man who does what men must. He is a saver of dollars and cents, a good husband, a lover of cats. He is a man in his own home, a maker of ways and means. He is a giver of tithes every Sunday, a believer in prayers over mashed potatoes and peas. He is a follower of God's ways, which are men's ways, truths written in a closed fist in the sky. If you pray hard enough, he believes, the fist will open. It will become a gentle hand, fingers stroking the back of your neck when you are afraid. When he says, "Trust him," he means God, he means Jesus, he means all holy truths. He means ones you breathe in, sweet as smoke, and they are pure and good, straight from the palm of the sky. Why, then, not give him my boy?

I have no photograph of this man, my father, as he knelt in the waiting room on the day of my son's birth, as he confronted what was unimaginable to us both. I have been told that he waited there, those many hours of my labor. He held my stepmother's hand. He wept. He searched through the waiting-room Bible for the exact chapter, the verse that would give him solace. Had he been a father? Had he been a man? "Forgive her, Father," he prayed. "She doesn't know what she's doing." Some days I want to be able to go there, put my arms around him, pray with him for a more merciful God, a more merciful time and place we can henceforth call our pasts.

The bottom of memory. I've tried to look there as a place to find proofs and reasons, justifications for my life. Can memory be proof? It alters with time. It's like water on a road you want to remember, a flooded road in the wake of a passing car. Memory is this image and the next and the one after that and you want to put your hand up to the air and say, Now, *say,* Stop, *and time holds still, holds all these images together, intact, a comforting whole you can understand at once and forever.*

I'm five and my father shows me how to take a hair, coat it with toothpaste. We drop the hair down in the toilet water, watch it squirm like a tadpole. This, my father says, is mystery. I am six and I've started elementary school, a building next to the high school where my father teaches. At lunch, I eat with him in the high-school home-economics room with pretty girls who will be decorators and dressmakers and wives. We eat with girls I will remember for their curled hair and the high-school pins on their collars and the way they slide over to make room for us at the lunch table, the way they are solicitous of my father.

"I wear the same shirt for a week," my father tells my mother at home. "They feel sorry for me at school," he says. "They're thinking about taking up a collection." The girls do feel sorry and they pour us coffee and milk. They touch the cuffs of my father's suit jacket and they give me a hamburger bun spread with peanut butter and grape jelly and tell my father I am sweet.

After lunch one day a girl, one with plastic glasses that slide down her nose, takes me and my father down the hall to the biology lab, a room full of metal and sinks and trunks labeled

HAZARDOUS. *She shows us things. She knows how to light a match under a glass cylinder and melt a paste that smells like rubber. She wants to impress me with slides under a microscope, one with a hair from my own head, magnified to look like a ladder made of cells. She bends down in her V-necked cheerleader's sweater and opens a refrigerator and lets out chilly frost.*

I tug at my father's trouser leg and whisper up to his face. I make him bend down to me where I can say, "Listen," where I can say, "Is it time yet?" I know it's past lunch hour, that it's time to head back to first grade and the spelling of words like once.

The room has begun to smell astringent, home-permanent sharp, and I know there's something inside this refrigerator, something cold and odd that I won't like, and I don't believe her anyway, this girl, don't believe a human hair can be that vast. But memory tells me it's true, that she and my father are kneeling beside me. They're holding out a long, thin spoon. They want me to touch it, and I do, and the spoon is icebox cold and it's filled with shapes. I remember them as beans, pods. I remember them as tiny and alive, their minuscule hands reaching out.

In my memory, my father is saying, "Possums."

They're possum embryos, a spoon full of them.

"Amazing," he says, and the pretty girl laughs, he laughs, and I laugh too, because I should.

I'm seven and my father shows me a science experiment. You take a glass, fill it with water, put a piece of paper on top of the glass, put your hand over the paper, and turn everything upside down. No water spills out. Is this a fact that can be proven or a memory? Cohesion and adhesion, my science books say, are properties of the same logical truth. Molecular attraction by which the particles of a body are united. My father tells me water doesn't spill at all. It trails after itself, a single, silvery mass, molecule upon molecule, fluid as time. Molecular attraction between the surfaces of differing bodies. He tells me paper, as fragile as air, can hold back water as it pushes down. "Feel it," he says, and puts my hand under the glass and the paper and tells me to marvel at it, how my skin comes away dry. "Miracles," he says. "They happen, and people just call it science, another name for the same thing."

I am eight or nine or ten and I am on a road trip with my father and we stop at a house I will later remember as white. Before that, we've been driving for hours on back roads, through small eastern-Kentucky towns, Neon, Hazard, Lynch. Hazard, my father tells me, is a game of chance, a risk you take when you can. It's also a coal town, and we stop there for lunch at a drugstore where I have a Coke with crushed ice and a pickle-and-pimiento-loaf sandwich on white bread. My father points across the street at the bathhouse and tells me how men once stopped off there before going home, to wash off the coal dust. He tells me this like he's been there, stoking coal in the ovens or on his hands and knees a hundred feet below ground. His own hands are dry and white and they make me think of chalk and blackboards from the school where he teaches, but I love him because he's shown me all the world I've ever known and because one day after lunch, he takes me on an adventure.

He takes me to the outskirts of Hazard, to a white house with a mimosa tree and a woman with blonde spit curls who comes out. Memory tells me this woman and my father have secrets. They have certain handshakes and stories of a past I am not in. They have cool drinks from pink glasses and I drink too, something sour and syrupy, and then my father takes my hand and says, "Here, I have something I want to show you."

What he shows me is out back in a tool shed smelling of peat moss and manure, or in an attic with a cedar chest and a dress mannequin stuck with pins. It is in a cellar with the potatoes, or it is in a side yard with a tire in a tree where he first swings me toward the afternoon sky. It is a bright fall afternoon, that much I believe, and I know I touch fur that is soft and sleek.

"I still don't hardly believe it myself," the woman says.

She's bending down and her laugh is like silver and she's show-ing us a cat. It's a cat that should have been in freak shows, in a *beside-the-road carnival with two-headed goats and a fat woman with a neck scarf you pay a quarter to tell your fortune and to dance you around and around. This cat belongs to a white house and a woman my father seems to know and he says, "Look, how wonderful, you've never seen the like."*

And I haven't. This cat is eight footed. Its secondary feet are nothing to dismiss, no useless flesh and claws hanging to one side. They are well formed, a complete second set with individual toes and tabby stripes. My father has me touch the cat's feet, each smooth, pink pad and the smoke-colored, sharp nails. The cat is docile, used to inspection and amazement. It preens, stretches its generous neck, licks its backside.

"You'll want," my father says, "to remember this."

I am nine or ten or eleven and my father and my mother and I are driving at night through Hazard. We've driven through here before, once with the water up to the hubcaps and households floating past. There'd been a flood and I saw a pillow embroidered with a hula dancer floating in a ditch under a streetlight at a truck stop. Or that's another time, another small town. That time is a flooding creek under a bridge by a house I don't remember, and tires and mattresses and the board cover of a well floating by in the night. Or that's the time the creek rose overnight and flooded our car and my mother stood at the bottom of the road, crying.

Or it's a time that never was. My father says this. We never drove through Hazard at night, with the roads treacherous and wet. My parents were not quarreling about visits home or about the other women my mother conjures or about the unsewn buttons on his dress shirts. There never was a flood, no water high enough for me to trail my hand through out the back as we entered that town he calls imaginary.

This town is in a lowlands so that the main street and the two blocks around it are the worst, deep with water and debris and police cars with their lights reflecting blue. The main streets are roped off and so we have to take a side road, and then another one, and then we're lost on the outskirts, going uphill and down, fast and steep into a skid of mud and rocks.

The road is bordered with coal camp houses and chain-link-fenced yards, side by side, and in one I remember a Styrofoam deer marked with arrows and a black jockey painted white. I remember a boy running out, his face pale and small. I remember his black hair and how there is, maybe, a bicycle with training wheels he is riding along the unlit road. Or he is just running, from this house to that one, following the sound of his mother's voice as she says, "Time for supper, get on in here, now." I remember my own mother, how she says, "God help us," and at the same time the sound of flesh on metal, soft and quick. I remember the road specifically as cinders and ash and we are standing there, and someone—a woman with an apron or my own mother, who wears pearls and a wool skirt and pumps—is holding this boy who is shaking, who is shaking himself out like a wet dog standing up and is saying, "I'm OK, I'm OK."

And then we're in a living room with a green horsehair sofa or a kitchen with a drop-leaf table, some place that smells of onions and burning coal, and my father is talking, his voice anxious, that voice I remember as a little boy's. He's been found out, he's sinned, he's done something he must bury deep like a bone in the yard, a haint that will come back to pick our pockets clean. He talks fast, with high-school math-teacher words, words I'll be able to add and subtract in my memory. "Cut our losses," he says. Or he says, "Offer compensation and suitable recompense." Or he says nothing at all. We're not in a room with a scared boy with a knot on his head. We're not beside a road or driving through a flooded town, couch cushions floating out.

None of this can be true, of course. My father confirms this fact when I describe my memories of places and events, my conviction about spoons and eight-footed cats. "You remember things," he says. "You do. You remember lakes and summer and the color of your mother's eyes. You remember stones from a river bed and the *taste of pawpaws from the tree above your grandmother's house. But memories," he says, "they aren't it." They're the sum total of nothing, the truth of absolutely zero. Time is a distortion like shadows on a wet road. It is spilled oil on water, thin as air bubbles from a drowning thing submerged. "That time," my father says, "simply did not exist." There was no boy, no bargain in a stranger's living room at midnight. And if they did exist, if that boy and that car and that moment of impact were true, then that, he says, is the responsibility of language. "We choose," he says. "We are adults and we can choose to forget." We can revise, remake our pasts. Our pasts are a map, a deluge of roads and roads and roads. "Pick this one," my father says. "Pick it once and for all."*

And yet, I am eight, I am nine, I am ten years old and already the truth is an echo in my head, a reverberation from my future, a haunting from my past. The truth is this. I'm ten and my father takes me to a junkyard on Abbott Mountain. He has me brace a rifle against my shoulder and shoot whatever moves and anything that doesn't. I shoot old washers and truck tires and once a rat with a thick, pink tail. My father beside me is tall and he holds the gun when it shakes in my arms. He steadies the world. I am eight and my happiest times are at my father's mother's house, where I do not have to believe my own home and my mother and my father exist, their quarrel words, their lack of love. The truth is I am hollow at my center. I am an empty box. I am a script, I am mere words, I am all the times to come, all the things that will be. I am seven or eight or nine and I am standing on the back porch at my father's mother's house and I feel a warm wind down from the hollow and I believe this is the hand of God. As sure as I am born I am already all that I will become.

It was July, then August of 1973 and I was living with my in-laws, their breakfast eggs sunny-side up, their laundry and their Sunday suppers. I was sleeping more and more. I slept through seven o'clock in the morning, when Joe's father left for his job as a game warden, and I slept through eight o'clock and Joe's mother's departure for her secretary job. Then it was nine, then ten. The sisters were gone to church camp, Joe was gone to his job as a grocery clerk, and I was alone.

It was summer and I spent the afternoons by the portable swimming pool in the side yard, or I spent it in the basement, where Joe and I had moved our room. Our room was cool and windowless and I napped under the damp sheets, beneath a poster-sized tarot card. It was the Tower, lit by fluorescent lightning, and inside the tower was a woman with hair as long as Rapunzel's falling into a sea.

Afternoons, Joe's sisters were home again from camp with Bible verses and houses made of Popsicle sticks, but since they stayed in the television room upstairs, I could crank the stereo full blast. "Ten years have got behind you," Pink Floyd sang. "No one told you when to run, you missed the starting gun." I had not eaten all day and I swallowed Pink Floyd and Black Sabbath, their words like cheap wine that made the knot that is my gut unwind, turned sadness into sweet acid rock spilling into my veins. I felt alive again with this sweetness and I fell asleep again until late afternoon.

I dreamed myself anywhere else. I was dancing on a floor made of lights. I was twirling and spinning. I was alive but I did not know why. I slept until the twins opened the door to upstairs and yelled down to me. They were watching soaps and eating cake batter right from the bowl and they said, "Quiet! Can't you please be quiet?" I slept through a chaos of sound, a slamming door, a guitar's whine.

I was asleep even at dinner, when I fed roast beef and gravy to a body not my own. Mother Rose made meat loaf. She made barbecued chicken and spareribs and steak. She was trying to fatten me up. I was Gretel sticking out her finger, and Rose tweaked my bones.

"Are you," she asked, "eating enough?"

I was the thin one in this plump family who opened their mouths, chewed, swallowed. I did these things, too. I sliced my meat and spooned in potatoes, but I had secrets they didn't know. If I had known how, I would have gone to the bathroom and stuck my finger down my throat and purged myself, but it was 1973, and I hadn't heard of that yet. Words like *purge* and *self-mutilation* still made me think of saints or martyrs, of hair shirts and birch twigs and hot coals. I was pure in other ways, and they suspected.

When I counted calories, they thought I was trying to *get my shape back*. I was trying to *come back to myself* when I kept lists no one saw, lists of every spoonful, every slice of bread. Three hundred calories, four hundred, five hundred, stop. A year, maybe two, and I'd weigh in at ninety-five, ninety, eighty-seven and counting down. No one spoke yet about anorexia or bulimia or any other mysterious disorder of body and food. A sad teen-aged girl was a sad girl and what should she do? *Get on with it*, they said.

I went back to high school, entered those pivotal years, 1973 and 1974, as if I had never given birth. I remember critical details of those years. I remember Watergate and the oil crisis and the aftermath of Vietnam. I can recall Richard Nixon's indiscretions, the width of his nose and the various modifiers of the name Dick—*tricky, shifty-eyed*. My friends and I heard about the oil crisis and imposed embargoes on ourselves. We gave up sugar. We marveled at yogurt sweetened with honey. My best friend dated a Vietnam vet, which was suspect, since we knew all about the immoralities of that war. He came to visit her between classes, in study hall. He was told to leave the premises and we watched his blue eyes turn to ice. He stood on the cafeteria table and screamed at us in Vietnamese. He stamped his army boots and waved his fist. "Make me," he said. "Make me leave, you motherfuckers."

Drugs no longer seemed delicious, but I craved them. Pot

made me brave. It made me laugh and eat club crackers right from the box, food I'd punish myself for later by eating next to nothing. I did acid again, little paper squares with comic characters on their fronts. I dropped blotter like this once and saw myself as Alice, with her long, thin neck, and I strummed the plastic strings of Joe's guitar and pissed on myself as I lay tripping on a trailer floor. I did a four-way hit of windowpane and left my body altogether for two days. I thought I'd found heaven. "Don't let it stop," I said to Joe as I peaked. I found more-exotic highs known only by letters. THC. PCP. Nothing satisfied me. The colors I saw were flatter. The crash came sooner. Drugs made me tired and hungry, and I grew thinner and thinner with the consumption of nothing but my own body and soul.

My friends, too, could no longer help. My best friend graduated early and moved to Columbia, my runaway destination. She enrolled in college and wrote me letters about drugs and boyfriends, and sent me hippie earrings in a satin purse with beads. In the auditorium the last week of school, there was a production, student skits about the last four years. The cheerleaders stuffed pillows in their dresses and did a sequence about unwed mothers, and the people I was sitting with laughed and then got quiet, just in time. Sometimes I got close to those who might have understood. The girl they called Buckwheat was supposed to have had a baby when she was twelve, but she was more furtive than I was. And once in the hall I saw a girl I'd known only as one of the elite, a cheerleader, who had had a baby that died at birth. Our eyes met in the hall and I knew her and she knew me, but we didn't speak.

Nights, on the carpeted living-room floor, I did sit-ups, twenty, thirty, fifty, a hundred. I did stretches and push-ups. Such exercise was ahead of its time, before fitness centers and workout videos, but I wanted to be ahead of time, behind it, so deep inside it I'd never have to come up for air. Time was me, standing naked in front of a mirror and seeing every girl I'd ever been. I was ten and my father took me to the junkyard to shoot rats and bottles and cans. I was fourteen and I hadn't lost my virginity yet and I admired my own body, the unmarked breasts and the hips and thighs and stomach with no map of scars. I was fifteen and I was riding at midnight on a country road. I was high on mescaline and stars and I was leaning out the window and I was shouting at the sky, "Forever, forever, we're on the road to forever." I was sixteen and I was in labor and I was lying on my side. I was riding pain like a car on a winding road and I wanted someone, anyone but myself, to hold on to, someone who would never let go. I raised my legs, sucked my stomach in tight, leg lifts, one and two and fifty and more, as if counting could make me whole.

Sleep was my refuge. In sleep, I told myself, I would forget pain and the way it felt to stretch open and hear my son cry, but already I knew that for the rest of my life his would be a body united with mine. Mine would be a body connected to his, to a body not my own. Time was an amalgamation, a refuse heap of memory. I lay at night and took out memories of my son one by one and touched them, as if they were real.

I often called my father, hung up before he answered, called again. "You've made your bed," he told me, "and now lie in it." He meant my life, that *it* I no longer understood. For years I went home to see him, as if he were the key to what I'd missed, to what I'd done.

For years, when I visit home, my father will tell me stories—ones about his boyhood or his service days in the Korean War or the time he flew back from Morocco with my mother's engagement ring in his back pocket. He will tell these stories on Saturday afternoons in the garage, that place filled with many third-rate wonders, castoffs, junkyard finds. There are toasters, lawn mowers, weed eaters, transistor radios. And there are the near-finds, the could-have-beens, things damaged nearly beyond repair. There is the 1965 Volkswagen he bought from my college roommate when I was twenty. The floorboards are rusted and the engine is shot and he is no mechanic, but when I visit some Saturdays I find him in the garage, making the things that don't work look their best. I hear the hiss of the spray-cleaner bottle, watch his back quiver as he works.

I try, on some afternoons, to ask him questions. Ones about my mother, about himself, about what he remembers of the day my son was born. He says very little, just a few words that sound hollow and quiet from inside the car. "That's just the way it is sometimes," or, "You just remember things different. Worse than they were." And he's right. We both have re-created the past. Held it in abeyance, undisturbed as dust on a dirt road.

Sometimes they're about men, the stories my father tells. About men or their ghosts. A ghost of a man. In some dreams, this man is a soldier from the Civil War. He is lagging behind long after the troops have gone home and he is lost in forests or beside creeks whose names he has forgotten. In other dreams, this man sleeps at night outdoors, jumps from the heights of bridges onto the backs of passing trains. He is an outlaw, a runner of moonshine, a mighty preacher who saves souls right and left. None of these men are merely myths, you must understand. They aren't the kind in campfire stories, stories about a one-armed man with a patch over an eye. They are all the ghosts of a man who is merely tired, who has failed to be all he once believed men must be, to be men. They are all ghosts of my father, that long-ago boy at night in the woods with a knife and a hunting dog. That long-ago boy who could not say yes to one way to be a man and who later could not say no to the terrible purity my mother brought to our lives.

And there are other stories, ones my father will never tell. Ones about an imaginary boy who must come to my father often, in dreams and unfulfilled desires and sometimes at a lake on a Sunday morning, just before dawn. His grandson, real enough to cast as far as a boy can. The two of them waiting out circles on the water, waiting out the silence, then reeling in with the whole weight of both of them against a bass the length of an arm. The boy, old enough to talk about women. Not just any women, mind you, but the ones that once made my father whistle between his teeth and raise his eyebrows. The ones my father knew in high school, the ones at the soda shop with tight sweaters and the fourth button down missing. Someday, my father could tell him, you will find women like those. Ones with sweet scents and handkerchiefs with red kisses blotted in the middle. The imaginary boy, dark-haired and tall by now, a young man working long days by his grandfather's side in the hot summer sun. Himself, grown small and vague. That imaginary boy-now-a-man standing behind his chair at the supper table and saying, It'll be fine now, it'll all be just fine.

And there are the stories we could tell, one to another. The stories he could tell about my past. He's heard, but he won't say when, about how I was sleeping with some married man, a service-station attendant, and that's when I got pregnant, that's why I gave my son away. He's been told, but he won't say where, that someone once saw my son at a crafts fair outside of town, a boy who looked just like him. There are things, but he won't say what, that I just don't know. There are ways, though he cannot describe them, that he could have been a man and saved me and himself, both. And me? I have stories too, ones I can't stand to reveal. About how I've wanted, as long as I can remember, for him to save me from myself. About why I could not lay my son's life in his hands. Some stories cannot be told. Some questions cannot be asked. Why wasn't every-thing different? Why did we choose as we did?

"Time," my father will say to me year upon year, "heals all wounds." The past, he will say, does not exist. You pick a course, life settles itself, and you go on from there. I will try to believe this advice. I will hold it in my mouth at night until I can't breathe anymore, until I forget how to feel. I will forget the weight of my *son inside me and the way my skin moved with his reaching out. I will forget the way my son pushed down between my legs, the way he was gravity, holding me fast to the earth, wanting me to be still, to remember, to remember. Neither my father nor I will speak my son's name, and yet I know that the child I birthed is as real to both of us as the blood we share.*

The truth, my father has said, is that I could have chosen differently than I did. It was I who signed on the dotted line and gave my son away. It was I who chose conception in the first place. It was I who did not choose, in 1973, to give up custody to my father and my stepmother and thus set the course of my son's life.

For days after the birth, there was that option, letting my son be my brother for the rest of our lives. My father visited Social Services, who told him the choice was mine, irrevocably mine. He called lawyers and doctors and state officials, anyone who would listen. He stood at the hospital window with balloons on a string and made faces just so, ones my son might remember for the rest of his life. He phoned me, night after night, begging me, demanding from me his grandson as his own. The simple truth is I could not see this as love. The truth is I refused. The truth is, most days when I think of that time, I am kneeling somewhere, behind a closed door, in the recesses of my own heart. I am praying for a reason that may never come. I was not quite an adult, not quite a child, but a shade, passing between the uncertain worlds of both. Neither my father nor I had the faintest idea how to obtain our salvation.

If the truth is then unalterable, the future was thus and thus. Six weeks after my son's birth I went to work at Holiday Inn, where I spent my afternoons with Pauline, who had a Texas accent and trained me to be a maid. "Can't trust those boys one bit," she said, raising her penciled eyebrows. She told me about how a jacked-up country-music band came through and spent the night partying, in her rooms too, and colored in all the little squares on the bedspread and crushed the water glasses with their cowboy boots. She pursed her cherry lips and laughed and called me honey, and while she talked, I stood at the nightstand with a damp rag and I wiped the insides of the drawer, a bottom shelf, the base of the lamp, the bulb itself. I wanted the world to be clean, but it exploded, a shattering of thin, hot glass.

The future unfolded, straight and true, and we moved, my boy husband and I, from one relative's house to another. High-school friends brought me wedding gifts, forks and knives and napkins with rings, and we moved to the attic of Joe's maiden aunt's house, to two rooms full of furniture I didn't know and summer heat strong enough to melt candles double. My cat hid in the closet, and just to prove he loved me, Joe built her a maze of boxes to climb through, but nothing was enough. I grew sick, so sick Joe came for me at the hotel one midafternoon, and I was shaking, curling into myself beneath covers and covers in the summer heat. Back in our room at his aunt's I hid under the covers in the dark, held myself in the darkest, warmest place I knew.

I was mourning. I was mourning how the top button of my jeans still wouldn't fasten. I was mourning the red stretch marks on my breasts, and the way a boy at school poked my stomach with a pen and said, "Putting on a little, aren't you?" and the way a girl I knew told him to hush, said, "Don't you know anything?" I was mourning silence, the hush down halls at the high school where I almost didn't graduate, the whispered words behind hands, the words people never said, but said all the same. *Mother, unwed, wasn't she?* I was mourning everything, every-thing but the son I had given up.

Soon the phone stopped ringing. My high-school pals didn't know what to say anymore to a girl who wasn't one. My father quit calling, quit asking me to change my mind. Six weeks passed, a year, more than the proper time to grieve, far past the legal time for me to turn over my decision about the adoption, and time, everyone knew, to move on. Joe and I moved to a used trailer near the county line, one with a roof that leaked and only just enough storage space for our record albums and Joe's radio repair kits. Baby gifts that might have been, a blue cloth bear, a set of bibs, sentimental gifts, lovely and blue, disappeared from closets, were given away in due time.

My memories of 1973 are sharp as cutlery stolen from a Washington hotel, and those memories are a tape I replay in my head for years. Tell me, *I demand.* Tell me the truth. *There is no proof my son ever existed. No baby shoes in bronze, no lock of hair and a satin ribbon and a little paper book that says,* Welcome him, our boy. *My womb, after 1973, was clean and pure. Clean and free, I told myself, of indiscretions, of the manifestations of wayward desire. And yet for years to come, for all my life, I will be able to close my eyes and remember. I will cup my hands over my heart and I will listen and I will be able to follow the sounds inside me down to the way my womb once moved, echoing with the unalterable truth of my son.*

I'm twenty and I speak with my father about the vicissitudes of responsibility, about the reasons time hurts and love is lost. It's 1973 and I'm sixteen and I birth a boy I will never see, the son I put up for adoption. Put up, *like green beans or beets in a jar. I'm fourteen and my mother leaves our home at gunpoint, or so she later says.*

I was eight when I spent two weeks with my father's mother in eastern Kentucky. It was summer, so hot some afternoons I went behind the main house to the root cellar for the cool. I loved its smell of potatoes and the slick, wet walls lined with canning jars. In one corner was a boarded-over spring that cooled this cellar, which we called the warm house. One afternoon, I knelt and pried up the cover and bent over the spring, close enough to let my lips and forehead touch my own shadow. The surface of the water rose and I held still, not letting my reflection break. The blackness made me think of locusts and tree frogs and of how I wished my mother were one to tell me stories about the look of trees at night when there is no moon. But my mother was odd-turned, as they said, and when she tucked me in at bedtime, she wore white gloves and her hands were not kind.

Cohesion and adhesion, my father once told me, are properties of the same logical truth. Molecular attraction by which the particles of a body are united. My father told me water doesn't spill at all. It trails after itself, a single, silvery mass, molecule upon molecule, fluid as time. I touched the spring water again and again with my lips and my palms, feeling my reflection approach and recede.

Time is present, past, future. I am in search of that one place, an unreachable moment, a truth my father calls the quintessential now *or* nothing at all. *Time is a carnival ride going fast enough to whirl up into the unfathomable sky. Time is a vortex in which I am spinning and spinning, fast enough for the world to vanish, leaving no sign of myself. I reach out and I want to hold on, to hold on and never let go. I want to find it, that one point, that one essential moment called forgiveness.*

CHAPTER EIGHT

Lovers

*Art, you tell me, is the only true opening. Art is a dark hallway
with a light at the end. Art is soul. It is a red convertible under a
starlit sky on the road to forever. It is breath and blood and sex
and a stranger's touch in the aisle at a country store. Through art,
you tell me, we reach ether,* quinta essentia, *the miracle that holds
together fire and earth and water and air, holds together our selves.
But in the months and then years following my son's relinquishment, I do not understand this. Two years later I do not yet know
how to weave and unweave past and present and possibility, how
to ride down those twin roads of pain and joy, how to slide with
ease up and back and around in that spiral called time, that birth
date I can't remember.*

    *My memory is a tape that unwinds, skitters and stops and
replays. I'm caught in a parabola of time. A glitch. A flaw I believe
I created and can never, ever fix. I'm as paralyzed as the quad-*

riplegic woman I knew who gave birth in an iron lung. I'm more immobile than that. I'm suffocating, breathless between what might have been and what isn't. Someday I'll write stories and novels and words and words and I'll believe they're a cure. But in 1975 I don't know anything about such power. About the splendor or the inadequacy of words.

In 1975, I was more worried about counterculture paraphernalia than I was about art or truth. I liked how my hair looked when I braided it wet, slathered it with Dippity-Do, then combed it out to resemble Janis Joplin's. I wore moccasins, halter tops, and a spoon ring on my middle finger. Because I'd written poetry on the backs of truck-stop menus and because I'd sat up all night doing acid and communing with spirits via Ouija board and incense, I believed I knew more than anyone else. I knew more than my husband's best friend, a druggie who feigned chords, hands held midair as he pretended to be playing hot rock 'n' roll. I knew more than my former history teacher, who told me to use my fine brain, and more by far than God, to whom I prayed only on momentous occasions.

For six weeks straight in the summer of 1975, I wore the same pair of jeans. I wore them for concerts and drug deals and for swimming in the Kentucky River on the night of a lunar eclipse. Joe and I took beach towels and a canning jar full of vodka, and someone else took a radio. It was the moon's disappearance, we told ourselves, that made the radio sit between stations, made us hear half of one tune and half of the next until we zoned out on static and rolled joints to smoke just at the height of the eclipse. The river slapped and sucked at the bank while the moon went from red to a thin slice of white in the black sky. By day, if you looked at an eclipse too long, you went blind, but that night I stared straight up. I wished it were day, a bright sun that would hurt me, from the outside in. It was times like that when I prayed. *Tell me,* I told God, as that white edge of moon wavered and threatened to black out the whole sky. *Tell me who I am.* I wrote a poem about it the next day. I had become, I wrote, an eclipse, a knife edge of light, one slowly disappearing. I hurt and I was in love with hurting, that fine liqueur. Drunk on hurting, I could ignore the closing of my own heart.

Joe and I were living, by this time, in a trailer park below a minimall, The Jett Town Plaza. Our trailer was brown and cream, 14 by 70 feet, paid for with a bank loan cosigned by his parents and with a down payment borrowed from my father, with interest, complete with a homemade repayment book. We were in a corner lot, right next to the road that circled a giant block of mobile homes just like ours. From the rear windows we worried about neighbors with telescopes, and in the front yard, which was gravel and pavement, we worried about jagged bits of glass hidden in the weeds, leftovers from the tornado that took the whole park two years before we came on the scene.

Nights, I worked selling fast food, and days I took typing tests and practiced shorthand, hoping for a secretary's job to supplement our income from Joe's job at Kroger, which he supplemented by coming home with his biker boots stuffed with stolen steaks and cans of peas and beans. Nights, when neither of us was working, there was the Jett Town Lounge, where the same band played over and over, Delaney and Bonnie, and Anna on drums. They played country and Anna had a faint mustache, but I still made Joe take me up there some nights to sit at the back behind all those tables and chairs and cocktail napkins. You had to be twenty-one to buy a drink, but I tapped my foot to the music and we slipped out to the parking lot now and then for tokes and shots of sloe gin. I wouldn't understand how for years, but on such nights I was learning to play at sex.

On one such night Joe and I were at the hockey table, spinning the wooden goalie and kicking the ball up and back. "Son of a bitch," Joe said, when the ball slapped so high it hit the particle-board ceiling, where Day-Glo velour stars shook with light from a disco ball. By eleven, Joe was sweating big, wet circles under the sleeves of his polyester shirt and sucking hard on his blond mustache hairs. He rubbed his blue eyes with his fists like a little boy and held his soft, hungry belly, wanting powdered-sugar doughnuts and a big, tall jelly-jar glass of milk. It was the munchies, I knew, and if I had been a good wife I would have gone home with him and heated up a skillet of leftover hamburger noodles, but I was not a Good Wife. I didn't even love him, though I told myself I did. I told him I did right at the door of the Jett Town Lounge, when he left, alone, at 12:35.

I told myself lots of things. How tonight I wouldn't get that far gone. But I was gone already. I felt my face begin to slip, my lips twitching with late-night bar smoke and a smile that wasn't quite right. I was going on eighteen and thirty at the same time and already I was stockpiling men, the way they noticed me, my bandanna halter top and hip-huggers and my post-baby gut. Tonight, the only man noticing was the one over in the opposite corner, and he was pretty shot himself. He was clean-cut, well combed, and decked out in a pin-striped shirt and penny loafers, a costume almost ridiculous here, in the midst of diesel mechanics and short-order cooks and jackhammer operators, but I liked that. Liked how he was ready to buy the last round for anyone who'd listen. He was nothing but a boy himself, a silver-headed albino boy, and from a distance softened by pot and booze I thought, *All right.* I thought, *Let's play this one for all it's worth.*

I liked how he had a fountain pen in his left front pocket. I liked how he looked at me in that significant way and how I might as well be part of the furniture, a chrome lounge chair, a bar stool that pivots, a tiny round table. I was not quite eighteen and I was jail bait, but I was also dessert, with coffee and sugar and cream. I liked how he made a spot just for me in the center of his lap, a hollow like a palm of a hand. I liked how I could sit there, just long enough. "You're a sweetheart," he said. "My little doll." He smelled like cigarettes and cherry candy as I stroked his face, let him touch the tip of my tongue with his. Let him take me just to the point of imagining a trip to the parking lot, a quick rendezvous in the front seat of his company car. I was young and I was old and I knew, for now, when to stop. When to head down the hill from the Jett Town Plaza with my keys and my cigarettes and my fidelity, thus far.

In the trailer kitchen I picked up an empty milk carton from the Formica kitchen table, did one more toke from a roach in the ashtray. This was the life I'd ended up with, black-light posters and shelves for my incense burners and my head-shop statues of the Buddha, and Joe thrown in the mix, part husband and part boyfriend and part father to the child I'd given away. I stood beside our bed and looked down at him as he slept, the tilted head and open mouth and snores that skittered and stopped, this husband weighed against a memory I had of a blond-headed boy who'd loved me for my moccasins and my hippie dress, the most beautiful boy I'd ever seen.

I thought of when my mother left and I stayed with my father and I could date Joe for real, right out in the clear light of a Sunday afternoon at the Kentucky River, the two of us floating down, stoned and touching, desire new and quick. He had the largest feet, square and long-toed feet I'd dive down under the deep part of swimming holes to watch, feet stroking water like scuba divers did in the blue, blue waters of countries I'd never seen. And then I was pregnant and I married him and we gave my son away and before I knew it, it was morning and I was watching as he ate. Breakfast. A whole loaf of white bread at one sitting dipped in runny fried eggs. Supper. Hamburger Helper right from the skillet and cookies by the handful and barbecued meatloaf, his favorite, sent over by his mother on a plate. Evenings, while I worked serving fast food, he sat home alone and built experimental circuit boards. Later I'd find tiny pieces of soldering wire, perfect silver drops.

I slid into bed and closed my eyes and I fixed my mind on someplace, anyplace to make the room stop spinning with alcohol and smoke. I was *stoned again*, I thought, a clever T-shirt slogan to fill in the space between me and the bed and me and him, this boy, this husband. Most nights were like this, one of us asleep before the other, one of us up and moving first. I had long since stopped wanting him to touch me and, for the most part, he complied. He turned to the wall or to the pile of comics next to the bed. He turned to heaped-up plates of potatoes and rice and puddings, starches that made him grow fat, insular, protected from himself, from me. He was immune to the questions I asked, the things I insisted we remember.

This night, as the room twisted and spun, I felt him catch hold. I felt his fingers slide inside the waist of the underpants I'd worn to bed, inside the bra strap that slipped aside. I was slipping aside too, a shade of myself that rose, hovered above the bed, watched as my sleeping husband rolled over, rode the waves of his own sleep. His knee fell next to my stomach, drifted across my legs, parted my thighs. I lay so still I was sure who I was would push no harder against his sleeping than wind against a screen, no more than the fall of a hand on an alarm clock. His body was fluid. He moved across me like a shadow, pushed into me, his breathing still shallow, unbroken. Up to that last moment, that last sharp intake of air, I didn't move.

In a year, in two, I'll look for a kind of touch I'll mistake for forgiveness and my trailer life will vanish, as completely as my mother did when I was fourteen, as quickly as did my son. I will find lovers to bring home, friends of my husband or night-school boys who can say smart things to fill up the silence when Joe and I speak less and less. Someday soon, we'll fight, hard words that shiver and break. Joe will break things I love, china animals on a wooden shelf, a vase made of blue glass. He'll yank the telephone line from the wall and toss the phone, an enemy, into the weeds in the yard. He'll say, "Yeah, yeah, they talk to you better than me? You want me to talk? I'll talk, all right."

We'll tack up a quilt, one my grandmother made, a wall of cloth and anger, right down the center of the trailer, dividing front rooms and back, his rooms and mine, two halves to inhabit. Two married children, we'll play games—circuit breakers on his side and lovers on mine—until the games wear us down, leave us tired and sad. I'll move to an apartment in town where I can hold on tight to new boys every night, and I'll go to college, part-time, and learn words and words to fill up the void that is becoming my heart.

Even though this marriage between children ended in divorce, in my memory the quilt still catches a summer breeze through an open window. It snaps and sways and flaunts its colors, reds and yellows, a pattern called Trip around the World. It bends and catches wind from an open window, catches light, and almost, almost catches us, catches me, that time, that particular place. Then it is still and that time is gone forever.

Art, I want to believe, is supplication. We send it out to the night, an offering, and it flames up, bright and true, and everything gets easier. Art is mysterium tremendum, *an invisible ladder to a finer understanding than we can ever devise with the most ordinary of lives. Art can take us above the subdivision, its houses and streets and family-sized cars. It can take us above memory, time, place, the touch of hands. It can hold us better than a lover, hold us still and comforted at an exact point in time and space from which we can watch ourselves, know ourselves, change ourselves if we only will. It redeems us from the past, helps us find the living present, pushes us forward into the future we might resist. I see myself, on some cold night with the pillow against me when I sleep alone in the bed, remembering other times, times of the ghost dance that is my life. Art is merciless and kind. Through the inexorable eyes of art I can, if I wish hard enough, see myself for who I really am.*

But I have it on the best authority that sometimes words are not enough. "Flesh," says the poet Marina Tsvetayeva, "it is far truer than poems." "Therefore," the Bible says, "comfort one another with these words." If I could, I'd put my ear to the earth of my own womb and I'd hear that crying there, crying of the child I've lost, the child I've been.

By 1976 or 1977, my marriage to Joe was ending and the reasons, I told myself, were discarded socks and toilet seats left up. He'd given me a list of foods, homemade bread and butterscotch pie and barbecued chicken, and he'd put a big, circled star next to meat loaf, his favorite. He'd left stray buttons and ripped boxer shorts on the kitchen table, with little notes that said, "Fix me," with a smile and two dots for eyes. These notes, I knew, were Helpful Hints. They were How to Fix Your Marriage, helpful as salt on spilled wine or ice on wax on a tablecloth. They were sacred wisdom, but all I could think of was putting them in my mouth and chewing to a papery paste, swallowing, feeling the words burn in my veins.

By day, I grew angrier at him. Angry that he hid out in our trailer, doing nothing but drawing comic-book sketches of space-men with transporters and superhero suits. He'd begun refusing to answer the phone, refusing to go to his new office job where, he said, he was nothing but a daytime step-and-fetch-it. He wanted more than that, he said. He wanted to be a rocket scientist, a computer wizard fifteen years too soon, a cowboy with Indians to chase into the sunset.

"Why," I asked him, "don't you do something about it, about you, about your do-nothing self, the way you sit there on your fist, reared back on your thumb?"

I was angry, too, at incidentals. How he didn't pay the light bill, the car insurance, the trailer payment. How he washed his jeans with our last hit of acid in the hip pocket and how he hitched up his baggy jeans, or how he left them hanging, low enough in back to show the crack of his ass. I was angry at how he left his blond hair shaggy over eyes that shone through, almost as angry as mine. I was angry at night, too, but he said that was another story, a whole new skillet to fry.

One Sunday, we were cramming our Plymouth Duster full of goodies from his parents' storage closets. Rose and Joseph and Mandy and Candi, the whole clan, were away on a fishing trip and we'd stayed the night at their place, where we could crank up the air-conditioning and watch cable and replenish our stores of laundry soap and canned soup. We'd also stolen undetectable quantities of Mother Rose's prescription drugs for heartbeat regularity and blood thickness, ones that substitute in a pinch for speed or downers.

The parents were due back any second, but we'd made time, like we always did, to get high. This go-round, it was diet pills, square tabs divisible into four neat parts, ones that Joe sometimes sold to buddies as pseudo–White Cross. I was speeding along, scurrying to fetch damp socks out of the dryer, loading the dishwasher, writing down, on my secret list, the calories for everything I'd consumed in the last two days.

"Peanut butter," I wrote, in a little notebook just for food. "One spoon. Two hundred calories. Jelly, stirred in, another hundred. No bread." I ate things like that, main meals with the substance left out. I ate a hamburger and fries and skipped the burger, had eggs and bacon but left the plate piled high, just the edges of the toast nibbled away. Food had become bargain and exchange. Too much chocolate and I gave up a tuna sandwich. Too much mayo and I skipped breakfast the next day. Meals were accompanied by a rhyme, one sure to ease the gnawing in my gut—*Step on a crack, break you mother's back, Skip a meal or maybe nine and your bones will feel just fine.* I liked it more and more, the sleek feel of my own bones.

I liked the way my cheeks were hollow when I looked at myself in the bathroom mirror, like models who pulled out their teeth to make their faces look thin. I liked the way I was nothing but sharp hips and shoulder blades when I lay beneath my husband's body. I was a wraith. I was Alice in Wonderland. I could turn sideways and disappear, if I really tried, and this was exactly what I wanted to do. I silently told Joe this, a repetition, a rosary, a mantra. *Leaving and never coming back, leaving and never coming back.* If I was thin enough, thin enough to feel my own sharp self, then maybe, just maybe, I'd be forgiven for the baby I sent away as easily as a too-full plate.

As I looked at myself in the full-length mirror in the hall of his parents' house, my head was spinning faster and faster with speed. I was spinning so fast I was a dervish, a Tasmanian devil, a cloud of dust that dwindled to nothing in the distance. In between trips to the Plymouth Duster with more of our loot, I felt myself getting lost somewhere between the frenetic energy of the diet pills and my body's weightlessness. I was suspended in time in the heat of a summer day, careening so fast between the girl I once was and the childless wife I was now that I was nauseous and I held on tight to the car door as I bent down with the basket laden with laundry, the shirts and jeans and under-shorts belonging to this husband I no longer loved.

I was ready to fight before I knew it. I was angry at how he was standing there on the other side of the car, shoving in another box, this one full of Furry Freak Brother Comic Books and books on how to play like Bob Dylan in ten easy lessons. I was angry at his sweat. His blond mustache and the hair on his forehead were drenched and the wet front of his shirt was straining open with his plump stomach and I was angry at this plumpness and at how, in his other hand, he was holding that thrift-store Harmony, the guitar he'd never learned to play but hauled from trailer to his parents' and back again like that would teach him to find chords and be a man.

What I was saying was none of this. I was carrying on, Joe said. I was complaining about how hot it was, about how much pure crap there was to pack up for just two days in a place I'd rather not have been anyway, his parents', the place where we always were, these days. I was going in and out, in, out, car to house and back again, and I was showing him, *thank you,* how easy it was to be organized, get our shit together in no time flat, with him still sitting in the house like he had all day and tomorrow, too, if he had his way. I was carrying on, he said, about how he wasn't good enough, never had been. And what could he do about it, he wanted to know, with me to haul around like a stash of stale pot.

He was angry too, though he was not as good at words as I was. He was sliding his reflector sunglasses on, so I wouldn't see how his eyes had gotten shiny with anger and too much speed and caffeine. He was slamming the car door, a resounding slam that punctured the day, sent it crashing down, limp as the dick he was saying I thought he was, a limp dick, not enough nerve to show me who he was, thank you, too, sweetie. What he couldn't say was that I was emasculating him with my lack of desire, with the orgasms I almost had but didn't, the ones I lied about.

What he didn't say is that I should go figure, how men need to stop at a certain point in sex, stop and just, you know, *feel.* Feel, I was saying, is just what he knew jack shit about, that and how it was, some nights, when I woke up with a taste in my mouth I couldn't get rid of, the taste of him. And what, he wanted to know, would I know about tasting anything at all, me with my head up my ass and him with no sex in six months.

He was moving, coming around the car, and he was no boy. He was a square shape that blocked the sun, a short, fat man who had wide hands with a white scar on one knuckle, and I knew how it got there, his fist punching the trailer wall. And he was moving that way now, with a certain deliberation, a heavy grace that moved him to the center of his anger, what he thought was its origin, me. I was backing up now, against the tree in the yard, and he thought I was afraid of him, only that was a lie. I was coaxing him. I was saying silently, *Pretty please.* I was saying, *Come on and take me if you think you can, if you think it'll do any good, if you think you know how, anyway, you with your cheap guitar.*

Was it then that my life shifted to present tense, shifted and stayed there and could not let go? I remember a fine music, a ringing in my head. I remember speed keening, high and sharp. I remember a yard full of heat and the shadows of trees, of one tree, bent in, teasing me with its shadow. I am in my memory the shadow of someone else, a girl I no longer know how to be. What I'd eaten since yesterday was one piece of white toast, fifty calories, and I am aching somewhere between my neck and my gut, sick enough to puke, but I hold on tight, the tree's hard bark scraping my hands. I am saying, "Yeah, that's right, hit me, you son of a bitch."

And I wanted him to. I wanted him to hit me so hard I saw stars. I wanted him to punch this aching that wasn't in my gut, though I wanted it to be. I wanted all of it to be easy as a belly-ache, about food or about sex or about a car full of clothes and borrowed soap. I wanted to come clean with pain that had a name. I wanted the aching to come from the crash of fist against skin and bones, the hair he'd grab, the shove and pull of me along the sharp, dry grass. I wanted us to get there, to someplace lower down, dirty and dark and honest as rednecks fighting in a bar at 2 A.M., voices drunk and suspicious, "Come on honey, show me what you're made of, right now, mister." And I was saying that to him, to my boy husband. I was saying, "Come on, sweetie, hit me if you think you're big enough."

Something did break, only it wasn't me. It was the Harmony, the guitar, as Joe swung it in a wide arc over his head. It landed with a twang, a snapping of plastic strings, a splintering of frets and notes that would never be songs now. He swung the guitar into the tree over and over and he was saying, "*This,* this is what you make me do," and I was cowering now, I was small.

I was small enough to lie down at his feet like a little dog and I was whimpering. I was folding my knees into my arms and I was shaking, waves of speed and what he thought was fear rising from my skin like music. He thought the song was this. *I'm sorry, baby, for the things I've done, come on and love me now, be the rising sun.*

I remember this moment years later and what I recall is a girl who was amazed. Amazed at how a guitar shattered so easily and at how splinters can fall with such grace through sunlight. I recall my face raised to that sunlight, a penitent seeking forgiveness, but not from my husband, whose face was angry, who was saying, "What do you think now, who do you think I am now?" I recall my husband, that boy, who thought it was serious, this moment, the next, moments as out of control as that friend of ours who overdid it on acid and danced naked on a tabletop in a family steak house. In my memory he thinks it's all about moving on and more, about supper in a couple of hours and maybe getting some before sleep and bacon and eggs and speed the next day. In my memory he still wants to make me say everything is OK, *forgotten, forgiven.* In my memory he is like me, two people in one—child and grownup-ahead-of-time. We're in some irrevocable present, Joe and I, as he stands there with the guitar neck in his fist, looking as guilty as a little child found out.

For years I have made an art of it, this loving of boys. I tell myself I have found, in these boys, an unalterable charm. They are malleable. They are capable of bending and swaying in my arms, capable of falling into my suggestions. "Trainable," a woman friend has told me. "With them, there's still hope."

They fit into me, my boys, with the ease of hand in glove, and I cultivate their love like all things bitter yet desirable. I am an actress with these lovers. I could be, I tell myself, a geisha. I know how to use my hands and my tongue. My smiles are certain to please, my laugh pitched just right. I am the master of the foot beneath the table, the accidental touch. My eyes seduce. I am delighted with how I drink them in, my would-be lovers, when I glance surreptitiously across a barroom. I am a performer, the creator of illusions. I know how to be the woman who isn't too old yet, the girl who's old enough. I am skillful and insincere, the only way I know how to get close. I know when to hold on, when to let go. I know how to lead these boys right to the edge of the abyss that has become my heart, how to release them just in time. I am not responsible if they fall hard and fast or if they disappear into the recklessness that is my loving. Their purpose is to sanction me, to pick me up and hold me as I grow smaller and smaller in their arms, hold me until I am complete.

This art of loving boys is about the body, mine and theirs. Boy-ness is not, of course, chronologically determined. There are boys of twenty-four and there are boys of forty-nine. I love it, this mystery of what makes them boys. I love the ones with soft hands, the ones whose upper lips are hairless and sleek. I love the ones who love me with an edge, a cruelty that passes as nonchalance, a casualness that masquerades as reserve. I love ones with tight hips and cowboy boots. I love the ones whose bodies are in some way wounded, in some way unformed. One has a testicle that didn't descend at birth. Another has a lazy eye. Still another has a gold tooth that I polish with my own tongue.

I love their innocence, the unending richness of who they might become. I love the ones who've fucked few women, two or three or four, at most. I love the ones who can cut their losses down to one or two. I can do a slow striptease with these boys. I can unwrap them, experience by experience, until I know what makes them tick. There's the boy from the Great Northwest whose mother flipped out when he was twelve and chased the whole family around the kitchen with a French chef's knife. There's the one with the pre-dictable mother who drank Bloody Marys every evening starting at five so she could berate his father over the well-laid southern dinner table. There's the one whose mother was a suicide, the one whose mother coughed demons into the toilet on a regular basis, the one whose mother gave him away at birth. I am the mother who isn't one who can fix anything, even a motherless, wounded boy. I am the mother who isn't one who wants to take the boy back, take him deep inside herself.

In return for my love, these boys make an art of me. One tells me how he keeps a special room, right in his heart. It's a veritable portrait gallery, where he keeps the likenesses of all the women he has ever desired, all of them pure as the Virgin Mary. It's 1994 and I am a dozen years older than this particular lover, but I, too, am hanging there, in this shrine of his imagination. I'm right in the temple of his heart, where he keeps other girl lovers, where I can join the ranks of fine cheeks and lips and blushes. There, I have no flaws at all. I have no stretch marks, no tiny spider veins. I have never given birth. I have never given away my son. I have no son. I have, instead, this boy lover, who lies down upon my body and never imagines who I really am.

I am incapable of receiving pleasure, but they've never heard of anhedonia, that modern malady. They don't know I'm frozen in time, my boy lovers. They think I am exalted by their touch and my body says I am. It says, Yes. I arch my back correctly. I purr and moan. I am a whore and an angel and damaged goods. "I eat men," the poet Sylvia Plath says. "I eat men like air." I devour them, these boy lovers, and they devour me, and still we are empty, empty and longing and motherless. Their love will leave an aftertaste, a taste I eventually won't be able to discard as easily as I once did a tie-dyed dress.

It's 1992. I'm lying on the bare boards of a screened porch in a cabin in North Carolina and I'm holding on to the waist of a man who has loved me. He's loved me in the Blue Ridge Mountains of Virginia and he's loved me in the front seat of his 1963 Valiant and he's loved me in the deserts of Rajasthan that go on and on with sand too hot to touch. He's traveled the world with me with a pack on his back and he's made a home with me, a place of quilts and flea-market tables and pets who lie on the rug. He's loved me even when I've gone away from him, to visit the family I can't love, to visit artists' retreats, to visit the ocean by myself, to find myself, I tell him. He's loved me for nine long years and he's loved me in this cabin, too, where inside at this very moment a stove burner is still on, heating soup he's made to fill up my bottomless need.

We've tried, for nine years, to commit to each other, but we've always fallen short. We've almost gone the distance, to vows at the altar. We've priced tents for the backyard in case we have a wedding and guests. We've told friends of our marriage plans and then never acted on them. We've gone through the paces, he and I. First I wanted marriage, and he didn't. Then he did, and I couldn't. There's a void beneath us and the only thing we can do to keep from falling in is fix each other, which isn't exactly love. Neither of us knows how to stay in or get out.

Nine years, after all, is as long as I've managed to hold on to anything. When I was seventeen and still married, my husband borrowed his parents' Service Merchandise credit card and maxed it out with gifts for me—an entire ensemble of star sapphires—and those gifts, once I was divorced, ended up by accident in the trash when I came home blacked-out drunk. I've held on to other gifts with just that much care, gifts of fine china and glass music boxes, things that shatter and can't be mended. Things I mourn once they're gone, but never protect until it's too late. Until moments like now, when I hold on for dear life to this lover's waist, his legs, the hem of his jeans.

Outside the screened porch there's a huge orange moon. We're surrounded by mountains towering above this home we've made. I want to pull them down around us, a quilt of earth and comfort, but it's too late for comfort, too late for the flowerbeds he's made with his own hands. The moon caresses these flowerbeds, the pistils and stamens and leaves and dirt, caresses with light so beautiful I want to cry, though I seldom do. I hold on tight to his waist and I want him to say, *Stop.* I want him to say, *Look around you,* like he always does, like he does on some mornings when I'm lying in bed, too sick with grief to move. Mornings like that he'll say, "Come on, come outside and see how lovely it is, just to be alive." Mornings like that I'll be too busy, too busy being haunted by the past to think of loving the present.

This day has been a perfect example. Friday, his day off, and I've wanted him out of the house, wanted him anywhere but here, where I sit in front of a computer screen writing stories, summoning ghost after ghost, a mother who mystifies him, a son I gave away he sometimes comprehends, lovers, real in the past or wished-for in the present, lovers who have something he doesn't, whatever that is. Friday, his day off, and he's tried and tried. Out of the house, like I'd wanted, long enough to buy carrots and summer sausage for soup from the grocery in town, long enough to meet me at a counselor's office, where we can talk, talk, get to bottom of the mire that is my past. And I didn't even show up, until later on, here, back at the house, where I mock him at his own front door. Stand in the kitchen and shrug off being late. Make him stand in the kitchen and listen to them, the latest recitations about my life.

For nine years I've handed him myself on a platter, chapter by chapter, always with a promise for the next installment. About the time when I was eight and put a pin, straight up, in my grandfather's hand soap. About the time I stole crackers from the cabinet while my mother was washing her hair. About the cup I broke. About the baby boy I gave away. I tell him these stories with just the right words and I love how careful I am in the telling, the way the words take aim at the heart, his and mine, the way our hearts break with these stories and how I've wanted him to be the one, always, to fit the pieces back, remake my life.

He also knows of my past indiscretions. He knows I have found lovers in the most likely, and unlikely, places. I've told him all the details of my previous life, how I've found boys in hallways outside of public restrooms or in checkout lines at supermarkets, and how once I saw a drummer in a blues band and danced in the center of the floor, by myself, until he followed me home. I have made an art of these divulgences, this telling of secrets and misdeeds, have told him these things with care but with little comprehension. I don't understand, yet, that high drama can never be a substitute for the truth. That excitement can never be a diversion from the vast absence that is my heart.

My lover of nine years is tall and thin and the details of my life make him shift and turn, make him swaybacked as he shoulders my burdens. Friends gave us a small Russian icon as a Christmas gift. It's a knight on horseback coming to save a beautiful princess from a witch with a poisoned apple. That, my lover has said, is him, my personal Prince Valiant. He's not good with words, but I've made up for his silence by telling him everything, with concrete details.

Now it isn't any good anymore. We're lying on the floor of a screened-in porch and somewhere in a tree at the edge of the hollow is an owl. Its talons are sharp, and it's ripping the living flesh from the belly of something helpless and small, and my nine-years' lover, who's nothing but a man, a young man, a boy who wants the sheer rapture of the believing world, says he's just like that, because of me. He's bleeding from the inside out. I've eaten his love alive, repaid kindness with unfaithfulness. He's had enough and more than enough. He's drained and small. His love is as used up as a retread tire and he's on his way out, already a ghost of his patient desire.

He says, "You're hurting me."

He pushes against me like a dog on a leash, like an animal in a trap that will eat its paw away, and I say, "Don't you? Don't you love me anymore?"

He says, "Part of me does. Part of me always will."

I don't get it yet, this about parts of a self. I don't understand this *always* he's after. I don't yet understand that he can't save me if I can't save myself.

I don't know it yet, but I'm already dead to him. I'm a spirit and I'm rising, light and negligible, toward the horizon and the trees. I'm nothing but a memory that hurts, but I hold on a little longer, to his legs now, the legs kicking and struggling, a child's, restless to get away. I hold on until he's running, out through the slam of the screen door. He's running and he's starting the truck and its tires spin and its lights grow distant on the gravel drive and I glimpse the truth, just barely. He's stronger than me, as strong as he was meant to be.

I call them boys, my lovers, because they are not big enough to contain my grief, because they try and they inevitably fail. They can't keep it together, these boys who want me, can't hold together all the parts and unfinished pieces of who I am. I'm a pattern made of delicate paper, and their human hands are big and clumsy. I'm a house with too many rooms and they wander from one to the next, calling out a name they believe is mine. I'm a tarot deck and they're reading me and try as they might to remake my future. I've already stacked the deck and I like it that way, with the Tower and me falling into the sea, my hair all lit up with flames. I'm a sonogram and they want to reach right in, massage the heart that stops and falters and stops, but what they don't know is that I've long since forgotten the meaning of that mere thing, that inadequate vessel for love.

Love, you tell me, is the only truth. You call it dassein, *the voice of the soul. You call it holy of holies, shadow of permanence, gentle opening into memory and light. You say that it is with love that we reach the safety called suspension of disbelief, the renewal of all desires. Love, you say, is art, and art is the manifestation of love. Art, that loving trickster, is grace, a communion, redemption's fine wine. Art is as good as Mary on a cloud from heaven where she stands ready to touch your forehead with holy water and forgiveness.*

With art and with love we glimpse the only real beloved, the spirit, but for years I will think of love as the clink of ice in a glass, as ephemeral as touch. For years I will be in love with memory as a terrible ghost. I will remember waking with my sheets circled with new milk. Waking to some strange, thin cry as my son is born and asking, "Is he all right?" That question, a sweet refrain replaying itself again and again and again in my blood. I will spend my life running from that refrain. Running via distance, via time, via the touch of hands.

How far have I run by 1992? How successfully? I haven't remarried. I've moved from town to town, state to state, Kentucky, Virginia, North Carolina, Florida, Georgia, a kaleidoscopic history of states and road signs. I've become a writer, but when I face my own words, I turn away from them, afraid of completion. What of grief? What of why and why? The day of my son's birth is a specific date my mind won't let me remember. If I write, truly write, will I come to the end of remembering, of grieving, and will there then be nothing left?

Winter 1998. The black night is cold and I light a fire in my fireplace and wait on this twelfth night before Christmas for my South Carolina lover to visit me. For several nights, I have dreamed this visit—sound of his vehicle in my drive, sliding of the van door, the knock. He is an old-time dance caller and I have imagined the way he could waltz me into Christmas, tango me into the new year, slow dance me, forever and forever. He greets me in the entryway with a glass of red wine and a kiss tasting of pipe tobacco and homegrown. Over and over I have fallen into this kiss, into his old-clothes scent and his excuses, and soon I am kneeling by a chair, unzipping, sipping him, wassail, riotous and too sweet. I am ready, like always, to forgive his two-days' lateness and the way the glass of wine at the door is a token of something not affection. His only Christmas gift for me is a giveaway poster from a movie theater, a film about a colorless town lit by the imagination with vermilion and fuchsia and magenta, colors as bright as what I wish for as I trace the lines of his empty palm with my tongue.

This is not, after all, the season of roses and comfort, but I try. I am wearing a green silk shirt and the strand of jet-black beads, my mother's, in honor of Christmas, and I have painted my lips a color called Brazen. We are sitting by the fireplace and I believe that light and wishing can make me beloved. With my fingertips I trace his thin lips and call them beautiful. I think words like *believe, adore, now,* and these words shame me, but I say them and I strip off my shirt and hold his hands against my bare breasts. *Sacrament.* Long before this night, I have let myself think this lover is a sacrament.

The dance between me and this lover was learned before any Christmas at all. It was learned in childhood, his or mine, before that, in the womb or the lungs or the blood, in the solitary heart of everything, the heart that cannot, will not, love. Call this dance fear. Or grief. Call it nothing. With this dance, there is no meeting of eyes, of true skin to skin. This night, I have said to my lover, "I love you," and this should take us above the abyss, above the chasm of loss to faith itself, but this is a place we are not meant to go.

"I love you," I say to this dance man, bringer of wine, my antilover. I know that love is a gift, freely given, not necessarily meant to be bought or sold or reciprocated. But the fact that he does not love me, that he says so, is a cold wind in me. It is a hollowness tasting of ice and bitterness. It is too sentimental, that a heart should break in the modern world, but this winter night there is the shrill sound of a fissure widening on frozen water. "I'm not in love with you," he says, and I feel myself ready to plummet into the opening I have made in myself.

I am lying awake, remembering the way my son's foot felt pressing inside me, against my ribs. I'm remembering the way my womb opened without my consent and how I bore down in surrender, how I gave birth, and how now I am somewhere, anywhere, and enough time has passed to make it winter, to make this a rented room above an alleyway, a room lit by no streetlight, no corner store. Below this alleyway, at the bottom of the hill, are railroad tracks, vacant coal yards, a river so muddy there is no bottom. Beyond that, above the valley, a fluorescent sign flashes, "Jesus Saves."

But I know it isn't true. Salvation, palms that bleed, that's too easy. So I sit alone at night filling up notebook after notebook. I write this: "She experiences a summation of emotion—that all she had wondered about, found difficult and pathetic and insurmountable, had only been part and parcel of all the things that must happen in any given span of years and she wished desperately that she could have any of it, just one hour, back again." Having written this, these words about myself, I open the window to the backyard and I lean out, the wind at night smelling of snow that will fall, and I feel, regardless of these words and words, that something is left undone.

In the winter of 1999 I am living alone and for months I have touched no one. I sleep alone with my two small dogs and feel my breath in rhythm with theirs. I have promised myself I will learn the art of solitude, yet I want a lover so much that I stand bare chested against a blank wall, just to feel touch against my skin.

In the middle of one such night I am standing alone in the hall. When friends later read the story I will write about this moment, they will say what I experienced was just loneliness. That it was nothing more than a quirk of sound and light, a power glitch in an old and poorly wired house. But I'll tell them how it was, for just an instant of time, to stand there in a hallway at night, listening to the sound of my own heart. How it felt for that moment in time to enter a place of darkness, of loss, to dive down into black water and night and emerge, slowly, into light and understanding.

The wall against my skin was warm. The air seemed to get brighter, so bright I could hear it beating in my ears, hear my own heart strumming a wild song. My heart was beating full tilt, so fast it melted, warm and opening, like an orgasm. In that opening that was at that minute the whole world, I glimpsed the faces of so many people I have loved, the faces of boy upon boy. I saw the face of the father of my son.

He was a boy, just a frightened boy, and he would have knelt there with me at that moment if he had known how, asking for forgiveness. Behind his face was another one, and another, a far-reaching sequence of sad boys' faces, and behind them all was the one face I will never see. My son's. My son, a baby, unformed and unreachable, suspended in light too hot and white to touch.

CHAPTER NINE

Maria Milagrosa

At her moment of quickening, your mother is trying to learn to drive. She's sitting in the car's front seat and your father's hand is on hers, guiding her along unfamiliar streets, taking her through the motions. There's no real chance she'll learn to drive, or keep her waitress job at a local diner, or be anything besides what the high-school yearbook predicted—in a nice little home in the West, right beside the one she loves best. This is Kansas, a whole new world, and it's all she can do to navigate, to see through the dust and down the highways, ones so much straighter than the road up Abbott Mountain. At night, she dreams planes from the Air Force base. She dreams your father, moving across her body. And now you, the shadow of that plane moving forward into her life. Already the pear-shaped uterus contains you. The buttonlike mouth that will open to spew you out already speaks your name.

She wants to be part of this miracle, as your father calls it. He places his hand on her stomach night after night, touching this earth that will bear his name. He says, "Listen." And she can hear it too, the way the sac that holds you is growing. By day she watches herself in the mirror in the apartment hall, how she is and isn't the girl she was before. Perky, they called her in school. She was the lightest one on her feet at the drive-in where she met him, your father. Now, her middle blossoms out. She uses safety pins to fasten her pedal pushers, pulls a sweater down over a little belly she sucks in. She writes her mother letters, in desperation. She wants to go home again, wants to hoe down row after row of beans in the hot sun. She feels that earth pull her back, but this earth holds her down, this round globe of her body.

She is larger than she could ever have believed. She wobbles now when she walks, sloshes, feels the ocean in her gut, the ocean she's never seen. She is fluid. All of her is floating out, reaching for one memory of who she used to be. She is twelve and she is drawing water by a chain from the deep, deep well. She is nineteen and she dreams of far away and she writes letters to a boy who says he loves her and buys her a diamond wedding ring from Morocco. At twenty, she is far away. She peers over herself, barely sees the pointy toes of her little slippers sticking out.

She wishes, most days, she still knew her own heart. She is alone a lot, in the apartment they call home. She washes the pink-and-black dishes, the colors she picked for Elvis. She switches the radio on in the hall and tries to find love songs, ones to remind her of why she is here, married at twenty and living in a foreign land. She wants to put your father's hand over her chest, hold her heart still, but she feels herself shifting. Feels the placenta blossom, grow minute branches, feels it reaching out, drinking her in. She is afraid. Her heart is different, is rising inside her, pushing against her ribs, even if the doctor holds the stethoscope and says no. Her heart is nearer than it has ever been, and she touches it, just beneath her breast, feels the beating rising to her mouth. Taste is bitter.

And then, two days before the birth, she lightens. In reality, she is heavier than she has ever been. It's the end of summer and her ankles are swollen and she changes from one of her maternity tops to another, one, two, and the buttons will hardly fasten. Her back is wet with sweat, but she is floating. She is so light she could drift out through the still windows of the apartment. She could float on the Kansas air, a hundred miles, more and more, settle at her own mother's doorstep in time for water to boil in a metal pan. Hands she knows could ease you out of the blue vulva's flesh between her legs.

Is that when you first think of each other? Do you open your eyes then and look up with hope into her face? Is that when she names you, middle name after a star she's loved at drive-in movies, first name one the baby book promises means "purity" and "truth"? Your worlds are crashing, one into another. Her uterus is light, grown thin and hollow. You are ready to be born, already a little girl dreaming of her mother.

Winter 1998. Winter, and not just a time of dark after five o'clock and snowless, frozen yards, but almost Christmas. I'm living in a medium-sized southern town with a reputation for evangelical faith and a church or a bridal boutique or an estate-sale specialist around every corner. This winter, I am in love, long-distance, with a photographer and teacher of traditional dance who plucks broken teeth from his mouth after years of nighttime grinding and calls himself a wounded man. This winter, yard upon yard of my town is decorated with Santas and Jesuses, mangers and sleighs, flashing rooftop stars. One house two blocks over boasts enough red bulbs to light the way to redemption. This holiday, like I always do, I'll travel to Kentucky. But not yet.

Redemption and the holiday both feel undesirable, brittle as foil. I have put up a tree, laden it with glass balls and blue lights. I have wrapped gifts and sent cards portraying silver foxes in a snowy woods. And each night for twelve nights, I have lit a candle to the Virgin of Guadalupe. "Merciful Virgin," I read from the back of the candle, "show clemency, love, and compassion to those who love you and search for your protection. May the sweet fragrance of roses reach your divine son, that he may hear our prayers, wipe our tears, and give us love and assistance." Prayer, too, is mere holiday decoration, and I fall asleep at night with the tree lights on, holding my small, black dog. We breathe together into sleep and I am lonely and full of self-pity. I change my answering-machine message to a blues song—"I want a Sunday kind of love." I call all my friends until there is no one left to call and ask them to tell me that I am loveable, that someone, somehow, will love me.

There has been an unexpected ice storm and so I have hibernated, inclined to influenza and isolation. The streets of my town shimmer, frozen and cold, and I go out only after the second morning, to chisel away at my truck's doors and windows. I'm later than I have ever been for my journey home, with Christmas one day away, but still I hold back, relishing cold and lethargy and my tree's blue lights at night.

I stay an extra day, make a trip fifteen miles outside of town, with a friend, to test the roads. We have chili dogs and root beer at her father's country store. I stock up on homemade country sausage, ostensibly a gift for my mother, although I know that this gift will waste away in my own refrigerator while I am gone, or in hers; she fears the erratic nature of frying foods, their sizzle and splatter. My friend and I drive home slowly, before dark, on roads now ice free, and as I watch the stars and angels and mangers glitter from roadside houses, I feel lethargy turn, widen in my gut. We stop at a grocery on the outskirts and I buy jars of jam for last-minute gifts and cheap champagne for myself. I tell myself I'll celebrate New Year's now, since Kentucky will be sin free, Southern Baptist dry. At home, alone, I drink too much, then call my dancer lover.

"Christmas Eve," I say and I pause, waiting for him to acknowledge me and the season both. "It's Christmas," I say again. "I wanted to wish you a merry one."

"You, too, gal," he says. His voice, his most seductive quality, is low, sleep-filled.

I know, from this endearment, this *gal*, that he's all right with me at the moment, safe enough in his own home, six hours away. At times of less security, there are long pauses on the phone, or he won't answer at all and I leave message after message, counting, later, the rings before the machine takes over, four rings or two or a variety, a sign, I believe, of whether or not he's checking messages, then ignoring me.

He tells me about his Christmas Eve, the movie he went to see, how cold it is, how he plans to make contact sheets later on, pictures of this dance or that or of last fall's road tour of northern California. I read beneath these words, looking for signs, symbols. Does cold mean he wishes for me, my body heat, my warm mouth? Does his reference to the ice storm mean he wants me there, in the relative safety of his desire? I read the story underneath, the one I know about from times he's let me glimpse his past—the Christmas, years ago, when his former wife left, and how beautiful his two daughters were, looking back at him from the rear window of their car. Or is it all a way to put me in my place, tell me my Christmas is here, his there?

He asks where I'm sitting, what I've done with this day, and I ease, just like that, into a familiar territory, a slick, transparent surface of only certain words, certain thoughts, a surface where we circle and glide, dance away from anything too real. But it's Christmas Eve and I'm giddy, drunk on champagne and my two-days' worth of lethargy, a heady mix that makes me want to dance faster and faster, skate at a dizzying rate until these usual words, words that make me think *polite, distant, cold,* shatter and I can look, make him look, beneath who we are. Show me, I want to tell him, show me who you really are.

Instead I say, "Do you?"

"Do what?" he asks.

I know he is fond of Appalachian ways of knowing and speaking, and that *do what* falls into this category as an interrogative, but I also feel him hedging my real question, which I myself have not yet expressed.

"Do you love me?" I ask.

I have already known, for a long time, the answer to this question. He loves me, as a human being, as a fellow artist, as a dear old friend. That isn't what I want, even if I don't know, entirely, what I want.

"Do you love me?" I repeat.

"Gal," he calls me again, more softly this time. "How can you love anybody," he asks, his voice not unkind, "when you don't even love yourself?"

Through the spin and shiver of champagne, I feel hurt. I feel hurt and so empty I do nothing but sit with the receiver for a long while. I touch my lips to it, as if it is his mouth, any mouth. "What do you know about it," I say at last. "What do you know about love?"

"You're just a girl," he says, "a lonely girl at Christmas time wanting her mother."

I remember being almost twenty when I visited my mother again, the first true visit in almost five years. Before that I had seen her only sporadically, for hours at best, or in passing, like a stranger with whom I am somewhat friendly. Once with Joe at a holiday, before our divorce. Once for an afternoon visit in the public library at a table near the paperback romances. Another time on the streets of the small town near where she lives, near a shop where she worked for a time selling women's clothing. My father had long urged our connection with surreptitious letters and phone calls my mother would later tell me about. "She's been sick now and then, he wrote, "but she's strong." "She's not done well in school, but you can't tell her much," another letter said. This visit will be for real. I'll eat supper, greens and cornbread and beans and fatback cooked twelve hours. I imagine I'll answer questions. Fill in blanks. I'll build a bridge between the life I've been living, which she knows nothing about, and the life she's been living, about which I believe I know everything. She has gone home again and never left and I believe I have it memorized, the house of brick and concrete that is her life.

My visit is in late summer, close to my twentieth birthday. In my memory it is my father who takes me to see her, parks down the road to let me out, far enough away so she won't see his Oldsmobile, or my stepmother in the passenger seat. In my memory the short stretch of road is hot and the asphalt burns my feet through the thin soles of my Chinese slippers. I hurry, climbing the steep driveway toward the house so quickly I almost don't see the drapes fall back into place. I knock and wait and knock and there's my grandmother at the storm door. At first, she just smiles at me with her gold-toothed smile, wipes her hands on the front of her housedress. Five years, I think, have made me that unfamiliar.

Before I know it I am standing in the living room of that house and looking at my mother's face as if I have never seen it before. I am studying her cheekbones, their angle, and I am trying to meet her green eyes. I'm thinking, Do you remember me? Have you missed me? Aren't you going to ask where I've been? *Her eyes are beautiful, as they have always been, and they are ringed with just a hint of soft lines. She has not, I think, changed at all, not her dark brown hair, its peaks and wings of hairspray and curls, not her dry hands that snag on my sweater as she hugs me, her back straight and wary. She is wearing, I could swear it, the same thicksoled house shoes she had always worn in our house.*

"Well," she says, and she laughs and I laugh and I think somehow of slivers of glass. Behind her I hear a radio playing country songs and I see a coffee table with an arrangement of plastic roses and an open Bible on a stand. My grandmother hovers in the

background, then hurries back to the kitchen, which smells of soup beans and salty ham and something sweet. From his green chair my grandfather says, "Don't you just look like butter on toast?" As I hug him, his whitish old-man eyes seem pleased, and I forget for a while that this man, so I've heard, once wanted to hold me down and cut off all my hippie hair. Behind me I hear the rattle of coal trucks on the highway past this house and shift from foot to foot and see my grandfather stare at my moccasins and my bell-bottom pants. "Well," my mother says, and brings two kitchen chairs for us. "We'll sit for a while," she tells me, "just us girls."

We are girls in my memory of that reunion day. My grandmother and my grandfather listen as we talk about candy and lipstick. We talk about how my father didn't love her enough, as if he is a boyfriend who has jilted her and asked for his football jersey and his ring. We talk about how hot July has been and how she's been doing nothing in the afternoons but run a cool washcloth over her face. We talk about how, on Wednesday afternoons, she meets her two sisters in town at the drugstore, where her favorite thing is a Coke with lemon and just a little bit of ice. She has had, I am surprised to hear, small adventures. She's seen Loretta Lynn at a concert at a local high school. She's gone back to eating her mother's cooking, complete with things that fry and sizzle, and her hands, I notice, have no cracks or bleeding knuckles. A girl. She is a girl again in her mother's house, and they are girls' stories she has to tell me, this day.

We talk about long-ago events, as if they are the only present that exists. There's the story of the drive-in where she met my father, the girlfriends she's now sure he had. Goldie, she says, is the one he never got over. The fast one, the one with tight sweaters and a rinse on her hair. She herself, she says, was always a good girl. Never let my father or anyone else put his hand on her knee or anywhere else. She was a good girl and her friends were good. There was her friend Mary Katherine, the one she took Home Ec with that time they made dresses and the teacher made her rip out every seam. There was Bonnie Burchfield, the one who wore rhinestone glasses, how she died in a car wreck, went through a guardrail and over a mountainside, and how they found her glasses later, lying in the middle of the road.

They were good girls, all of them, though goodness, she says while she files her nails, is not to be counted on. Not in this world. She whitens her nails with an orange stick. She smoothes her hair and tells me about her last permanent wave, how it's been almost six weeks. "I'm almost the same as I was back in high school," she says. Her weight, she means. And she talks of this weight, its own goodness, the one hundred pounds she's maintained, one hundred two at most. She does laps every day, she says. She walks the circle of rooms that is the house, and she watches what she eats, too, she says. But it isn't easy. Ice cream, she says, that's mostly what she has for lunch, though her mommy bakes biscuits and eggs and cornbread and all that fattening food. The mess and fuss, she says, but she's kept herself small. She can wear the same clothes she did in high school, even. The very same ones.

After a while I go into the kitchen for a glass of water. My grandmother is there frying cornbread and I look at her ankles, their rolled-down socks and her tiny feet in their tennis shoes. I look at the radio sitting on a windowsill, next to a hand mirror I'm sure my mother uses to make up her face. "The Kitchen," a plaque says, "The Room Closest to Heaven." As I sip refrigerator water I walk past the back door and into the room that is my mother's bedroom, where I stand for a while.

Her bed, covered by a polyester throw, is so neatly made a coin could bounce from its center, and at the head of the bed, on a little shelf, are the icons of my mother's life. There's a Billy Graham reader called Reflections on Today and Tomorrow. There's a candle, rose scented, that has never been lit. There's a photograph of me in a tiny frame. I'm small and I'm walking down a sidewalk *and I'm holding my mother's hand. I touch each of these things, put them back carefully in their individual, dustless spots. A spy, a covert daughter, I then inch open the dresser drawers. There are neat rows of white cotton panties, and beside those, equally neat boxes of makeup and polish remover and hand lotion. In a closet beside this dresser, there are more boxes, larger cardboard ones. "Bedroom," one says. "Living-room knickknacks," another says. "Garage storage," still another says, and I realize, with a start, that I'm reading my own father's writing. This tall stack of boxes, still taped, never opened, are boxes from my mother's other life, the one she led with us. I close the door to this closet as soundlessly as I can, then slide open the door of a free-standing wardrobe. My mother's clothes are here. Some are veiled by plastic dry-cleaning bags, each bag carefully knotted at the bottom. I imagine pedal pushers and three-quarter-sleeve sweaters. I imagine the full-skirted dress she wore at her wedding.*

I wonder, briefly, how such clothes can breathe, and then I stand for a long while, staring down at the bathroom scale at the foot of my mother's bed. I stare down and wonder about my own weight, about the tiny pouch that is my belly, the place the son she knows nothing about once lived. Then I hear a kitchen chair slide back in the living room, my mother's footsteps. One, two. Her voice, asking me where I am. I swallow the rest of my cold water, fast, and ask myself which piece of evidence I should remember longest. Which small fact that will tell me, for years to come, how it is that my mother leads her life.

Home. At the holidays, 1998, I am in one, a house I call home. It's a house with two dogs and a festive tree and a kitchen sink, although holidays take me elsewhere. At Christmas, sometimes at Thanksgiving, and for a week in the summer, I take Interstate 64 through West Virginia, via Beckley and Charleston and Huntington, then on from there to eastern Kentucky, to the little town where my mother lives, to my mother's house and to the house of her sister. Both their houses I have by this time come to call places of secrets.

I, too, inhabit a house of secrets, lead a life my mother only suspects. I am by 1998 a writer and a reader of books she vaguely calls novels, a category that for her includes romances and old movies and one long letter she reads to me again and again, one my father wrote her before their divorce. "Long enough to be a novel," she says of these ten pages, itemized reasons my father wanted out. I am a college teacher, and she imagines me in a school yard with a bell, ringing in classes for children after recess. My growth, this body turned from girl to woman, is a mystery to her, its breasts and desires.

This winter, this Christmas of 1998, I am determined to shed my greatest secret, shed it like a snakeskin, like an undesirable and heavy coat. *I'll tell the truth,* I say. *I'll come as clean as spring water.* I'll go forth, I tell myself, having sinned and confessed. I will be absolved forever at the feet of the Mother. I will tell her I have a son and that hidden piece of myself, that fragment sharp as a sliver of glass, will be plucked out and I will then, I tell myself, be whole at last.

I hit the West Virginia Turnpike by midafternoon, a time at which everything seems rhetorical. Bare wires and bulbs from Christmas lights drape over everything. Houses and churches and barns advertising Mail Pouch Tobacco, transformed by night, are now nothing but dispirited Santa's workshops and unresplendent roofs. Every roadside diner and gas station is a testament to those of us who are part of this holiday, and not.

I stop at a BP in Marmet for a bear claw and coffee and talk for a while to the man at the counter. He has small, red eyes and a nervous way of sucking at his lower lip. He offers me free soft peppermints and tells me he's worked every Christmas, New Year's, and Fourth of July for the past fourteen years. He smells like sweet wine and winks as I pay for my coffee and a pack of cigarettes. I'm not a smoker, and he's maybe not a drinker, but we're celebratory, high energy, and it's nearing the zenith of this holiday—one o'clock, time for turkey and dressing and reruns of *It's a Wonderful Life*.

I'm late, and I know it. But I drive slowly, thinking of my mother and her sisters. Of Ruby, who died in an auto accident a number of years ago. Ruby had secrets, the greatest of which was the exact nature of her illness. Seizures? Manic depression? She was on her way home the night she died. I imagine her in the car on her way back to her apartment in that concrete block building with a guardrail along the halls and a persistent smell of something medicinal and sanitary. My grandfather was driving. I imagine how they came to stop sign. Ruby might have looked off to the right, to a field and sign with praying hands and a promise, "Jesus Saves." Or maybe she closed her eyes in those last seconds before the other car crashed through, striking just as they pulled ahead. It was she who died, not my grandfather. Was that death like her dreams of a Holy Ghost with her own face?

Ruthie, the youngest sister, lives up the winding stretch of asphalt called Mining Hollow, outside of town. She also leaves home less and less, since her son shot himself in the back room of their mobile home. That was a dozen years ago. Now, she spends her days tending house and the grave of her son, which she can see from the trailer's kitchen window. When I went to visit there one August, Ruth's husband was leaving to go squirrel hunting. Just joking, he waved his rifle in the air, pointed it at us. From the couch, Ruth said, "I can't stand it when you do that." She didn't get up. I remain unsure why my cousin killed himself. Depression, they all hint darkly. And drugs, too, ones that sent him once to an unnamed hospital, *one of those places*, they called it. The night of the shooting is called *when that happened to him*, or *the night that happened*, and no mention is made of death itself. It is at Ruth's house that there'll be Christmas dinner, if I'm in time.

I reach my aunt Ruth's by four o'clock, having missed this traditional dinner. My lateness has thrown everything off, their twelve-thirty dinnertime. They waited, a half hour, an hour, before giving in, feasting without me. Now, my dead cousin's daughter sits in the post-ice-storm warmth of the patio, rocking in the porch glider, her patent-leathered feet scooting up and back. The rest of them are inside the trailer, where there are still pots of green beans and sweet potatoes on the stove, and the refrigerator is packed with foiled pans of turkey and ham. But I can see that it's over. My uncle has already stripped the Christmas tree, an artificial one, and I can see it lying naked in the living room, a few icicles straggling on its branches. Dishes have been washed. Pa sits in his usual spot by the door.

"Hello stranger," he says, his whitish bird eyes looking me up and down.

The television is blaring football and the mother of my dead cousin's child is lounging with her second husband, sock footed, with their other three kids, one of whom is short necked and crippled, son of his own grandfather. My uncle, who is loud and white-haired and a former radio rock 'n' roll performer, welcomes me.

"Well," he says, "look who the cat drug in. Were the roads bad?"

I tell him the ice was still around, a little, back in Virginia, but that here the roads were good. My mother is at the table in the adjoining dining room with my aunt. They're talking blood-sugar levels and hairdos, but they stop and my aunt gets up and hugs me. She's wearing a negligee, and she smells like hair spray and White Diamonds cologne.

"Were you careful on those roads?" she asks.

I've brought her a flavored-coffee selection for Christmas, but I can smell Maxwell House from the kitchen, and my gift suddenly seems off, the hazelnut and cinnamon dwarfed by the plethora of things in this trailer. To the side, along the floor of the dining room, are plaster statues—angels, dalmatians, chickens, rabbits, a windup monkey that plays reggae. Most of these were gifts from my uncle to my aunt, who seldom leaves the trailer to buy herself things. A table by the back wall displays a Bible, open, and photos—my long-dead cousin, the aunt killed in the auto accident, my grandmother, who died a few years ago from complications of pneumonia.

"Were the roads bad?" my mother asks.

"Them roads weren't a bit bad," my uncle calls from the other room.

I mention the ice and Virginia and the warm spell and as always, I am struck, when I first see my mother, by her smallness. She has a delicate face, large green eyes with the same darkness beneath I'm getting, at forty-two, and the knuckles of her small hands are swollen with arthritis and housework.

As I take my place at the dining-room table, my aunt offers me leftovers. "Ruthie," my mother says, "has been up since 2:30 A.M., basting the turkey and peeling ten pounds of potatoes for her potato salad and you wouldn't believe the dishes they've washed." Soon I'm sitting with a paper plate of turkey and dressing, the potato salad, and the cranberry sauce I've liked since childhood, sliced, garnet-colored jelly, edged with tiny ridges from the can.

While I eat, my mother has a second helping of dessert, her favorite. She piles her own paper plate with vanilla cream pie and chocolate cake, cheesecake with strawberry sauce on top, all the while telling me she's lost some, that she was at 101 when she weighed this morning, as she does every morning.

"I believe you've gained a little," she says. She looks at me speculatively, takes a bite of pie, her mouth open wide, to save her lipstick. "How were the roads?" she asks. "They looked good over this way."

I tell her about the ice storm and how I chiseled open my truck, and the warming trend since yesterday. I eat slowly, tasting fatback in the green beans, viscous marshmallow in the sweet potatoes, pickle, mustard, and Miracle Whip in the potato salad. I feel my stomach widening, my hips expanding, the untimeliness, ungainliness of me, eating, late.

"Now, she ain't fat," my uncle says. He bends behind my chair. "Just getting some of that middle-age spread," he says, nuzzling my cheek with his beard.

He whispers into my ear. "Don't you have a little sugar for your uncle?"

This is the way of this afternoon, five o'clock now, Christmas ebbing. We talk of lipstick brands and permanent waves and innovative eye creams, and after my mother finishes her cake, my aunt goes to get her blood-sugar test kit. I decline, but they solemnly poke each other's fingers, testing the rightness of their blood. Soon it will be dark outside, and I will drive my mother and Pa home along Mining Hollow, then head home along Highway 23. I think of roads, iceless roads, connecting house to house, aunt's, mother's, my own, my own house now devoid of blue tree lights, softly dark, waiting for the certainty of my return.

Absolution, that's what I really want when I say I want love. I am a lost soul, waiting to be cleansed. I absolve thee, the waters say, and I am a girl again. I am seven years old again and I am at the house of my great-grandmother and I am standing in a backyard listening to the sound of an underground spring. Its waters are pure and sweet and I know that if I taste them, my soul, if it departed right then, could ascend, full of loving-kindness. I am a girl standing on the boards of a covered well, and I dance, my feet drumming time on the hollow board. The hollow sound makes me afraid, and under my feet the well is deep, a black mouth in the earth that could drink me in. The well is forever and I'm afraid of its waters, afraid of the waters of forgiveness. Why didn't she come, my mother, and lift me into her arms and comfort me?

Fear. All of us suffer from it, my mother and her family and I.
My aunt Ruth suffers from relentless dreams and memory, a grief
that won't let go. And Pa, some part of himself is lost forever down
a bottomless hole in the floor of his very own house. And there are
cousins: The one who is a product of incest. Another who weighs
three hundred pounds, insulated from the sad, outside world. Of
course, the one who put a gun in his mouth is released from fear,
unless hellfire and the aftermath of sin have made that impos-
sible. My mother suffers from fear, from what diagnostic manuals
would call obsessive-compulsive disorder. Or I believe this, based
on my own conjectures, my own limited knowledge. I know that the
illness manifests in the midthirties, and I have looked, again and
again, at a photograph of my mother standing near our car in the
drive of the house we lived in until I was fourteen. I am a shoul-
der, a glimpse of hair in this photograph, and I live her obsessions
vicariously. I am them. Already, in this photograph, I know about
hand washing. I know about fear of the body, of sex, of love.

Suffering. This. A winter night, 1998. Christmas night, follow-
ing food and family conversation, following discussions of beauty
and the purity of our blood. Five-thirty and dusk, and we're head-
ing along the narrow road called Mining Hollow, past trailers and
debris and dogs worrying turkey bones and paper sacks, past the
Church of the Pentecost and the ghost of my cousin, which follows
us, taps at my window, wondering where I'm from, where we're
going, if he can go too, hitch a ride, find his way out of ghostdom,
forever. Where we're going is home.

I've always written about home. When I was nine, an eastern-
Kentucky friend played guitar and we wrote songs and poems—
pretty ones about transparent moonlight and wind in poplars
and hollows. Now I write prose, less pretty, but no less filled with
the ghosts of eastern Kentucky. Some years ago when I visited
home, I'd go running up a road called Lick Fork. I'd pass someone's family cemetery and occasionally stop on my way back to

look at the gravestones. I used to imagine the ghost of my great-grandmother, Beck, who was grandmother to my mother and Ruby and Ruth. This ghost wears a cotton dress and she smells like face powder. In real life this great-grandmother spent the last ten years of her life in one bedroom off a gas station that, in an unpublished collection of stories of mine, became the Black Cat Diner. Her daughter, my great-aunt Della, dressed her up like a doll baby, and she died without much protest, having almost never left that room.

"It's the Lord's will," Beck said about most everything.

My great-grandmother is only one of the ghosts, now, in the boxes in my mother's bedroom closet. In a photograph she sits in a booth at the gas-station diner, the pop machine and the cigarette shelf at her back. She is wearing a loose, apricot housedress, she is holding her favorite pipe, and her face, wistful and strong, is already a spirit between mountains and heaven. The boxes hold other ghosts—announcements of weddings and funerals, pictures of anniversary cakes. There are photos of births and of graves and of high-school graduations. The boxes themselves are ghosts, never-unpacked ghosts of my mother's move back home, after her divorce from my father, more than twenty-five years ago. I too am a ghost in these boxes, many ghosts. I am a baby. I am an eleven-year-old in an orange dress, my expression both absent and sad.

We are both ghosts this Christmas night as we unlock the door, enter this house. It is the same house as always, this house my mother almost never leaves. It is where my mother once daily put rouge on her mother's cheeks, set her hair, clipped her nails, where now she still decorates my dead grandmother's walker with plastic flowers and does forty minutes of laps through the immaculate rooms past an enlarged photo of my aunt Ruby, her dead sister. It's six-thirty or seven and I think, *Four hours until I can lose myself in silence.* At first the house is quiet as it settles for the night, floor furnace popping, breathing, in and out, of the paneled walls. She goes from window to window, plugging in the single blue candles she's set out for the holidays. Soon the quiet will dissipate, filled with voices of then and now, words said, unsaid.

On television tonight is my mother's favorite movie. Doris Day is in a hotel room, deciding between twin beds. She wears shorty pajamas and brush curlers, but she is cute, perky, alert to the least sound, the coy knock on the door to the adjoining room. She knows Rock is in there, bare-chested, dark hair slicked back with butch wax. They are antilovers, pure as vanilla cake icing. They are destined for twin gold bands and a honeymoon at Niagara Falls.

They remind me of the twin pictures in the back room of this house—a teenaged boy and girl, both in blue, with giant eyes and bell-bottom pants. Throughout this house are other pairs, other couples. On a shelf in the kitchen are little china puppies, joined by a chain to their china mother. Two glass chipmunks have fake fur tails. On the coffee table are two plaster hands, offering up the prayer inscribed at their base. "Set me as a seal upon thine heart, as a seal upon thine arm: for love is as strong as death."

"I don't believe in this stuff," she says to me. She's sitting in the same kitchen chair she always sits in, on the other side of the end table from where I'm sitting. She's filing her nails to soft, white rounds. "This love stuff," she says. She peers at me, waiting for my answer.

"What do you mean?" I ask.

"You just can't trust people, that's all," she says.

"How?" I ask. "Why can't you trust them?"

I know the answer to this, the same answer as always, but I ask anyway. It's part of the ritual, as traditional as mistletoe or candy canes, and I can tell she's waited for this part, the retelling of the past.

As the movie unfolds, she recites for me, as she always does, a litany of loss. There was the Christmas, she says, when my father went to work at his office, when he took me and left her home alone, and the two of us, without her, ate cornbread stuffing and chess pie at a cafeteria and didn't come back until five o'clock. Don't I remember that?

Don't I remember the time he gave her nothing but a cheap bottle of cologne, nothing but a pin made of metal and gold paint that flaked off on her palm, nothing but a coat too big or pants too small or a nightgown no decent woman would wear, no less her. Don't I remember? I don't know who is remembering, she or I, but there is winter upon winter, Christmas upon Christmas, our subdivision home, a Christmas crèche with no holy family inside, home with no Christmas tree, no Santa in the night. I remember the cold under covers and the sounds of voices, theirs, quarrel words rising like heat and I tried to catch hold, warm myself on their anger. And it was winter, too, when he left her, made her leave, she says. At gunpoint.

I listen, as I have listened for almost thirty years, to her stories of the past gone wrong, her stories of what might have been and never will be, now. While I listen, I feel inside the collar of my sweater, count the beads of my necklace—of her necklace of jet-black beads. On impulse, I reach back, unfasten the clasp.

"Do you remember this?" I ask. I place the necklace on the end table.

She's finished her nails by now and she's been peering into her hand mirror. She's been touching the lines underneath her eyes, and when she's not looking, I watch this small act, her look of inexpressible sadness. "Where did you get this old thing?" she asks as she scoops up the necklace, studies it under the lamp light.

"It's yours," I say, so softly she can't have heard me.

"Well," she says as she touches them one by one, like a rosary. "So it is."

We're quiet for a while as Doris sings, voice clear as wedding crystal. My mother sighs.

"They don't make these like they used to," she says, and I wonder if she means movies or beads.

"Don't they?" I ask, but she doesn't answer. She's staring into her hand mirror again. She's busy planning her nightly routine of soap and water and creams for her skin.

"There isn't any such thing," she says at last.

"What thing?" I ask, though I know, like always, she means love.

Some women, I know, die in childbirth. The life expectancy for women of childbearing age in some third-world nations is thirty-seven years. I can recite a litany of possible outcomes, the mortality rate for women over forty-five who bear children, for girls under fifteen who give birth, for women predisposed to complications, women with particular sexual histories, women not inclined to follow all the rules of pregnancy, its foods and prohibitions and monthly sessions of listening to the fetal heartbeat. And what about women who simply fear birth?

My own mother. She grew up fearing sex in the first place, the dubious nature of men, the inexplicable ways of hands and unmentionables. No self-examinations in a hand mirror for her. The region of birth is down there, far away from the averted eye. The Bible, she knows, begins with darkness on the face of the deep, the sin that lieth at the door. The womb and its darkness are the deepest place of all, unpredictable, full of gushing blood month after month and the possibility of pain so great women whisper about it, one to another.

This is why, I have come to know, we need rituals. Don't let a pregnant woman look into a mirror after her sixth month. Don't let a pregnant woman go walking, in the rain or the forest or up any steep hill. Pay attention to her dreams, to the shape of her handwriting, to the way the color of her eyes shifts. We need ritu-

als, the lighted candle at the graveside of an ordinary woman,
the rosaries before the likeness of the Sacred Mother. We need
cemeteries and their plastic roses. We need plaques and cups and
hand-embroidered samplers. Mothers, they say, light the way in
this dark world. It is rituals that keep these mothers safe.

Since love is no seal upon our hearts, my mother has made other
seals, written other songs, rituals that carry her, smooth as a
sleigh on snow. Carry her through days and months and years.
Tonight she brushes her teeth, thirty minutes, while old films
give way to sitcoms, happy ones about families and dogs and
streets with trees. Eight o'clock, eight-thirty, and she talks to
me through paste and cleansing. Sometimes, she tells me, she
falls asleep while she is cleaning her teeth, wakes when the
brush hits the floor. There are other rituals. At our feet, the torn
linoleum gleams, cleaner than clean.

Tonight I will sleep beneath sheets washed tissue thin, sheets
from the beginning of her marriage days, while others, warmer,
thicker, Christmas gifts from me in years past, stay unopened
in their new packages. Hers, the litanies of clean, of folded, of
the spotless plate, the unblemished cheek. Tonight I will hear
her, for an hour or two after I myself have gone to bed. She will
cleanse herself, the small face, the delicate face. She will enter
her own sleep pure as ice.

Nine o'clock, nine-thirty, and we unwrap our Christmas gifts,
saved for the very last. Mine, an envelope, twenty dollars, a card
that says, "Love, Mother and Pa," and "In Loving Memory,"
with the names of my dead grandmother and cousin. Hers, earrings, dangling gold ones with small, inset pieces of red glass. I
take them from their box, point out their best feature—they're
hypo-allergenic, with stainless-steel wires.

"I need your help," she says.

I push back her short hair, look at her small ears and the tiny
holes. She's talking again, about the roads from Virginia, about

last Christmas, the next one, about how faithless my father was. She's happy enough with this gift, this evening, but I can tell she wanted more, the necklace of freshwater pearls she has said my father never gave her, some new cologne from Estée Lauder. But I stand behind her chair, bend down, ready to guide the wires into her soft lobes. I'm gauging how hard this will be, to put earrings in someone else's ears. I'm gauging whether the moment is now, to tell the truth.

"Do you ever wonder," I ask.

She's looking into a compact, examining her front teeth, which she fears have chipped at their edges. She touches an imperfection on her nose.

I prod with the first earring wire, searching for the other side of the hole.

"Do you wonder," I start again, "why I married when I did?"

"I'll never be able to get those in by myself," she says. She reaches up, dabs at her ear with toilet paper. It comes away clean.

I try again, more gently, and the wire slides through.

"What did you think," I say, "when you didn't hear from me for so long?"

The second earring is harder. I try once, again, a third time, and there it is, a pinpoint of red when she blots with the tissue. I hand her the alcohol bottle, watch as she dabs and examines.

"Do you want me to stop now," I say. It's not a question, but an affirmation of what I really, already know.

She looks anxious, and she peers closely into the mirror, turning her head this way and that, watching the way the earring dangles.

"I don't know," she says. "Do they make me look too young?"

She glances up at me and our eyes meet and I know, for just

that long, that it's not the earrings or the mirror image of herself she's questioning at all. I see her, just a glimpse, but I see her. She's frightened of the way it could be, the words I could say. She shifts in her seat, a girl who became this sad woman, ready to hear a truth she may have suspected all along.

"We've gone this far," she says, and she tilts her head, poised, waiting for the next earring.

I have gone far, farther than I ever have, inside myself. I've seen how easy it would be to say them, those few words. *I have a son*, I could say, and it would be finished, as easy as happy-ever-after. Truth, that sinuous wonder, could wind its way through this safe house, could pull long-unread letters from envelopes, could open drawers and boxes, rattle the bones and blood of secrets never told. Could open the door to this house forever and let in the cold, cold Christmas air. This house. One as safe as she has been able to make it against the way her life has gone. How hard it is to tell some truths and feel them settle with ease into someone else's life.

I do not tell her. Not now. Instead I tell her how beautiful she is, tell her how these earrings sparkle. I tell her they are like garnets or rubies, that they are a namesake for her sister, a sign the past can be kept alive. I tell her they are like real jewels and that they add color to her cheeks and, even though she won't understand, I tell her that they are a metaphor, that they are like this season, this winter and others, lovely, full of fire and remembrances, beautiful remembrances, at the heart of ice.

Someday, I will reveal my secret. It will be summer, and roses will be blooming on the graves of sons and mothers. I will be sitting with her doing the customary things, the cleansing of teeth and hands, the rites of evening, of before-bed. In the background will be the sounds of television comedies, ones she's seen a million times. She knows them by heart, Lucy in Hollywood, Buffy and

Jody in the park, sentimental versions of the past. In the midst of such ordinariness, I will not intend to tell her the truth. I will have accepted the necessity for discretion by then, but nonetheless I will speak.

"Don't you realize," I will say.

And I will fill in the blank of years with the name of my son, the reason I married so young. I'll speak words she's never heard. Adoption. Relinquish. Surrender.

At that moment I will believe. I will believe in the good witch of the North, descending from the sky. I will believe in the long enchantment's end. In miracles and revelations. My mother and I, released from silence, will be transformed. Presto. The cost of years, redeemed. Forgiveness at the feet of the only mother who counts.

But that isn't how it will happen at all. I will watch her, at the moment the truth spills out. I will see it, what I most expect, the shadow that crosses her sad green eyes. She will tell me how her heart aches. She will tell me of her disbelief. She will give me an itemized account of my father's past sins, the way they made her life and mine. And that will be it. Except for the script I could write, if you wanted.

One in which music swells in the background, lyrics from a musical with a carousel. In this script the heroine drives away on a morning after Christmas, oblivious to ice and the wonder of sunlight over the mountains. Tragedy strikes, a desolate chord, a sultry blues song from beyond the next curve in the road. There is an accident, an unmistakable sound of metal on metal. And the ending? A rescue, perhaps. The sound of an ambulance, the cavalry, a lover's song. A lover kneels at the heroine's side, gives her breath, gives her manna in the wilderness. Later on, the heroine is miraculously healed of all injuries, of all past sins. There are afternoon walks in a civilized setting, reunions with a long-lost son, interviews on talk shows. Time, that video camera, rolls back, and mother and daughter walk in the park with a baby carriage.

There is forgiveness and a family reunion. A sequel. An unlimited number of possibilities.

None of this is more true than anything else, no less true than any other revelation from a past that never ends. The truth will be told, someday. It's inevitable. The truth will be told and it will fall back into my own open hands.

Eleven o'clock and one hour left of this holiday. My mother and I lock the doors, front and back, turn back the covers to our respective beds. Outside my mother's house, night is here and Highway 1492 is still, waiting for after-Christmas, for loaded coal trucks, for cars laden with after-the-holiday returns. One last time, I look out the living-room window, down to the road I'll take in the morning, the highway out.

I haven't told her what I never tell, about my own secret past, mysterious as the boxes in her bedroom closet. I don't tell how it felt, that winter of her disappearance from my life, how I sat for days with my grandmother, my father's mother, working jigsaw puzzles of the lakes and snow and wondering how it would be, in two weeks, in a month, when I went home, alone with my father, my choice, since the law gave me that power at fourteen, the power to choose a parent. I don't tell her about the next five years, those missing pieces between me and her, how I grew to despise her, her clean hands and floors, her purification of me. How I gave birth to a son neither of us has known.

There is a river on the other side of this highway, and down the road is a swinging bridge. My mother used to walk there, early mornings. I think of her in 1954, unmarried, in pleated skirts and bobby socks, waiting for the school bus. I think of her now in the back room, readying herself for sleep, her dry hands laden with lotions, her permanent wave safe in a netted cap. She will sleep on her back, hands folded across her chest, covers neat, unkicked, this sleep an inconvenience, a temporary stay against wakefulness.

> CHAPTER TEN

A Gift, Freely Bestowed

Magic

My mother's family believes in magic, or superstition, as your defi-nition goes. Cats suck breath. One gray hair pulled sprouts three more. Immersion in a body of water means salvation. A great-aunt I never knew, whose name was Stella, was odd-turned. Does that mean insane, or tending to believe in magic? I've only heard fam-ily rumors, but I've imagined a crazy girl who heard chimes hang-ing on the front porch and believed they were rung by God.

Is it magic that gave my grandmother, my mother's mother, a fear of deep places, water holes and wells that smell of sulfur? She interpreted so many things as signs—stray hairs on a pillow slip, a shadow crossing a grave, broken mirrors. Or is it magic that makes my own mother fear the swishing tails of cats? Magic, her cleans-

ing of teeth, her cleaning of hands and house and self? Magic, the rituals that keep her safe in this world?

In 1990, while I was working on my fiction in a small writing program in Virginia, I began to take an interest in a genre called magic realism. Magic realism, also called magical spirituality or the miracle of existence, is about "looking inward to the magic that already exists." This is what Franz Roh, one of its conceptualizers, said in 1924. And one of his contemporaries, Alejo Carpentier, called such magic "a kind of return to the ancient mythologies underlying a modern world which thinks it has outlived their uses."

Magic? I read books to find it. I read about girls born with green hair and insurance salesmen who believed they could fly, and I began to summon magic into my own words. I wrote about a fat girl who levitates at a church revival. I wrote about a woman who believes Jesus literally holds her in the palms of his hands when she dives to the bottom of an algae-covered pond. And my interest in magic also began to take very concrete forms. I took up Runes and I Ching readings. I phoned psychics for their free five minutes and stood in grocery lines reading women's magazines for their horoscopes. I paid twenty-five dollars for a session with a quadriplegic fortune-teller who divined the future in photographs. I began a friendship with a poet who still believes in the magical powers of the number thirty-three, which represents good fortune and is found in everything from a lottery ticket number to the name of a Louis Armstrong song.

I also became a believer in dreams. In one dream at that time, my mother handed me a tiny, perfect cathedral made of ice. In another, I was at a table in my mother's house. My aunt Ruby and my mother and I were eating a mountain favorite, salad drizzled with bacon grease, and the house, uncharacteristically, was a chaos of unwashed dishes and clothes. Asking about this in my dream, I was told that we were all moving to a house made of glass. During the end of this period of time, I had a dream about a long tunnel through which I fell and ended up in a bookstore in my mother's house. At the sales counter, I asked for my own manuscript and was refused it, again and again. After a number of requests, an unidentified person handed me a bound volume with the words photography—memory—light *on the cover. I'd think of light, years later on a winter day, when I almost died.*

Light? You've read the stories. They're set between this world and the next. People who are as tissue-thin as breath float through these stories after near deaths. They glide and hover, undecided, until they're swept back from that decisive moment, that quintessential edge between life and death. What do they see in such moments of transformation? Light? Or darkness that blinds them, leaves them too afraid to die? Do they think of love, a person, a day, a time in summer they floated in pond water, buoyed up by warmth and sunlight? Or do they believe, at last, in love, that elixir both light and dark? "Grace," the Bible says, "is poured into thy lips; therefore God hath blessed thee forever." Is that it, the only real magic?

Loving-Kindness

Friday. Autumn 1993. Eleven-thirty in the morning. I'm driving through Atlanta via Highway 78 when Stone Mountain rises out of nowhere to the left of the road. I've passed fast-food joints and convenience stores and traffic is everywhere, but now there's a mountain, enormous, bare moon rock. You can climb it at night, they say, and be at the edge of forever, between a panorama of stars and city. I could stop there now, but it's two hours past the time I was to be this far along toward my destination, Knoxville, Tennessee. Minutes, years, months, past, present, future—all are lost in a timeless few hours where nothing matters very much anymore. Time is as palpable as a taste, the inexplicable taste of before.

I've set out without watch or map or plan. I was to be in Knox-ville at four-thirty and already there was no way to make it. I'd taken back roads to Interstate 85, toward I-75 and Chattanooga, stopped at a discount shopping mall for new music, stopped at a rest area, stopped for strong coffee and toast. My friend has been anticipating this weekend with me, when we'll have our usual conversations about her printmaking and my new fiction. She's at work on a large piece of fabric, a shroud of the Virgin Mary, and I'm at work on a novel about a man in central Florida who's lost his soul, but now I'm two hours late and still I drive slowly down back roads. I'm listening to the Song of Solomon set to music. "Awake, O north wind; and come, thou south; blow upon my garden, that the spices thereof may flow out."

I'm indifferent. Indifferent to my lateness. Indifferent to the emotional death of a nine-year love, two years ago now, though I hold on to my sadness, precious enough to tell me I still can feel. Indifferent to the passing of other attempts at love since, to the death of renewed faith, to the dubious redemptive power of passion. Indifferent, most frightening of all, to the power of words I've been writing since I was nine. Words powerless to heal, to reveal the faltering heart, to go beyond it, to discover the truth of love, of more than love, of all our lost spirits. *Between, Rosebud, Suwanee.* I pass through little towns I've never seen, indifferent to extra miles, a circuitous route heading north to a friend I long to see yet to whom I have nothing to say. I am totally indifferent, yet curiously at peace. So much time has passed, so much of it so beautiful, beautiful enough to taste, and I can't ever, ever have it back again.

Seven-thirty. On my friend's front-porch railing I see red balloons and a huge welcome sign and I think, *Here I am, right here, right now, love gone, can't get it back again, can't get anything but words.* I sleep on her couch without sheets or blankets, any-thing that is too much weight, and I dream for the first time in a long time. I dream of a trip I took to Knoxville twelve years ago, of driving there with a busload of Upward Bound high-school students to see the World's Fair. They all wore red jackets and disappeared into the crowd as soon as we parked. It was summertime and there were so many rich, warm, bottomless summer days. How have I forgotten it, this being alive?

Fruits of the Spirit

I am not always indifferent. For years, I hold on tight to letters and postcards and scraps of paper that say "Remember the smell of sage in the desert" and "look for the clear, unadulterated version of a face, a hand, an eye." I keep Christmas wrapping paper and envelopes with addresses for people I no longer remember. I decorate my shelves with feathers and shells and colorful fragments of broken glass, and I am reminded by these things of days and hours, of exact moments in space and time that I must not forget.

I am devastated when a blue cup I have loved shatters in the kitchen sink. I am angry when I discover my nine-years' lover has washed reds with my whites and I scream things at him I don't mean, "Fool, can't you do a damn thing right?" We're in a laundromat and the other customers stare while I hold on to my white cotton shirt, furious that the fabrics have bled and run and that what I have loved is unrecognizable. "You'd better take a look at how you're acting," my lover says. He's whispering and his lips are white and he's angry, too, and what he means is that I'm overreacting. I'm crying now and I'm holding together the frayed edges of something neither of us understands. *I'm in search of a language,* I'd tell him if I knew how. *A language to fill up the holes in myself.*

I begin to write stories about women who are lost. In one story, the embryo of a horse is a central image. The embryo is brown, as small as a bean pod and as perfect as a shell or a smooth stone, and a woman holds this thing in her hand when she tells her lover she can't, can't love or remain faithful or feel joy. In another story, a woman leaves a bar at midnight and nearly has sex with a stranger in a pickup truck. We last see her kneeling in the parking lot, holding on to a handful of earth, wishing she knew how to be alive. "What," a fellow writer in a workshop asks me, "is this silly business about dirt?"

There are other stories—about women's ghosts and roadside graves, about women trying to go home again to cities with names they can't recall, lost women, women who dream of drowning children they can't save, women who give more than they know how to receive. One such story has as its epigraph a mountain saying. "To dream of something absolutely white," it reads, "is a sign of death." I am seeking a sign. A story that is everything. A name I ought to know but can't remember. Directions to a time or a place. An exact definition. One word. The only word to describe a blank at the center of myself that has never been filled.

Then my body begins to write its own story. It's the beginning of summer and I wake up late one night drenched in sweat, my womb clenching and unclenching. The next summer comes, and the one after that, and I wake up at the same time, the same series of summer nights, the same contracting of the uterus, enough pain to make me faint lying down. I wake up with the sheets soaked with a fluid that might be urine, but with a scent that's pungent, disturbingly alive. The scent is ocean water, fish and vaginal membranes. I want to wash these sheets and dry them, the temperature turned as high as it will go. I want to burn away this foul smell that reminds me too much of my own body, its secretions, the parts of us we wipe up, throw away, hide. The insistent parts that say, *Wake up. Look around you. Look inside.*

It's obvious, I tell myself, why I'm waking up when I do. It's my own sinful self. I'm the beautiful boy who ages in a self-portrait and never in the real world. The painting becomes corrupt and hideous while he stays the same, youthful and good. I've stayed the same, too. Haven't married again, haven't given birth again, haven't latched on to a place or a life I call home. I'm fainting because that's what I did ten years ago when I got up in the night in pain and fell, dead weight, on the bathroom floor. It was July and I'd had an abortion that day. Given in to it, the desire for a lover greater than the desire for a child. Desire for the child from before too great for me to give birth to another child now. I waited hours that day for my womb to open. For my quiet, polite insides to name themselves. *Womb, cervix, fetus.* An abortion. A sliver of pain upending in me, glass set on edge in my womb, and I wanted to scream. That, surely, is why ten years later I wake up in my own piss and blood. Why fainting repeats itself at the same time, summer after summer.

My body doesn't agree. Magic steps in, gives a name to what has been forgotten. Summer again. I'm at the apartment of one of the students in a writing program I've just begun. None of us knows much at all about any of the others, nothing about family or love life or even the way each of us writes a sentence. None of us are friends yet, but that might happen. Our host is doing the Ouija board for all of us, our first get-together. There are the expected questions. *Does he or doesn't he love me? Marriage? How many children? Will I be a success in all new undertakings?* When it's my turn, I don't ask anything at all, since I'm not sure what it is I want to know. I just hold the pointer and wait. What we're getting, she says after a few minutes, is a garbled message, something that makes no sense at all. It's like, she says, a child's rambling. *I'm all right*, this message says. *I'm OK.*

Who, I ask myself later, was speaking? This new friend, intuitively aware of my past? The child of my abortion? My son? Summer after summer, June, July, and a voice wakes me up in the night, pushes me over the edge into darkness and sorrow.

Remember, it says. *Remember*. And I wake again and again with the scent of birth, of afterbirth, of unspecified, sloughed-off memories. Which child am I remembering? Which unspeakable, unnamed part of myself? Who, after all this time, is all right?

Miracles, Prophecy, Tongues

Spring 1994, and I am living in Georgia, working on writing in a new town and at a new school, and I have become a believer in signs and revelations, in words right from the mouth of heaven, and I am living, by then, in just the right place and time. Georgia has been home to visionary artists such as Howard Finster, and I've gone to see his paintings of heaven and fire. In the nearby town of Conyers, an ordinary woman named Nancy Flowers also has visions, on the thirteenth of each month. She is the vehicle for the Holy Mother, who sends her signs and messages about the arbitrary state of the modern world, messages she delivers to believers.

On the thirteenth of one month, I wake early in the arms of a new lover. We have made love again and again throughout the night, and as I dress, I trace a map of pale bruises on the insides of my thighs. This lover, like so many others, has touched the outside of me, entered me, yet left me unexplored, an unknown and feared country. I still remember his dark eyes above me in the night, the slightly flat, boy's nose, naked upper lip, one raised brow with a slanted scar, the careful and mocking way he answered my questions. This early morning, we will drive together to see the Virgin Mary.

A stretch of Highway 20, west. With the traffic heavy, we stop for breakfast at a country store selling white bread and bologna by the pound, and all the religious paraphernalia you could want. Hot-pink rosaries. A giant scented candle shaped like Jesus, wick sprouting from his thorned head. My boy lover buys me a snow globe with, at its center, a miniature Bethlehem and a sweet, blonde Mary, hands held out to receive the gift of plastic snow.

After a slow mile, we park in a field jammed with vehicles and on-foot penitents. At the edge of the field crowded with lawn chairs and blankets on the grass, Hispanic migrant workers chant the Magnificat: "My soul proclaims the greatness of the Lord; my spirit rejoices in God my Savior. For he has looked upon his handmaid's lowliness; behold, from now on will all ages call me blessed." A businessman tailgates off the back of a Mercedes. A very pregnant woman, the side of her face a silvery scar, aftermath of a burn, is already in tears. "My third visit," she says, "and no answer yet. Not a word."

Everyone, we find, has come to possess his or her own soul's secrets. This event lays all of us bare. Holy litanies are broadcast from loudspeakers in the trees while hawkers sell pop and photographs of various sightings of the Virgin. She is a shadowy face on a rock by a creek. She is a thin angel opening her wings over Conyers. My lover buys three of these photos, saying they will look good in black light on the ceiling of his room. I let go of his hand and push my way through shoulder-to-shoulder people until I am near enough to catch a glimpse of a small white house behind a fence. Already I see the sky opening to the hand of God, a woman standing in his palm. "Hail Mary," we say. "Blessed art thou among women. Blessed be the fruit of thy womb."

The air has a scent of roses, and cameras click and flash as worshippers photograph the sky. They want that sky to be the color of flesh. They want to find the Virgin's face behind the sun. They say, given just the right intensity of light, the right moment or angle, a camera can capture a glimpse of the Mother as She steps out of heaven with a begging bowl large enough to hold all the worthy. I am humbled by the sight of the little house, on its back porch a circle of nuns and priests kneeling in prayer. We push past each other with prayers on slips of paper to lay, with gifts of roses, on the steps of the porch. I reach down, find a lost petition. "Forgive me Mother," it says. "I have sinned, I have forgotten, I have sinned again."

It's almost noon, time for the holy presence, but I have no camera. I hold my bare hand up to sun so bright I think of watching an eclipse through a pinhole. Words, whole litanies of my own, hum inside me—*bright love descending, wings of fire, hope of desire, remade, remade.* In and out of cloud shapes, we look for signs. "These shapes," a woman standing near me wearing an ornate manta says, "contain Her, are Her, if we know how to look. That one, there," she says. She points to a cloud drifting away from us. "In it," she says, "I see bleeding hands, and I see Her ankles. She is settling to earth."

Then, at exactly noon, more clouds appear from nowhere. As I look at them, their shapes of hands and faces and wings, I believe, still believe, and I experience a pure moment. White light is reborn in these clouds and I close my eyes, breathing it in. "She is among us now," a voice says. I don't know if the voice is from the loudspeakers or the woman of the manta or my own heart, but I peer into the sky. Shadows of clouds move forward through my spread fingers. I imagine a woman, a girl really, standing at the door of her parents' house, arm curved up, hand steadying a water vessel on her head. Light speaks to her. It says, *Hail, favored one. The Lord is with you.* The voice quickens in her belly. She sees herself as she will soon be, her sleek belly heavy and ripe. She is a virgin giving birth, lost in an ecstasy of pain she does not fully comprehend, a pain delicious and huge. She contains this moment of birth forever and forever. She is a mother looking up to the sky as her son leaves earth, his spirit rising, light as a balloon, and she must let go. She is a mother and not one for all time, and this is a metaphor for a love so vast she must repeat it again and again, a rosary in her own heart, until she understands.

What she felt settles in me. I see my boy lover's face in the dark, the delicate skin of his new-shaven upper lip. I see years past and other lovers, none of them beloved. In the clouds I see the shape of my own womb. It is tipped forward and emptied of its fruit. "Forgive me," the petition I have brought this day asks. "Forgive me," I say, and I turn my face up to receive light spilled from the palm of the sky.

Turning Away from the World

Another time, in summer, my dogs and I are living alone by the ocean. Days, I'm working on a novel about an eastern-Kentucky woman who finds her voice only through God. Evenings, I run for miles along the empty shoreline, find pieces of shells, strands of weeds filled with seawater, and once, five small, dead sharks laid out neatly in a row. I run for points in the distance rather than for time—the two gazebos, the white birdhouse with the red trim, the end of the long row of beach apartments, the entrance to the national park.

I have long felt a need for water, for rivers and lakes, for laps in swimming pools in the middle of the city. I keep a map on my wall of lunar geography and the names of the seas on the moon— *Tranquillity, Moisture, Fertility, Crises, Dreams.* I'm fascinated when a friend sends me a bottle of liquor from France called Eau de Vie—*water of life*—and I save it for years, protective of the perfect, whole pear suspended in the fluid. Another friend takes me canoeing on Lake Jocassee in South Carolina and I swim the length of the lake above an entire submerged village, its houses and businesses and its church steeple that reaches toward the watery light. Still another friend tells me of taking her infant son to the ocean for the first time, how he crawls again and again to the edge of the water, drawn, she tells me, to his origins, to water like amniotic fluid.

I am as obsessed with these birth waters as my mother is with her daily rituals of cleanliness. I have come to the ocean this summer to be alone, as I often am now. Yet by mid-July I'm friends with a man named Wild, a trucker and a hunter and a teller of stories about alligators and snakes on the Apalachicola River. I am lonely and I am drawn to his honesty and his pit bull named Sassy, and so I sleep with him, only once, complete with the necessary protection. But I am certain I've become pregnant, as I have often been certain. I keep the friendship but end my intimacy with him, and then I wake each morning wondering. Like always, I am half fearful and half hopeful, wondering whether I'm pregnant. I am like the young character in a novel I once read whose husband must go to a leper colony. She accompanies him and lives through this time, but she spends each evening for the rest of her life meticulously checking her body for signs of illness. I, too, am meticulous. I check my underwear again and again for telltale signs of blood, buy at-home pregnancy test kits and test myself early, just to be sure, until the blood gathers and spills out, salty and fecund smelling. This time, too, I imagine the life that could be—my waitress job at the ocean, my little house and my dogs, my life alone with a child.

For weeks after my period starts, I continue to think of pregnancy and I secretly luxuriate in what birth could be like, this time. This time, I tell myself, I'd eat only vegetables washed in rainwater, bread made by hand. I'd love my full body and I'd lavish my stomach with gifts—oils and lotions and the touch of my own reverent hands. I do not imagine who would father this child. I do not think of the pain, only the way I'd open, like Buddha's mother, and give birth from my side. I want to be Mary, pregnant without sex, yet completely sensuous and ripe with birth giving. I'd fall on my knees to pray, thankful for a child whose history I'd follow, photograph by photograph.

Some years before, I traveled to Greece, where I picked fruit, lived on the beach, and dreamed one night that someone lovely and godlike came up from the ocean to touch me while I was sleeping. A dream lover to make me whole? My son, a man now but with his spirit wandering the world in search of his first mother? My son, a man who forgives me and urges me to forgive myself? My mother and her white-gloved hands, still visiting me as I sleep, thousands of miles from eastern Kentucky? That dream comes back to me now as I run on the beach, and some evenings it is my own self I see rise from the ocean, born again, and I am my own creator.

I wait for the sunset, wait for my body to cool with sweat and saltwater, to relax into no-time and forgetting the past, to say yes. Yes, not only to running and beach and the inestimable gift of time, but to something, something with no name at all. Call it an awareness of the heart's blood. Call it breath. Call it being alive. Or ecstasy. But that's a huge word, one to be used cautiously and with humility, even when your spirit wants to shout what it knows to the ocean and wait for the waves to bring back your self, transformed.

Proof Thereof in Practical Effects

In the summer of 1997 I'm at my father's house for a visit home, both of us say, though by this time I'm not entirely sure where home is in space and time. I've begun to suspect that *home* has an amorphous definition, akin to blood and bone, as insubstantial as ether. I'm lost inside my own skin and I want something to blame, some time and specific memory to pin me down, keep me from spinning.

Nevertheless, I am home, in my father's house, where I have dreams about bulls with golden horns and nuns with lassos, dreams about myself, pregnant and afraid to go outside. I sit with my father in the kitchen, over coffee. We talk about the new house he's built, about cherry jam he's made, about a story he's wanted to write, one about the ghost of the Confederate soldier he's sure he's seen more than three times over the past ten years. "Did you ever," he has written me in a letter, "catch a glimpse out of the corner of your eye of something in the house and for a moment think it was someone watching you? I had a shirt on a chair in the front room," he writes, "and for a moment I thought it was someone, a friendly intruder, watching."

Now that I'm home, we talk. We talk about our own past lives, though he assures me it's always better to live in the here and now. "Your mother," he says when I ask him about the way she cleaned house, the way she cleaned our lives. *Your mother?* He seems vague, fragile, and I think about the socks he wears at holidays, ones my stepmother bought him, embroidered with trees and bells. He stirs his coffee, which he likes weak and black, with a silver spoon.

"We had a good life," he says. "As good as anyone else, I'd say. As good as can be expected."

"And my son," I want to know. "Do you remember that? Do you know the date he was born?"

"I'd be lucky," he says, "if I remembered the date of my own birth."

At the end of several days at home, I'm panicking. I've gotten a long-distance call offering me a teaching job in Virginia, but I can't make up my mind. I've already imagined two more years in Georgia, where I'll live alone in a little yellow house with a garden and continue to live on graduate-student wages. I'm caught between worlds, at a crossroads. I'm losing myself in the dust of all the cars I've driven down this road and that, all the turns I've taken here and there, all the directions I could take next. It's then that I decide to visit the hospital where, twenty-four years earlier, my son was born and placed for adoption.

I keep this part of my visit home a secret from my father and my stepmother, tell myself I have my reasons. *My own decision; my own knowledge, not theirs; my own sadness, not theirs; my own, my own, my own.* Because my plan to visit the hospital is a secret, I don't know until the minute when I'm facing an empty parking lot that the old hospital has been torn down. *Reconstructed,* I'm told when I call the hospital number from a pay phone to get directions through a morass of new roads and signs to the New Hospital Complex.

The inside of the New Hospital is a morass, too. Blue lines lead to Emergency. Green to Lab. Red to X-ray. An information desk gives me directions to OB-GYN, where, I'm sure, they'll be able to give me some information about my records. I tell OB-GYN a partly true story about my need, for health reasons, to find some records of a past birth, and they send me to Record Keeping. Record Keeping sends me to Patient Care Services, and I am, by that time, losing it. I'm light-headed. I'm starting to get angry. I'm on the verge of tears and I hate the curly-headed woman with a gold chain around her neck and red fingernail polish who tells me there aren't any records, not that far back.

"What do you mean there aren't any records?" I ask.

"No records," she says. She taps a pencil on her notepad. "Records after 1975 were stored on microfiche."

"And before 1975?" I ask. I'm insisting. I'm leaning forward, close enough to smell Avon and hair spray.

"We did," she says, "have some minimal storage space. For older records from the previous hospital."

She says she'd have to look into it, but she looks doubtful, even a little fearful as I lean in closer, slap a piece of paper of my own in front of her. I've written down *Brian Keith McElmurray,* the only name I know; my own name; and a range of dates, late June to early July 1973.

By then I'm drawing a crowd. Another secretary from across

the hall and an orderly on his lunch break are in the waiting area. They're whispering back and forth, studying me, a wild-haired woman in shorts and sandals who's starting to smell acrid and sweaty, who's ready to cry.

I fall back on health reasons—my history of depression, my mother's family's history of depression, my second cousin's bouts of Tourette's and mysterious seizures, anything I think might be a reliable reason for me to be given records. I say anything I can think of until, at the last minute, I confess. I fall back on their pity. I tell them the whole story. I placed my son for adoption. I want some proof, any proof, of the date of his birth, a date I can't remember.

The woman looks down at her pad and pen and sketches what looks like a human hand, then draws a line through that, and another line, and then she looks up at me guiltily, as if she's been caught having a nice, clean life when I've been bogged down in something she's never confronted before. I feel dirty and ashamed. I feel found out. But at last she writes down Sherry in a neat hand followed by a dash, slips me a card with her name and phone number and promises to look into it. She'll find out how far back the records start, where the boxes might be.

She'll find out, she says with a wink, what information is suit-able, for my circumstances.

Once I'm outside the hospital, I decide it's up to me to deter-mine the circumstances. I head two streets down to visit Doctor's Park, which now includes the offices of the OB-GYN specialist I saw when I was sixteen. This office is less elaborate than I remember—smaller waiting room, comfortably worn tweed chairs. My pulse slows as I drink two cups from the water cooler, and I approach the women at the reception area calmly.

"Sign in," one of the receptionists says. "Date and time."

"I don't really have an appointment."

"You want to make one?"

She wheels around quickly in her desk chair, poised to enter the computer data.

"Which of our doctors do you see?"

"I don't see one regularly. Now."

"Now?" She smiles, still pleasantly.

I smile too, using my best college-professor assurance.

"I'm actually wanting," I say, "some information. About a previous experience. Some years ago."

"Years?"

"Nineteen-seventy-three, to be exact. I received prenatal care and I need to see the records. For a current health matter."

I am, of course, being sly. I lean casually against the registration desk, wait as she disappears into the back room with my name and the approximate dates of the services I received. When she comes back, it's a different story. She has the file, but she's shielding it against her body and she's whispering to her co-worker at the desk. They glance up at me conspiratorially.

"I'm afraid we're not allowed to give you any information about this file," she says at last.

I already know why, but I ask anyway. "Why?" I ask, and the whine I was developing at the hospital creeps back into my voice. I realize I'm sweating again and I feel drops ease down my spine.

"Why?" I ask again.

"The records," she says, "aren't usual. There were extenuating circumstances."

She knows and I know what these circumstances are, but neither of us says it, the word *adoption*. She's not smiling anymore, either, and I'm beginning to feel like a lowlife. Trashy. Like the Harlan County people with thirteen children my mother said were unclean. I'm beginning to beg in earnest. I'm saying, "Please, just a look," and I feel like I'm asking for the distribution of contraband substances, access to the records of the criminally insane. I want, I say, just to know a date, a time. I want to know my son was born with two hands and feet. That I really gave birth, after all.

They don't, of course, tell me anything. They're worried about legalities they don't understand. They're worried about keeping their receptionist jobs and what they're supposed to do or not supposed to do, and I understand that, since I'm subject to enough uncertainty myself to compensate for all of us. The best I can do is leave an address and a phone number, and I'm grateful, a week later, after I've left Kentucky, when a woman from the same office phones me up. I knew her, it seems, when I was in high school. She remembers me, very clearly. She doesn't say so, but she remembers my *situation*, how unfortunate it was, and how cruel kids in school were to girls like me and that other one, Buckwheat, wasn't it? Girls with reputations. She doles out a date for me, and I thank her and promise, cross my heart, never to reveal who gave me the information. This date is July 7, 1973. Not at all the date I'll be given a few months later.

By that time, I'm trying to settle down in Virginia, where I've accepted the college teaching job after all. After unpacking boxes and hanging up pictures and sorting through my files, I run across the card with Sherry's name and number at the New Hospital and decide to give her a call. I'm put through to her desk right away and I hope, I say, she'll remember who I am. Hope she'll have found out something. And she does remember me.

"Unfortunately," she says, "they were destroyed."

"Destroyed?" I ask. "What do you mean, destroyed?"

She whispers to me on the other end of the line, a confidential secret, a little *in* she's giving me at great risk to her position, her tone indicates.

"Once we had the new building," she says, "we burned them all."

"Burned them?"

"The records. Anything previous to 1975."

"Burned them?" I repeat.

"Well," she says, "maybe not burned. Disposed of properly. For the sake of economical storage capacity."

When I hang up the phone I close my eyes and see trails of smoke made of burning words. I see the crane and the steel ball crashing into the walls of the hospital where I gave birth, so that even the ashes of the records that proved my son's existence are buried, deep and finally. But I do not give up. The very next morning, I dial Kentucky again, this time the Kentucky Department of Social Services. I demand to speak with Record Keeping, and I demand information about one Brian Keith McElmurray, date of birth in June or July of 1973. This time, I am told that no such name exists, and especially no such name for the dates I am indicating.

"What does this mean?" I ask. "What do you mean no such name exists?"

I'm speaking with a social worker and she is vague and officious, in a suitable balance that I find maddening. She is doing her job, but I demand my rights. I am, I say, the birth mother. I have a right to know at least that much, at least the date when he was born, so I can locate him in memory, so I can know when to mourn, what to blame for the way my womb contracts and expands with remembering at a certain time of year. Before I know it, I'm crying into the phone. I'm begging, and my voice reaches a pitiful obsequiousness even I don't like.

"That's exactly it," she says. She pauses, delicately, clears her throat.

"It?" I ask.

"Why I can't give you specifics. You're a birth mother."

"But isn't that exactly why I *should* know?" I ask.

She quotes, book and verse, from the Good Book of Information and Rules about which I know very little.

Birth parents, I'm told, receive little or no information concerning the situations of adoptees, unless extenuating circumstances, or the specific request of an of-age adoptee, demands release of such information.

"Besides," she says, "the reasons could be very straightforward."

"Reasons?"

"The reasons there aren't records."

"Reasons," I repeat. I'm tangling and untangling the phone cord. I'm backed into the corner of my bathroom, crouching down in the floor between trash can and sink. I'm curling myself smaller and smaller.

"He could have been placed in foster care, which could explain a discrepancy in dates." She pauses.

"Or there are other possibilities," she says.

"Like?"

"He might have died," she says. "At birth."

And again I hang up the phone. I hang it up tidily, the cord untangled, the receiver carefully laid down, and I tell myself, again, *I won't give up.*

In the days following, I tell myself I'll hire private investigators. I'll sift through the ashes of the hospital, the ashes of my life. I'll wear black pants and turtleneck and I'll sneak into Social Services in the middle of the night and I'll ransack files and drawers until I find the truth. The truth is, I fill up notebooks and scraps of paper with drafts of stories and journal entries about loss that is never understood.

The truth is, I fall back for a while on indifference. Or if not indifference, this time around, an apathy that is familiar, a fine wine I can sip at night, alone. It comforts me, my aloneness. I am as perfectly alone as a sphere made of glass suspended in the void that is the center of my chest, and if I don't move too close to anyone else, I will remain as I am. I am a body no one really knows how to touch. I am a mother and I am not a mother and I love a son who is not my son, a boy who is a man I have never seen. It is much easier, I still believe, to keep my grief intact.

Then I get a letter marked *Confidential*. It's from the Kentucky Department of Social Services and it's what they call *nonidentifying information*. According to what is permissible under Kentucky adoption law, KRS 199.570, I am told that my son's date of birth was June 21, 1973. He was adopted one year after his birth, by a family of math professors in a reasonably large Kentucky town. One math professor, the father, born in 1936, had advanced degrees, and the other, the mother, taught at a smaller, nearby college and enjoyed being a housewife. Both, this nonidentifying information tells me, enjoyed good health and had more than adequate resources to provide for a child. A paper trail. One I could follow, my nose to the ground for clues and stray telltale signs that my son is out there, living the life I sent him to, a life well intended, happy even. A paper trail I could pick up and follow until he and I are reunited. *Mother and son, son and mother, let no man put them asunder.*

The truth is, what I end up with is a new language, compliments of the Kentucky Department of Social Services. *Adoptee:* the only one who has the right to search. *Birth mother:* me. *Adoption worker:* an employee of the cabinet designated as such by the secretary for human resources. *Voluntary and informed consent:* condition in which, at the time of consent, the consenting person is fully informed of the legal effect of the consent, that the consenting person is not given or promised anything of value except those expenses allowable under KRS 199.590 (6). *Confidential:* subject to copy and/or inspection only on written order of the court. *Authorization:* application to the court by adult adopted person for information identifying biological parents and/or for consent to inspect all papers and records pertaining to the adoption. *Nonidentifying information:* may be released to adopted person eighteen years of age and older; includes date, time of birth, weight at time of birth, and reason for the adoption; minimal information provided to birth parents. *Disclosure:* legal condition under which, traditionally, birth parents receive little or no information about their child's placement or progress.

I'm also allowed, I'm told, to write a letter to Social Services. They will, they say, place this letter in a file, to be seen if inquiries should ever arise. As a birth mother, I'm allowed this much. I'm allowed a letter for a file I'm not allowed to see, to a child I have never known, a man leading a life I can only imagine:

Dear Son:

It feels more strange, awkward, sad, hopeful, overwhelming, joyous . . . more of everything, to write that word, "son," than I could say in this letter.

I've tried now for about three or more years to write a letter I might send you, if I knew where you were, or if you'd read these words. One of the problems has been that I don't know where to begin. There is, really, no beginning. The only one that counts, I guess, is that I was sixteen years old when you were born. I was confused and scared. I couldn't imagine how I could take care of you, or me, or the life in which I found myself. That time would be one beginning. But there is so much more—the family that made me, made me unsure of what being a mother meant, frightened of mothering, being mothered or giving or receiving love.

I do know that I love you. I have loved you all this time, without direction, place, person, or face. I have missed you beyond any missing I have known or can describe. You have been a hole in my spirit I have never been able to approach. You have been a question, a longing. I would so love to meet you.

Now, in my life, I am a teacher and a writer. I live alone with my two dogs in Lynchburg, Virginia. I teach creative writing at a little college there. It has taken me years to find a direction, look at the heart that has created so many consequences.

If you read this letter, please know I'm trying, and reaching out to you. I want to meet you, to talk. I'd give so much to have you be real.

Gongs and Bells

Birth, I know, is not easy. In high-school gym class we watched the whole thing on film—contractions, the bloody head crowning, the expelling of the afterbirth. Of late, I have expanded upon my definitions of birth. There is light in a tunnel after death. There is rebirth in a new body in a foreign city where the language is unknown. Life after life after life. Or not.

My mother has told me about it again and again. She has told me about the night of my own birth in a military hospital in Topeka, when she and a lieutenant's wife were both in labor, both of them, as she says, squealing throughout the night. "It hurts," she says. "Don't let anyone tell you anything else." She tells me this even after she knows, after almost twenty-seven years of silence concerning the birth of my son. These are the rituals we share—pain, lovelessness, the way we are all abandoned when we look into our hearts. These repetitions, easy as a charm you say under a ladder, are ones she believes keep you safe from the path into a future you can't trust. Safe even from the truth about my son that I finally told her in the summer of 2000. But it was winter 1998, the day after Christmas, that I call the day of my own birth.

On that day, I've just left my mother's house in eastern Kentucky. We'd spent Christmas like always, at my aunt Ruth's, with turkey and the trimmings, and blood-sugar tests at the kitchen table afterward. She'd given me, like always, an envelope with twenty dollars and a note that said, "Love, Mother," though she had told me, like always, that she didn't trust it, that ineffable thing called loving, that unpredictable thing called the heart. She'd told me her mantra, her safe phrase, "love can't be trusted," it forever comes and goes. She watched me back out of her driveway, that daughter as mysterious as other towns, as unimaginable as a foreign country.

As I head west, I think about her, how she's even then putting away the season, lights into boxes, gifts into drawers. I think about how my most recent lover has told me he isn't *in love with me*, that fine difference between being there and not. I'm repeating to myself, *doesn't love, doesn't love*, as I watch coal and mountains and houses that promise "Crafts 4 Sale." I'm lost in absence. I'm seeing my mother's hands stirring honey and butter on a plate, the fork turning over and over as she says, "There's no such thing, no such thing as love." Morning and mountains, a flashing star on a roof, praying hands lit in red and green and reaching up from a yard. No such thing as love, but chimneys send smoke out into the world and cars start, sending families home. Children, none of them mine, are laden with gifts. I almost believe it. *No such thing as love.*

Christmas has ended, and I should go home too, but for years I've not been where that is. I'm headed to Christmas Stage Two, at my father's brick Cape Cod house in the Kentucky piedmont, where we'll unwrap gifts and give thanks to the Lord. I'm headed out of the mountains on the Mountain Parkway and all the signs point west, but I'm dreaming of sleep and time passing, an hour, two, a nap at the roadside. My mother's uncle died that way, asleep in an old Chevrolet, breathing fumes, his head resting against the seat. I wonder how I myself will die. Softly, I want to believe, just like sleep.

The sky is snowy and it lulls me and I know I could pull off at a rest area, take a nap, quick and hard, just enough to help me shift from Christmas to after, world of mother to world of father, mountains to beyond. I could dream of love and wake with the taste of salt. I could dream of the way my son once left my body, long ago on a date I can't remember, how I was floating, looking down on myself, a body I didn't own. Why, I ask myself now, did I give birth at all? My son left me and I left him. The opening that was me shut, and my heart remains without love.

In a zippered Bible I was given when I was nine, Paul is on the road to Damascus and the sky comes open then, too, but it's made of fire and chariots of God ride down. My sky's opening is on the interstate, just where the mountains leave off and the bluegrass begins. It's an absolutely beautiful moment, this. The sky is soft with winter, a color between rose and gray, and I'm listening to Etta James and the blues. I'm drinking them in, songs of sorrow, songs of joy. "I want a Sunday kind of love," she sings, and I imagine that, a love both unconditional and kind. I imagine reaching back inside myself, taking out every memory I own, the fine china of my past, the way I could dust and shine, make everything new again. Or not. I could give up, once and for all. I could surrender. Wasn't that the hymn they'd always sung, in the church of my father, in the Church of the Lord, Redeemer? "All to Thee, I surrender, I surrender all."

That's when the sky crashes open, just for me. The road is long and flat, so if I'd looked in time, I would have known, could have stopped. But I'm reaching down for lip balm. I'm touching my necklace of jet-black beads and I'm saying Hail Marys. I'm reaching in for memory. I'm thinking of Christmas a long time back, of a tree made of pink foil that shines. I'm thinking of a lover's hands. I'm thinking of the feel of a baby's mouth on breasts not mine, the scent of hair still new. I'm thinking of my mother's hands in gloves at night. Gloves, a beauty treatment.

And then I crash full tilt into the car ahead of me, a bright-red sports car going fifteen miles per hour behind a truck. It's this moment you want to be able to describe, later. The way you're lifted up, protesting how you're seized and shaken, told the importance of disregard, the sanctity of all you are or can be. The impact is the scrape of tires along pavement, the neat and sudden slam, speed ending here and now. The impact is dark and quick, a span of time that might be hours or a minute, quick and black time in which you're absent, suspended from yourself and saying, *Go back, replay this just once more. Oh God help me,* I'm saying, and I don't mean just now. I mean forever, but I can't yet conceive of that, the way the sky reaches beyond the earth, the way a hand held out means hope.

I don't wake up for some minutes, but when I do I'm at the steering wheel, face down into a ghost. It's the air bag, white and balloonlike and set loose on impact, but I think it's my own spirit, ajar from my body, waiting to decide between life and death. My face is against the steering wheel, my glasses askew, one lens missing so I'm half blind to the scene on the road. I'm right-side-up, but the front of my vehicle steams and hisses, the hood twisted back and around as easily as foil. Etta James is still playing and I reach over automatically to switch off the sound and then this sound is me, calling for help. The door pushes open stiffly and I kick against it, my leg throbbing. Beads from the broken necklace fall from my lap and then I'm falling, listening to sirens and radio dispatch.

What happens is this. I'm lying beside the highway in the gravel and I'm being held in a stranger's arms. "Help me, help me," I'm saying, and I'm reaching up, into these arms I don't know, stranger who will later follow the ambulance, just to see if I'm all right. He smells of aftershave and fear. He's afraid for me, for the crash that had almost been him, and his wife comes too, lays a blanket on my body, and they both talk to me. "It's all right now," she says. "You're all right." They all say that, the driver from another car who slips me a note with his address, in case I need anything, hard evidence or a face I might remember. The ambulance driver, when I'm lying on a stretcher and someone is placing a wet cloth on my forehead and I'm cold and hot and cold. This person strokes my cheek, as if with love.

I'm raced down a highway, toward a hospital that will tell me I'm alive, and I'm looking up at thin winter sunlight, and I'm thinking, *How lovely and white.* The ambulance tires keen along the asphalt and I'm shivering now, my body as buoyant and light as water in sunlight, as insubstantial as air.

It's that moment I'll call *it*, when I realized I had wanted to die. There'd been no bottle of pills, or shotgun beside a chair, or noose made by hand. I had wanted to simply stop, there and then on that instant of highway going toward the future and away from the past, neither of them, I believed, made of love. What saves us in such times? The kindness of strangers? The mercy of God and time? Time is nebulous. I'm in a truck beside a highway and I'm that close to it, crash of metal on metal, metal unto death. I'm in an ambulance and then in an emergency room, waiting for them to tell me I'm OK. I drift and come to, and blame myself for what I have been, for what I have not. I do not think, quite yet, of that word, of *forgiveness*. When my father comes at last, I cry in his arms, for the first time I can remember.

The truck was having engine trouble, the police officer later told me, and the driver was inching it toward the next exit, in search of a service station. His daughter and son-in-law were traveling close behind in the sports car, shielding the truck's license plate from view. The officer told me this when he visited me at the emergency room and when I was filling out papers to say what happened. My rate of speed: 65 MPH. Destination: Shelbyville. Point of contact: Right front of vehicle one hits left midsection of vehicle two, with minor injuries to vehicle three. Injuries: broken ankle, minor concussion. No fatalities on either side. The father of this family I'll never know was pacing in the waiting room when I was wheeled past. He was praying and thanking Jesus.

What can never be recorded is the exact way the sky took me in that day. In some versions of moments like this, there are hands belonging only to God, ones large enough to reach down, grab a shirt collar, a stray hem, haul up any reluctant soul. Or there are other stories. A bird careening down against a mountain and then circling back against the sky, and the boy who did not believe listening to the sound of an echo. A woman standing beside a pool of water, stick in hand, stirring leaves and fish on a summer day. Thunder comes and lightning circuits through her body and she thinks, *That's it, the voice of life and death.*

And I wish it were that easy, how we learn the definition of grace. We are struck down by tragedy. The Hangman comes in the night and takes our beloved off to his death. The Angel of the Afterlife knocks at our door and we are afraid. I am a sixteen-year-old mother and circumstances conspire to make me surrender my son to a life I believe will be happier, a life without pain or sadness. *Sanctification,* they call it. Grace is a divine virtue coming from God; it is mercy, pardon; it is a privilege, a reprieve, a breath-fine moment before we are forever lost. I can no more assure myself of my son's eternal happiness than I can assure myself of safety in this tentatively beautiful, mortal world.

Time unfolds after this accident. Past folds into present, present into future and back again, to the beginning of who I am and who I might become. Early mornings I will wake into a familiar notion of my own body, a body I have long believed has no weight, no intent, a body nothing but a book of visions, a body not worthwhile. And then I will hear it, the kick and kick inside me, and I will think for just a minute that I've gotten him back, my son. I'll think, *It's happening at last, a blessing floating down, contrition right from heaven.* Is it possible to take back into the womb? Is it possible to forgive, and not to forget?

And then I'll be completely awake. I'll be alone in my room in the house I have come to love and I will know where I am and I'll touch my legs and belly, my own hands, with thanksgiving. *Oh,* I'll say. *I'm alive.* And so, I'll believe, is he, that son of mine so long gone into a world I cannot predict. He may be, I know, a man I would not like, but a man I would love. His life? Saving mortal souls across the continents, unraveling mysteries of heaven and earth. He may be far less kind. He may be cruel, a man who inflicts hurt and does not repent, does not ask for forgiveness.

Or he may be something more ordinary, a man you and I may have seen every day. He is closing down a cash register at night in a little country store. He is standing on a porch after he has locked all the doors for the night, for one more night, and he is looking out across a field of farewell-to-summer and ironweed. He is saying *thank you* to nothing larger than the night itself. He is saying good night to a woman he does not know. This may be me. This may be that love for which he has long wished. These things may be one and the same.

He is saying good night and fare-you-well, and I want to believe he's saying this to me. I am alone many nights and I am nothing but glad, in the end, to be in this world, among the living who may, after all, embrace my son. Forgiveness? How can I say? I am only listening to my own heart tell me how to begin.

Beauty

Grace, you say, is ecstasy. It is our folded hands held up to heaven. It is a prayer dance in the rain. It is light before the cloud moves in to cover the sun, the smell of rain, the scent of a new lover's hands. It is part and parcel of the known, sensed world. It is the chalky taste of sadness, the certainty of broken glass and departures. It is you, falling on your knees before what you can only trust is God. You're saying, Enough. *You're saying,* Lift me up. *And you're afraid no one will, but still you believe.*

Grace, you say, is the juncture of past and present, elusive promise of the future. It cannot be understood as easily as a mathematical equation. Lie on a bridge at night under a clear summer sky. Count the first of all the stars that fall. Multiply the time it takes between the first star and the second and the third and so forth until you have it, the proportional equation for, henceforward, the number of stars that will always fall, forever and forever. Can you then estimate the limits of your own heart? Is there such a thing as a measurable quickening of the womb? When and in what quantity does the spirit leave the body? What is the correct time for mourning? For the heat of desire? Is there another name for grace?

Imagine you've slipped out at night with no particular place to go and you're driving on a road you've never seen before and the windows are down and it's raining and you're facing into the musky wind. The earth exhales, sweet and delicious. You pass street after street, windows lit for evenings of dinner and television and sometimes sleep and then you look over and you think, Where, how, what's that?

What you're seeing is not that unusual. It's steam from a pipe hidden under the ground or it's smoke left over from the last pile of leaves burned in someone's yard. But for just a second you stop the car and you remember. You remember a story from your great-grandmother or your aunt or from a library book you never took back. The story was about souls. Sometimes, the story said, you can see them. You'll see a whirl of dust on a road in the sun. You'll see mist on a stagnant river. And just for a second, you'll remember last fall or the one before that or the one to come next, anything full of possibility, of what's to come. Souls, the story went. Waiting to be born.

Afterword

Come fall 2001, I have been reborn, in ways I never expected. I have chosen who I will love and who I won't. I've learned to say no to lovers who fail to see me, or who hesitate to see themselves. I myself have chosen, John, a Monacan council chief from the heart of Virginia, a lover who becomes my best friend as well. I have come, at last, to trust that writing is my vocation, if not my profession. By day I teach, this fall at a small liberal-arts college in northwest Georgia. These students, and the ones I've taught in other towns in Virginia and North Carolina, are, I often tell myself, my family. There is the girl who writes of an auto accident that almost killed her several years ago. One side of her face is slack, the muscles lower and half of her mouth slanted. "I'm not pretty anymore," she writes, and I tell her of her own deep and abiding strength, that beauty that can never be altered. Another is an ex-high-school jock. He writes stories about a football player who, in secret, plays cello, "songs," this writer says, "for the soul." Still another writes about anorexia and we talk about hungers that can never be filled, and those that can—with love and time and memory. Memory, I tell my students, has the power to heal. It is possible, I tell myself, to live in the present tense, in the true present that embraces us, comforts us with each rich moment. And yet, in almost every college class I have taught, I've imagined my son's face, third seat in the second row. In these imaginings, he's everything, and some things I'd rather he weren't. Sometimes he creates landscapes with paint made from red desert sand. Sometimes he's a neo-Nazi, or a corporate executive who moves columns and figures and lives. What I haven't imagined is what really, remarkably, comes true.

Come fall 2001, I'm worried that I'm stepping back in time, to a limbo of-the-season I don't like. I'm again between holidays and families and, this year, between states. John, now my fiancé, has unexpectedly remained behind in Virginia for a few months while I've gone to Georgia to be a writer-in-residence. Everything is good, really, but both love and my writing life feel ambiguous. My memoir has been finished for almost a year but has been delayed in its publication by a small southern press beset, like the rest of the nation, by economic fallout from the terrorist attacks of September 11. I've begun to recognize the similarities—waiting for a book to be born and waiting, almost thirty years after his birth, to see my own son's face. *When*, I ask myself, will there be the happy ending movies promise, the mother and son reunited and riding off into the sunset? Come spring, I remind myself, there'll be love and a book and all good things I can see and touch, but right now everything feels like it's waiting to be born.

Then, on Thanksgiving Day 2001, my life takes charge and pushes me forward in a way I could never have predicted. For weeks, since I purchased a new laptop, I've been obsessed with e-mail, and Thanksgiving is no exception. I've checked messages five times already, waiting for *the* holiday greeting, when I open a file that makes my world come open:

Dr. McElmurray,
I stumbled upon a web page looking for a book for a Christmas present. At the bottom of one of the pages I saw your picture and I was stunned. The resemblance to someone I know very well is shocking. I then continued to read that you had a son that you gave up for adoption in 1973 and that you were from Kentucky. My, fiancé, Andrew, was born in 1973 somewhere in Kentucky and adopted. I have his permission to write you. . . . He is a little nervous to do so himself. He is, however, very interested in finding his birth mother. I hope it does not anger you that I contact you. Have you already found your son?

Sincerely, Jennifer Williams

"Oh my God," I say to John, who is visiting and making corn pudding. John hurries in from the kitchen and I imagine sinking to my knees, hiding my face in my hands. Later, I'll think about my Introduction to Creative Writing classes and my beginning short-story writers who describe moments in which protagonists receive extraordinary news and sob uncontrollably into their toilet paper. Or experience terrible shocks and fall like lead onto floors, or slide helplessly down walls or the sides of refrigerators. Could this really happen? I ask them. Don't we feel things more subtly? Don't we just get quiet, or go lie down, or watch too much bad television for too many hours in a row? Anyway, I say, wouldn't it hurt like hell to fall so hard? Show me, I tell my students. Show me what really happens when we feel extremes. Give me sensory details—the tastes and scents and textures of love, of grief, of desire.

A pen rolls from the edge of the desk. My heartbeat rises and falls. My mouth tastes like sweat. John hurries in from the kitchen and we stand there, reading secondhand about a young man named Andrew who has wanted to meet his birth mother. I don't accept these feelings easily, of course. John tries to hug me, but I push away from him with both hands. "No," I say, but I'm not sure what I'm denying. I want comfort and I don't. I want my son in my life right now, and I don't. I want the baby who came from my once girl's body and not a man who can be just as afraid as I am now. I want this message to be true, but every reason it couldn't be comes to mind. That admirer of my novel who wrote me two years ago, and kept writing with new e-mail addresses until I moved away. It's really him, I tell myself, masquerading as my son's fiancée. Or something simpler. A mistake or a well-meaning stranger who's seen my memoir described on some web site for a conference and who now wants to make my life all better. I'm pushing as hard against the truth as I am against John as he holds on to me and tells me he loves me and tells me he believes it's happened at last. *My son and I have found one another.*

This is the truth, though it will take a month of phone calls and more notes and a packet of photographs for all of us to believe it. The truth is that my son, born on June 21, 1973, was indeed adopted by two math professors in a college town in central Kentucky. Their birth years match those in my Social Services nonidentifying information. My son's name, today, is Andrew. *Andrew.* The same name I'd chosen for the central character in a novel I'd finished in 1997. Andrew, who wrote his first e-mail message to me a few days after Thanksgiving:

I don't know what to say. All that Jennifer has said to me, shown to me, appears to fit with what I have come to know.

I stand speechless, and somewhat reeling, with mixed euphoria, dysphoria, and confusion. I've felt, for some time, the need to find an origin, but have always pushed the notion aside, waiting for a more opportune time in my life.

Now a possibility has fallen upon me.

Perhaps I ramble, instability beckons. I would like, with some trepidation, to contact you less electronically, or perhaps for you to contact me. I'm unsure how to proceed.

The swirling potentials are so new to me.

Andrew

I'm swirling, too, in late February of 2002, when I meet my son for the first time. I can't sit still and I'm pacing, though I've managed to play hand after hand of crazy eights with John, whom I wed in December and who has come at last to live with me and start our life together. It's a Saturday, and Jennie and Andrew have promised to drive from Lexington, Kentucky, to Mount Berry, Georgia, where we'll have dinner and get acquainted. *Reunion,* such an event is called by adoption discussion groups on the internet. It's one of the stages of adoption, the professionals say. *Surrendering of parental rights. Reunion. Aftermath.* Self-help books describe all such rites of passage in the world of adoption. The books also offer advice on all the residual effects, everything from anxiety to relationship difficulties to poor self-esteem. Between card games, I scour my adoption collection, fliers and books and organization magazines. I've even clipped quotes I like best. "Adoption Loss is the only trauma in the world where the victims are expected by the whole of society to be grateful." Nowhere do I find any specific advice on how to greet the son I've never seen. What's the proper etiquette? Should I hug him? Shake hands? Or should I follow my true inclination, which is to hide somewhere, in the apartment bathroom maybe, where I can peer through the blinds and catch a first glimpse of him as he steps out of the car?

Andrew and Jennie promised to leave Lexington early, and I've imagined *early* as synonymous with *eagerly*. I'm so eager that I've been up since five, cleaning our small apartment and filling the bathroom walls with tiny glow-in-the-dark stars that seem like the perfect light touch for a visit from the child I gave away. I imagine Jennie and Andrew up early, too—six-thirty, seven, seven-thirty at the latest for the five-and-a-half-hour drive south. I have the timing down to a science, of course. If they left at, say, eight, by noon they'll be near Chattanooga, which gives them an hour and a half, two hours with lunch, to drive from there. By, say, one-thirty they'll be near Cartersville, which exits onto Route 20, which leads to Mount Berry. That means that by two-thirty at the latest—unless they're drawn to one of the strip malls on the outskirts of Rome—they'll be here. For good measure, I give them until three o'clock. Or three-thirty.

By four-thirty, then five, I'm biting my cuticles until they bleed and we've gone from crazy eights to spades and back again. The cards slap down and the suits switch, hearts to diamonds to clubs, and I'm aware of how old the deck is, the cards soft and pliable. I feel soft and pliable myself, since I starting sipping an elixir of health-food-store nerve tonic about one, then switched to Shiraz, my favorite red wine, about two. I'm managing to be calm, I tell myself. I'm together enough to ration my eights from every suit, save them up for my last two cards so there's no turning back and I'm sure to win. John is letting me win, anyway. He's letting me win and fetching me wine and lapsing into frustration, because I'm *hopeless*, I'm telling him. It's been almost thirty years and *this*, I say, is what Andrew will find, and I mean a forty-five-year-old, a nervous wreck, a nail biter and a writer without a home. "This," John says, stroking my hair. "This is what he'll find."

Just after five I head down to the yard to talk to my neighbors, Jim and Susan. The whole clan is there—their two kids, their out-of-town guests, and Anabelle, their dog. Everyone is playing touch football and I linger at the outskirts, feeling like an uninvited guest. Anabelle, who is a Carolina dog, races in circles and leaps after the ball as the kids kick it. All of them, even

Anabelle I'm sure, know the importance of this day for me. On Thanksgiving, after Andrew's e-mail, John and I ate turkey and stuffing with Jim and Susan and all of us speculated on what Andrew would be like. "He'll look just like his mother," one of them said that day, and I felt all them looking at me, waiting to see how I'd respond to the testing of the waters. *Mother.* They look at me curiously now, a mother waiting to see the son who is twenty-nine years old and now several hours late. The boys and Jim drop-kick the ball toward their house and Susan lingers with me for a while. I like her. She smells of something clean, soap and good intentions, and I trust her enough, now, to tell her I'm going out of my mind. "Where is he?" I ask, my voice like a tired child's. I am nearly crying as this question, weighted as it is against years of waiting and against this late afternoon, hangs in the air between us. Susan hugs me. "It'll be fine," she says. She repeats this, twice, and looks at me with her clear eyes. I can tell she doesn't know what to say, or how, but that she's doing her best. There isn't anything, neither wine nor friendship nor love, that can comfort me.

It's six o'clock. Six-thirty, and we're back upstairs sitting at the kitchen table. I've straightened pillows on the living-room couch and washed the last fork in the sink. I've thrown the I Ching and the tarot. My future card is the Six of Cups. *Riding the waves into shore, the horses and their riders experience joy and pleasure, a full-out expression of emotional intensity.* Intensity. I know about that, have known about it all my life. Today alone I've looked out the window 364 times and I've drunk another glass of wine and I'm tired now. I want to lie down and curl up with my dog. I want to call the whole thing off. I want it to be over with and I want it to start again and then we hear a car in the gravel parking space beneath our window. John is already standing there, because it was his turn to watch the road. "It's them," he says. Just like that.

It's like this. The sixteen steps down to the landing and to the outside door are the longest I've ever taken. Other books, not adoption ones, but saccharine romance novels and paperback mysteries, describe such moments. *Her hands gripped the rough-hewn wooden railing as, one by one, she inched her way down the steps to the landing where who knew what enormity awaited her.* Absurdly, I'm thinking lines like this. I'm thinking *lines.* So, *Andrew,* I'll say. *How were the roads? Was there much traffic?* I'm thinking I'm becoming my mother. I'm thinking of glass beads on a string. Absurdly, I'm thinking of a heady treatise, *An Enquiry Concerning Political Justice.* Glass beads are the metaphor there. We string them together, William Godwin says, the accumulation of our experiences of right and wrong, good and evil, like beads on a string made of our lives. That's what I'm doing.

Impossible, they say, to think all of this down a mere sixteen steps, but that's the way it is, the way I'll remember it. I'm sixteen and I'm wearing a hippie peasant dress and I'm walking in a meadow full of yellow flowers. I'm pregnant with my son, and someone, a friend's mother, tells me I'm the most beautiful sight she's ever seen. I'm sixteen and I'm laboring, forty-eight hours' worth, and I'm high on pain and fear. I'm thirty and I'm incapable of love and happiest at my Granny's house, where I lie on her couch and pretend I'm small all over again. I'm forty-five and the door is opening and I'm seeing his face, my very own son's, for the first time ever, the last or the first glass bead on a string of moments I've accumulated until now. I wish I could tell you, you who expect so much, that this moment was exquisite. That we reached across the distance from steps to car, took each other in without reservation. I wish I could tell you that this moment was inviolate, a testament of love from son to mother, mother to son. You must decide how it was or choose to see how it wasn't, your own reunion story.

My first memories of my son are of a young man. Obvious, you say. Less obvious, that he is no longer a baby to hold in my arms, but an attractive man with blond hair. He is standing at the bottom of the outside steps, his face averted, his feet in black shoes I ridiculously find stylish. The shoes are pointed carward, ready to help him slip away. Like me, he wants to hide. Like me, he slides his hands deep in his pockets, stands to the side, awkward, uncomfortable in his own fair skin. His skin, I notice right away, is ruddy, the skin of a blond man with light blue eyes who *is* Joe, my boy husband of years and years past. He is Joe, and me, and someone else, my father maybe, with my father's build, his chest and soft belly. I do not see my mother in my son's body, do not think of my mother at all. I do not even think of *myself* as a mother, but for a space of seconds I am a woman outside myself, a woman vulnerable to desire, and I'm thinking, *How handsome he is,* and I'm thinking I'm his mother and I'm not and I am. What did an anonymous mother say in one of the adoption books I'd bought? The only way, she said, she could really have him back in her womb was to be his lover. My womb aches. That much is true.

"Let's go inside," John says as he takes my hand, and my son and his sweetheart follow us in.

Andrew and I have, after all, ridden into a sunset in the same West, at different times. I went to Arizona in the 1980s to work in tourism at the Grand Canyon, and Andrew lives today in Tucson, where he is a graduate student in archaeology and classics. There are other clues—the similar colorings of our hair and skin, the sameness of our faces in our childhood photographs. Other evidence is subtle—the proofs only he and I or the ones who care about us would notice. We have similar ways, his fiancée says, of holding our hands. We end our statements like questions. We bite our nails. We have vivid dreams. He fears abandonment. I fear losing things or people I love. My heart has been glad each time I've heard his voice, which is both young and a man's, both hesitant and eager. Nevertheless, I know that so much more is to be said and felt. So much more is waiting to be born. I've told my mother, at long last, that I have a son. "A son," she's said in disbelief, as if *son* is a word from a foreign country, as if *reunion* is the word for a language she doesn't speak. We've sat, Andrew and I, at lunch with my father, who, concerning this reunion, rides the cusp between joy and sorrow, between love and uncertainty, as do Andrew and I. I have twice been to Arizona to visit Andrew, where we've had adventures. We've walked across the border into Mexico to eat chicken with mole. We've gone to a Tucson pet store and bought a kitten and taken it home to his apartment. We've sat on his deck and drunk wine—Shiraz, his favorite—and I've asked him to forgive me. "There's no need," he says. But I know need is there, nonetheless. I long for him to walk again through the rooms of this apartment where I'm living, to look at my books, my photographs, to hear the same music I dance to with John sometimes in the evening. "I want a Sunday kind of love," Etta James sings as I dance in my husband's arms. Andrew and I will also, I imagine, someday listen to blues and sip wine and come, at last, to know one another. Or not. He is a young man on the threshold of the world and I am a woman who still longs to hold my son on the day he was born. So much is possible. Possible, that Andrew and I will forge a relationship. Mother and son? Two friends with a common history they have only uncovered? Impossible, that he can ever be the real baby I have longed for, or that I can be the real mother. Yet it is possible that we might someday send notes signed with that most tentative and beautiful word, *love.*

What has been born, I believe, is the power of words. By what coincidence did I name my novel's main character Andrew? By what coincidence did I dream, for years, of a strong, clear-eyed young man who looks at me today from a photograph on my desk? By what coincidence does Andrew study archaeology, the unearthing of cultures, the discovery of the past? There are no coincidences. There is no separation of the power of words and this thing called a memoir, no separation, in the end, of writing and living. Writing, after all, is salvation. I have birthed this thing called a book, and called to life the lost past I have so wanted. I have remembered the past and wondrously summoned what I hope is the future.

Karen Salyer McElmurray
Mount Berry, Georgia
February 2003

Acknowledgments

I'd like to acknowledge several people for help with the birth of this book—Lee Smith, who first suggested my own life was a story I ought to tell; Betty Cox, my son's mother, with whom I have found a true connection of the spirit; The Hambidge Center, for more than once giving me a quiet and lovely space for writing; my women friends—among them Cindra Halm, Carlyle Poteat, Judy Long, Rosemary Daniell, Wendy Miles, Virginia Craighill, Meg Keaney—who have listened again and again to my often lonely heart; Maura Mandyck and Amy Zipperer, who used their red pens lovingly; the Association of Writers and Writing Programs for giving this book their award for creative nonfiction and the University of Georgia Press for their support of this memoir; Patty Moosbrugger, who has had enough faith in this book to be my agent; and my mother and my father and all my family, both new and familiar.